Getting to
INNOVATION

Getting to
INNOVATION

How Asking the Right Questions Generates

the Great Ideas Your Company Needs

Arthur B. VanGundy

American Management Association
New York • Atlanta • Brussels • Chicago • Mexico City • San Francisco
Shanghai • Tokyo • Toronto • Washington, D.C.

Special discounts on bulk quantities of AMACOM books are available to corporations, professional associations, and other organizations. For details, contact Special Sales Department, AMACOM, a division of American Management Association, 1601 Broadway, New York, NY 10019.
Tel: 212-903-8316. Fax: 212-903-8083.
E-mail: specialsls@amanet.org
Website: www.amacombooks.org/go/specialsales
To view all AMACOM titles go to: www.amacombooks.org

This publication is designed to provide accurate and authoritative information in regard to the subject matter covered. It is sold with the understanding that the publisher is not engaged in rendering legal, accounting, or other professional service. If legal advice or other expert assistance is required, the services of a competent professional person should be sought.

Various names used by companies to distinguish their software and other products can be claimed as trademarks. AMACOM uses such names throughout this book for editorial purposes only, with no intention of trademark violation. All such software or product names are in initial capital letters or ALL CAPITAL letters. Individual companies should be contacted for complete information regarding trademarks and registration.

Library of Congress Cataloging-in-Publication Data

VanGundy, Arthur B.
    Getting to innovation : how asking the right questions generates the great ideas your company needs / Arthur B. VanGundy.
        p.   cm.
    Includes bibliographical references and index.
    ISBN-13: 978-0-8144-0898-8 (hardcover)
    ISBN-10: 0-8144-0898-2 (hardcover)
    1. Creative ability in business.   2. Creative thinking.   3. Organizational change.
4. Problem solving.   I. Title.

    HD53.V359   2007
    658.4'063—dc22   2007000392

Printing number 7 8 5 8 9 7
10   9   8   7   6   5   4   3   2   1

To my daughters, Sarah and Laura,
and my granddaughter, Chloe,
and
in memory of my parents,
Arthur B. VanGundy, M.D.,
and Sarajane Miesse VanGundy

Contents

Preface

Anyone who has followed management trends for the past forty or so years knows that there always seems to be the so-called Next Big Thing. In the 1950s, basic brainstorming was the rage, with countless articles written about it, some good and some not so good—for example, "brainstorming is nothing more than cerebral popcorn!" In the 1960s and early 1970s, sensitivity groups (or "T-groups") were in vogue. Group leader gurus would "lead" groups of managers by *not* leading. That is, after some broad, brief opening remarks, they would silently sit there waiting for someone in the group to say something. After that, they mostly would just facilitate and try to clarify. Supposedly, the "inner manager" somehow would emerge. Again, more research would follow with inconclusive findings. The 1980s ushered in the age of the quality movement (although some would maintain it began earlier) with the implementation of quality control, quality circles, Kaizen, Six Sigma, and other related approaches for enhancing worker performance.

Although the quality movement still exists, the 1990s saw the beginnings of corporate innovation as the next "it" approach, emerging from components of the emphasis on quality. Innovation has hit the corporate world with a force unknown in previous generations of business trends; however, profit-driven organizations have not been alone. Globalization of technology, media, cultures, commerce, and the new economy have created a momentum to forge new directions with customers and clients. Managers in profit, nonprofit, government, military, or educational institutions all now face the unenviable task of innovating like never before. The call has gone out for new ideas, fresh perspectives, and unique approaches to resolving old problems. In addition to the need for institutionalizing innovation processes, all organizations must confront the realities of how to define the challenges they face.

As my experience and knowledge base have grown over the years, it has become clear to me that the major challenges affecting organizations are not always those involving a lack of creativity. Unlike some thirty years ago, when I first started in the field, there now are hundreds of methods for idea generation available in increasing numbers of books and especially on the Internet. There are more creativity and innovation courses, training seminars, conferences, and consultants than ever before. Although idea execution remains a fertile area for future research and application, an even more important part of the innovation process requires urgent action: framing organizational innovation challenges at the outset of a project.

To define an organizational innovation challenge is to frame it. Perceptual frames create meaning that guides behavior. The purpose of this book is to demonstrate the art of framing innovation challenges to help organizations chart the best innovation courses possible. It is not another book on how to do strategic planning or how to institutionalize innovation; rather, it emphasizes the process of crafting organizational innovation challenges and organizing and mapping them conceptually to enable organizations to act strategically. Strategy provides context for this book, but it is not the primary content.

This book is organized into two parts, both based on the creative problem-solving process developed by Alex Osborn and Sidney Parnes.[1] The first part forms the core and looks at the essential elements involved in transforming organizations by using innovation challenges. It covers what is known as the "fuzzy front end" of the innovation process. The second part presents information on the middle and back end of innovation that involve, respectively, idea generation and implementation. These are activities to use after framing one or more challenges.

Part I discusses how to:

- View organizational innovation challenges in the context of strategy.

- Involve stakeholders in generating multiple strategic perspectives using "Q-banks" (questions) and "C-banks" (challenges).
- Use seven essential criteria to evaluate challenges.
- Write positioning and rationale statements for each challenge.
- Link together multiple objectives in priority frameworks.
- Create visual, conceptual maps of these frameworks.
- Plan and conduct organizational innovation challenges.

Chapter 1 presents an overview of the concept of innovation framing and its importance in organizations. Specifically, the point is made that generating great ideas for the *wrong* challenge can be even worse than generating mediocre ideas for the *right* problem. Most successful organizations have learned to devote resources to reframing their challenges in order to align better with and achieve their strategic objectives. One way is to test assumptions about organizational objectives and decide what order in which to achieve challenges.

Chapter 2 provides a look at how organizations should initiate innovation challenges by generating and answering questions. Q-banks are used to gather a large number of important questions about an organization to provide the context for innovation efforts. They also are designed to involve key stakeholders in the process by requesting questions and responses from a diverse population and providing all with feedback from the other participants. This is a planned effort involving strategic due diligence—that is, stakeholders are required to surface key assumptions they may be making and to test them for validity by comparing perceptions with each other. A list of more than one hundred sample questions is presented, involving areas such as core competencies, customers, the company as a brand, competitive positioning, markets, and overall goals.

Chapter 3 provides an overview of the challenge bank ("C-bank") process. C-banks build on the results of Q-banks. That is, they use stakeholder responses to the final Q-bank challenge(s) to generate a list of potential innovation challenge solutions. This process is similar to that of Q-banks, in that stakeholders also are involved in one or more rounds—the focus, instead, is on ideas and not challenges.

Chapter 4 discusses how to write (frame) innovation challenge questions. Once an organization has done its due diligence and analyzed responses from the Q-bank and other sources, the results can be used to generate lists of potential innovation challenge questions. This chapter describes how to use this information to frame challenge questions so that they are best suited for productive idea generation. An important part of this chapter is a discussion of the seven criteria for effective challenges. The use of positioning elements also is described in terms of how they can position a challenge in the minds of those generating ideas. Numerous case studies are used to illustrate this process. Finally, this chapter presents more than one hundred "preframed" challenges, all of which can be applied directly to a variety of organizational strategic topics. They also can serve as examples for creating challenges for specific situations and are grouped by application area—for example, customers, products/services, branding/marketing, and human resources.

Chapter 5 capitalizes on the fact that many people are visual thinkers who can understand complex relationships among conceptual variables better if they are presented graphically. This chapter describes how to draw manually or use computer software programs to create cognitive maps of innovation variables and their interrelationships. Step-by-step instructions are provided to guide the reader in creating these visual roadmaps of innovation challenges. Business examples also are used to illustrate how to map multiple challenges.

The focus of Chapter 6 is on how to plan and conduct innovation challenges within organizations, governments, and associations. Topics range from integrating challenges with strategy; selecting who to include; setting up internal communications; using employees, experts, and consumers for divergent input; and taking advantage of enterprise software for the systematic collection and evaluation of ideas. Numerous examples of previous innovation challenge competitions in a variety of sectors are provided.

Part II looks at how to:

- Use idea management and creativity software.
- Generate creative ideas using specific individual and group techniques.

- Design and facilitate brainstorming retreats.

- Evaluate and select the best ideas systematically.

- Anticipate implementation obstacles.

- Create action plans to implement ideas.

Part II begins with Chapter 7, "Idea Management and Creativity Software." In this chapter, readers will find a description of major computer programs designed to process vast quantities of ideas plus some directed at facilitating the creative problem-solving process. After reading these descriptions, readers will be able to make more informed decisions as to which idea management programs are best suited for their needs. Readers will be able to compare the unique features of various programs and how they can benefit users.

Chapter 8 presents a "A Crash Course in Generating Creative Ideas: Individual Methods." There exist at least two hundred formal methods for structuring idea generation by individuals and groups. This chapter presents a step-by-step description of numerous idea generation methods, including the author's top ten list of idea generation techniques and examples of how to use these techniques, including sample ideas when appropriate.

Chapter 9 provides "A Crash Course in Generating Creative Ideas: Group Methods." Brainstorming and brainwriting are discussed briefly as categories of group methods along with their advantages and disadvantages. The remainder of the chapter focuses on step-by-step descriptions of eight brainstorming and eight brainwriting methods.

Chapter 10 presents tips for designing and facilitating brainstorming retreats. The two keys to successful idea generation are preparation prior to a brainstorming session and the use of a process structured sufficiently to ensure a constant stream of ideas. This chapter describes how to conduct the research needed to generate the stimuli used to trigger ideas and how to create a structured, yet flexible agenda. There is also a list of tips for facilitating the process, as well as other helpful hints.

Chapter 11 looks at how to evaluate and select ideas once they have been generated. The purpose of this chapter is to show how hundreds of ideas can be reduced in number through a process of systematic evaluation and selection. Several techniques are described for choosing ideas in a step-by-step format.

The best ideas are of little value without an effective implementation plan. To help structure this process, Chapter 12 presents several techniques, including approaches involving weighted decision criteria, a multistage model, and potential problem analysis. General guidelines for ensuring successful implementation also are provided.

NOTE

1. Alex F. Osborn, *Applied Imagination,* 3rd ed. (New York: Scribner's, 1963); Sidney J. Parnes, *Creative Behavior Guidebook* (New York: Scribner's, 1967).

Acknowledgments

I first must note that I am indebted to all those before me who laid the groundwork for the creative problem-solving process, especially Alex Osborn and Sidney Parnes, who also founded the Creative Education Foundation and the annual Creative Problem Solving Institute. I would like to thank Victoria Cliche, executive director of the Creative Education Foundation, for her many helpful comments. I would also like to acknowledge the organizations I worked with on framing challenges over the past years. I especially appreciate the support and input I have received from Anil Rathi and Kenton Williams of Idea Crossing, Mark Turrell of Imaginatik, and Jeffrey Baumgartner of JPB in Belgium. I would like to thank Nancy Grande for her dedicated work in helping me edit the manuscript (P.S., you, too, Panda!). I would like to express my deep appreciation to AMACOM acquisitions editor Adrienne Hickey, whom I now have had the pleasure of working with on another book. Finally, I would like to thank Erika Spelman for her copyediting expertise.

PART I

The Frame Game

As discussed in the preface, this book contains two parts. The first part represents the primary focus of the book: the process of framing innovation challenges to understand better where to allocate resources for generating ideas. Some describe this as the "fuzzy front end" of the innovation process.

Part I will discuss the organizational context of how assumptions organizations make about challenges can impact the success of their innovation efforts. Six chapters will describe how to involve stakeholders in question banks (Q-banks) and challenge banks (C-banks) to identify strategic areas requiring innovation. Other chapters in this part will focus on the essential criteria needed to evaluate potential challenges, how to write challenge briefs, ways to create conceptual maps depicting relationships between challenges, and how to plan for and conduct innovation challenges.

Framing Innovation Framing:
An Overview

We are creatures of habit. We sometimes resist change just because it is change. It is easier just to stay within our comfort zones.

"THAT'S THE WAY WE'VE ALWAYS DONE IT!"

What company wouldn't want to reduce its costs, save its customers time, and increase its customer satisfaction, all while growing its business? Well, it turns out that many companies act as if they do not! Instead, they keep doing things the way they always have, even though that might not work for them or their customers. They do it because that's the way they always have done it. And, perhaps, because that is how other companies in their industry have always done it. We are creatures of habit. When an employee asks why something can't be done, the patented response often is: "Because that's how we've *always* done things!" It is difficult to argue with logic like that!

Where has all the innovation gone? It has disappeared into black holes of fear and uncertainty, swirling and meandering about, seemingly without bounds. It has been reigned in, flipped over, tied up, and wrapped into neat little packages of meaning that present happy corporate faces to the outside world, while struggling and suffering internally and for shareholders. It has disappeared in some companies that seem locked into conventional ways of doing business, in spite of undesirable results. Just as some people seem to persist in behaviors that produce unproductive outcomes, so do some organizations. It is as if they cannot help themselves.

These companies lock themselves into self-created perceptual "frames" that prevent them from innovating. There is a certain degree of comfort in operating within familiar, comfortable frames. Such frames reduce uncertainty by establishing known boundaries that also help to create meaning for us and, therefore, become our realities. Yet, it is this same sense of knowledge and meaning that presents the biggest obstacles to change and innovation.

"LET'S TRY SOMETHING DIFFERENT!"

The fact is that companies *can* help themselves, but they first must make a conscious choice to change the status quo. This is exactly what more companies now are choosing to do. For instance, Fujitsu decided to do away with the accepted industry model of customer service. Although the company wants to reduce costs, save its customers time, increase customer service, and achieve growth, it figured out that things would have to change—that it would have to reframe the conventional model of doing business in its industry.

James Womack, author of *Lean Solutions: How Companies and Customers Can Create Value and Wealth Together,* notes that Fujitsu figured out a win-win way to change the conventional model of customer help lines. This part of customer relationship management (CRM) represents one of the outsourced business processes that have been the subject of increased attention in recent years. As used by most companies, help lines seem to stand between companies and their customers. For some companies, help lines appear to serve as the means to get rid of customers instead of retaining and acquiring new ones. The traditional help line frame is one in which operators are paid a flat rate for every complaint they handle. The faster they can get a customer off the line, the more money the operators can make and the higher the margins for the companies. So, the incentive is very clear for operators: The more customer complaints you field, the more money you will make.

One thing left out of this equation is the lack of any incentive to *reduce* the actual number of complaints. After all, wouldn't such a frame be counterproductive? Fujitsu analyzed this model and decided that most customers would rather not need to call a help line at all. An astonishing conclusion, isn't it!

So, the company contacted its customers (Telcom and large computer providers) and told them that it would rather be paid by the potential number of complaints instead of the number actually handled. And, Fujitsu said that it would prefer to focus on the vendors' problems than those of the vendors' customers. In other words, the company wanted to learn *why* customers even called and then figure out a way to eliminate the need to do so altogether.

Fujitsu reframed customer service by training representatives to work with customers to determine why their problems arose and who would be the best people to resolve them. In addition, the company decided to create a positive experience by using its help lines to tell customers about product features they might not be aware of or to ask them what else they would like in a product or service. One immediate result was many new product ideas. And new ideas, of course, often translate into innovation and higher profit margins.

Now, if you proposed this model to some managers, they immediately would point out how much more expensive this approach would be. (Besides, if they haven't been doing things that way, then how could it even be considered!) What they might overlook, however, is the potential long-term impact on the bottom line. In the case of Fujitsu, costs gradually decreased as the number of calls declined. The turnover of service reps was only about 8 percent, compared with an industry average of around 40 percent. So, the company saved consumers time, increased customer satisfaction, reduced costs, and increased the company's growth rate—all by reframing the conventional model.

THE PARADOX OF PARADOX

One thing Fijitsu did was to employ paradox to redefine a basic business process. This seems to be a characteristic of many organizations perceived as being innovative: When faced with challenges, they have the ability to reframe them into new, more productive and innovative ones. In essence, they have learned the power of testing all assumptions, including even the relatively simple and trivial ones often taken for granted. As Douglas Adams, the creator of *The Hitchhiker's Guide to the Universe*, said: "The hardest assumption to challenge is the one you don't even know you're making."

A *paradox* can be defined roughly as any statement that appears to be true while also having the ability to be false—in other words, a contradiction. Seemingly contradictory statements have been the basis for much inventive thinking. (In fact, an entire industry based on perceptual contradictions has been developed based on TRIZ—a Russian acronym known as the Theory of Inventive Problem Solving.) Contradictions help us test any assumptions we make, especially with respect to conventional thought patterns. For instance, consider what has been accepted as true in the automobile insurance industry: high prices, mediocre service, and complex bureaucratic procedures. This was the norm until Ohio-based Progressive Casualty Insurance Company tested these assumptions.

Instead of doing business in lockstep with the major companies, Progressive CEO Peter Lewis noted that the company would do things differently and offer faster claims adjustments, work on weekends, and—gasp!—offer price comparisons with its competition! Although the auto insurance industry had been in the red over the last five or so years, Progressive increased its revenue more than 36 percent—a rate six times that of the industry.

Other examples of *frame busting* abound in academic and popular literature.

• When Steve Jobs returned to Apple Computer as it was spiraling downward, he started using the tagline, "Think Different!" [sic] and then tested assumptions about what a computer was supposed to look like. More recently, he illustrated the power of reframes by completely upending the traditional model of how music is sold. With iTunes, consumers now can download music, videos of television shows, and movies.

• Michael Dell of Dell Computer contradicted the old frame of computers being high tech, involving expensive research and development (R&D), and being high-margin products sold in stores. Among other things, he created the market leader in online sales of laptops that were sold directly to the consumer, instead of through a third-party vendor, with an emphasis on volume and purchasing efficiency.

• Plantronics tested convention by increasing collaboration between engineers and designers. Instead of designers having to create products after engineers produced the technology, management decided to involve the designers throughout the process. This way, designers no longer needed to focus on how to overcome technical obstacles and could devote their attention to meeting consumer needs. The result was a 31 percent return on invested capital.

• In a now infamous decision, Coca-Cola executives decided to rebrand Coke as a sweeter beverage known as New Coke. Based on blindfolded consumer focus groups who compared sips of old and new coke, the company concluded that consumers would prefer New Coke and then launched it, with disastrous results. Coca-Cola then reframed its perceptions and retreated by bringing back Classic Coke. So, it initially appeared that consumers preferred a sweeter drink, but the contradiction was that they also did *not* prefer a sweeter beverage. This contradiction arose because the market tests did not reflect how people actually drink Coke: They don't wear blindfolds and they take more than one sip. Thus, they liked it but they didn't like it—a logical contradiction!

• In the early 2000s, McDonald's Corporation realized that its previous, successful frame of "one size fits all" was no longer effective as consumers began demanding healthier foods. By recognizing consumer trends in this area and reemphasizing service, McDonald's experienced a 10 percent increase in in-store sales in the first half of 2004 and an 11 percent decrease in complaints.

• A few years ago, Sirkorsky Aircraft Company was asked to bid on a contract for the *Air Force One* presidential helicopter, a contract the company had held for about fifty years at the time. Any business relationship that has lasted that long constitutes a frame about future expectations. Perhaps the company used thinking such as, "We've had our contract renewed over half a century and we'll always have it." The company also might have assumed that its product's features would remain constant and viable as seen by its customers—for example, helicopter size, time to market, and communications technology. In fact, the Sirkorsky president at the time supposedly said he would jump out of a flying helicopter if the company didn't get the contract. Instead, the Lockheed Martin Corporation won a six-year, $6.1 billion contract. (No word yet on the helicopter jumping!)

IDEAS IN SEARCH OF PROBLEMS

Many organizations practice what I call "horse-before-the-cart innovation." They rush into generating ideas on how to become more innovative before they clearly have identified and articulated the most productive challenges. We have been trained and conditioned to gloss over the specifics of our challenges. As a result, we often make implicit assumptions as to the exact nature of our challenges and their priority with respect to other challenges. And then we jump right into generating ideas.

Most of us tend to be more solution minded than problem minded, as industrial psychologist Norman R. Maier used to note. Although lip service may be given about the need to "define the problem," relatively few people do it well. The very best ideas to the most poorly defined problem might as well not even exist. Anyone can have an exciting brainstorming session with hundreds of ideas. Frequently neglected, however, is devoting as much time and attention to clearly defining a "presented" challenge as is given to idea generation. As famed photographer Ansel Adams said, "There is nothing worse than a brilliant image of a fuzzy concept."[1]

Creativity consultant and business professor Chris Barlow, in discussing the role of redefining problems for brainstorming, observes that idea quantity is more likely when "deliberate divergence" is used as a way to define problems. That is, defining problems should have far greater priority than we give it in relation to generating ideas. The ideas will come if we first consider more options for problem definitions.[2]

We frequently expend a lot of time and energy using our creativity to generate ideas when we first should devote that time and energy to generating challenge statements to guide ideation. Instead, we often assume that we know what the problem is and just dive into brainstorming sessions. Why? Because that is what we have learned from experience and conditioning. It doesn't matter if research shows that we can generate significantly more ideas by taking the time to define a challenge and then deferring judgment during idea generation. What appear to matter more are the choices we make to persist in doing the same things the same ways we always have done them!

As a result, what often happens in a lot of brainstorming sessions is that ideas are tossed out that do not seem to make sense. The reason is not always that they are bad ideas; rather, the ideas different people think of may be based on varying assumptions as to what the "real" challenge is. Perhaps you have been in such a session where—after generating ideas for a while—someone says something like, "So, now exactly *what* is our problem?" Even groups that start with apparently explicit challenges may choose one so ambiguous as to complicate things even further. You just can't expect to generate useful ideas if you don't start with a clear-cut challenge question.

Undoubtedly, many organizations also may use such an approach to innovation initiatives. For instance, corporate managers often frame challenges based mostly on broad, strategic outcome objectives—for example, profitability or market share—along with some secondary goals such as generating new products and enhancing marketing and branding.

The best route to achieving any of these objectives is *not* to merely generate ideas but to first construct tactical maps to lay out the strategic terrain for all objectives. The old saying still holds true: "If you don't know where you want to go, any road will take you there." It also is true that even if you think you know where you want to go—an often costly, unchallenged assumption—you must create a map of goals to achieve along the way. These maps frequently are based on the premise that the objectives are stated clearly, known, and understood—often an erroneous assumption.

Most organizations do a good job of collecting research on how and where to innovate. However, Doblin, Inc. estimated in late 2005 that only about 4.5 percent of innovation initiatives succeed! One reason might be due to poorly framed innovation challenges. Unfortunately, there still are few resources on how to frame challenges for ideation. Before looking at the process of framing challenges, however, it is important to think first about the general concept of perceptual framing.

"FRAMING" FRAMING

When you have finished reading this sentence, you will have been "framed." The sentence conveyed some form of meaning to you by creating intentional or unintentional cognitive boundaries. What you understood at the time is what you chose to think. What you understand now may be completely different because this additional information created a potential "reframe" for you. And, right now, your frame may be different again, ad infinitum.

There is a considerable amount of research on framing, most of which deals with how frames can be used to send messages designed to influence others. According to Schoemaker and Russo, there are the following three types of frames:

1. Problem frames used to generate ideas
2. Decision frames to make choices
3. Thinking frames involving deep mental structures and prior experience

This book will focus on problem frames as they are used to clarify strategic challenges for generating ideas and creating innovative solutions to organizational challenges.

Failing to devote attention to how we frame innovation is a failure to test assumptions and, more than likely, adopt less than optimal perceptual frames. How we see and define things determines how we behave. If we do a less-than-adequate job of framing a problematic situation, we are less likely to resolve it. Thus, the more we understand about the general nature of frames, the better challenge solvers we will become.

According to Robert M. Entman, professor and head of communication at North Carolina State University, "To frame is to select some aspects of perceived reality and make them more salient in the communicating text, in such a way as to promote a particular problem definition, causal interpretation, moral evaluation and/or treatment recommendation for the item described."[3] According to Russo and Schoemaker, frames in the context of management are "mental structures that simplify and guide our understanding of complex reality—[and] force us to view the world from a particular and limited perspective."[4]

My definition of a frame aligns partially with these two. I define *frames* as "experience-based sets of cognitive boundaries we construct that define a given situation and create meaning." A perceptual frame is a fluid, dynamic, ever-evolving boundary of meaning, inference, and assumptions. As it morphs, twists, and turns, it alters our perceptions of what we have experienced, what we are experiencing at a given time, and shapes the assumptions we make. Thus, a frame is our reality at any given moment. It also can determine how we are likely to view similar situations in the future.

Frames help us to understand and to focus our thinking, thereby reducing uncertainty and enhancing human communication. Framing also is an exclusionary process in which we consciously or subconsciously include or emphasize some information at the expense of other information. That is, an ideal framing process helps us to deconstruct perceived ambiguous situations and clarify and create focus so we can achieve our objectives—especially our strategic ones.

There is a lot of research on how people will perceive identical situations differently, depending on how they are framed. For instance, research suggests that people given a preference for meat that was 75 percent lean versus meat that was 25 percent fat invariably chose the former, even though the choices were identical! This reaction describes how people often tend to assign more importance to negative information than positive. Such frames also have been found to attract more attention. Another type of perceptual framing involves attempts to persuade others to think a certain way or do certain things. Political advertising and public relations are two common examples of this type of framing.

Most attempts at classifying frames represent *prescriptive* or persuasive framing in that there is a conscious intention to get us to align our thinking with a specific point of view—to tell us how we should think. Persuasive framing, however, is not the only kind. There also is *descriptive* framing (also known as "semantic framing"), although it receives much less attention than the persuasive variety. In descriptive framing, the only intention is to clarify and make salient specific components of a challenge so that it might be resolved more easily. Descriptive framing, in contrast, attempts to generate alternate phrasing terms. Thus, the framing process involves describing what *is* instead of what *should be*.

Clarification of current and desired perceptual states, along with how to close the gap between the two, is the basis of all problem solving. Challenges are created when we perceive a gap between these states; challenge solving, then, is the process we then use to make the *is* like the *should be*—that is, we make a conscious attempt to transform an existing state into an ideal one using innovative means. So, if you are dissatisfied with your current error rate in processing customer claims—thus, believing it to be less than you desire—you would resolve this challenge by using activities to close the gap.

The ultimate goal of innovation framing is to state a challenge in such a way that it will produce the most innovative, optimal results. In this instance, there is no intention to persuade someone how to think; rather, the focus is on clarifying some desired innovation challenge involving perceptions of current and desired states. Another example would be increasing brand awareness about a new line of products. By implication, the brand awareness currently is lower than desired; the desired level then would be some predetermined level of measurable awareness. In this case, the frame might be stated as: "How might we increase the brand awareness of our X line of new products?" (Measurement of the degree of change would be an evaluation criterion and should not be part of the challenge. This concept will be discussed more fully in Chapter 4.)

Such a statement is relatively simple and direct, it doesn't obscure intent with criteria, and it clearly identifies the objective. Contrast the statement with the following modified real-life example from a major, global corporation: "How might we create state-of-the-art solutions to ongoing attacks that jeopardize endangered species more than other attacks while satisfying key stakeholders?" Or this one from a large government organization: "How might we create a new product/service/process or an enhancement to an existing product/service/process that will increase revenue involving current/new customers and may involve developing new marketing/partnership opportunities?" Both of these statements are overly complicated, ambiguous and contain unnecessary and confusing criteria. The need, then, is to deconstruct them so that they can be used for productive idea generation and achieve strategic objectives.

THE IMPORTANCE OF FRAMING INNOVATION STRATEGICALLY

Although most companies invest heavily in R&D, the effects on bottom-line innovation are questionable. As noted previously, the success rate of innovation initiatives across all industries is only 4.5 percent. It is unlikely that this low rate is due to a lack of innovation processes or access to intellectual capital. Instead, poorly framed innovation challenges might contribute toward this low success rate.

The August 2005 issue of *Training & Development* magazine published an article on "Strategy Blockers"[5] as seen by executives, vice presidents or managers, and directors. They were asked, "What gets in the way of strategy execution for top leaders?" The most frequent obstacle was "the past and habits" (35 percent). This seems to imply that rigid perceptual frames can block the execution of strategic plans.

A failure to frame and reframe strategically undoubtedly has multiple causes, such as inaccurate market data, tradition, the organizational culture, market uncertainties, managerial apathy, or an inability to multitask in a rapidly changing environment. Sometimes we are so busy that it's just easier to do nothing and stay on the original course, assuming the best will happen. Thus, we may keep cranking out ideas to maintain the current strategic direction without considering if the direction is correct.

It also is possible, however, that one cause may be the inability to ask the right questions. As nineteenth-century author G. K. Chesterton noted, "It isn't that they can't see the solution. It is that they can't see the problem." It very well may be that innovation fails far more often due to faulty problem framing than faulty idea generation or execution. Most of us have been conditioned to accept a problem as given and immediately jump into a search for solutions.

Renowned management theorist Ian Mitroff notes that it is better to solve the right problem incorrectly than the wrong problem correctly. At least you would be working toward the "correct" end state. And, in an article from *Innovation Tools* electronic newsletter, Imaginatik CEO, Mark Turrell, observes that in companies with large revenue growth gaps, it is especially important that they "invest effort before the front-end stage of innovation to identify opportunities and *frame their initiatives*"[6] (italics added).

The strategic challenges top management devises guide ideation and implementation. Starting in the wrong direction almost guarantees failure. Too often, however, we tend to assume we know what the "real" problem is without testing all the potential assumptions involved. *Business 2.0* magazine asked management guru Peter Drucker, "What is it that executives never seem to learn?" His reply was that ". . . one does not begin with answers. One begins by asking, 'What are our questions?'"[7] With a focus on ideas, many managers are more likely to lock onto the first problem definition and stick with it, often with disappointing results.

It is very easy to acknowledge this, but very difficult to take the time to frame challenges carefully. *Getting to Innovation* will help structure the questioning process and make it easier to design strategic innovation frameworks. A review of unsuccessful business frames reveals symptoms of an underlying inability to test assumptions and knowledge of how to frame situations productively—and competitively. Numerous examples exist of how some companies are able to reframe a market and become more competitive. Some of those companies have been described previously in this chapter, but here a few more:

As noted previously, when Michael Dell started his computer company, the prevailing frame was that computers were high tech, involved expensive R&D, and were high-margin, low-volume products. He reframed these assumptions by using low-tech, minimal R&D, and low-margin but high-volume products. He also took advantage of Internet-only sales and soon captured market share for personal computers.

Even strategic frames that were previously successful need tweaking as conditions change. For instance, in the past decade, General Electric's growth under Jack Welch was reported as 5 percent based on a strategic focus on cost cutting, increased efficiency, continuous improvement, and similar performance-based objectives. Under new CEO Jeffy Immelt, GE's profits grew by 24 percent based, in part, on the concept of reframing the company's energy business model from gas turbines to wind and solar power. Also consider IBM, once the IT technological leader. It now is embarking on a new frame involving a transition from technology to being the leader in business process outsourcing. So, it is just as important to identify frames that do not work as it is frames that do.

Perhaps the most compelling case for framing innovation was made by IBM CEO Samuel J. Palmisano in an interview with *Business Week* magazine about an IBM survey of CEOs of top companies and government leaders. A focus on business model innovation was at the top of the list of concerns by the respondents. According to Palmisano, an increasingly competitive environment increases the need to identify and deal with challenges in business models. In fact, he notes that such challenges can help jump-start organizational innovation. Technological advances, such as infinite computing capacity, have created new opportunities to address new challenges. For instance, IBM now is trying to become more global, pushing down decision making, and trying to develop new ways to collaborate with external groups. Thus, a major challenge is how to foster such collaboration within an organization and between it and other organizations.

None of this should be surprising to observers of corporate performance. Yet, the struggle continues for organizations to achieve corporate objectives, to increase market share and shareholder value, and to defend the bottom line in a complex and changing environment. The answer put forth by this book is not more ideas. The answer, instead, is *more questions*—especially the *right questions*, and how to generate and fit them together into meaningful, conceptual frameworks.

This book is designed to serve as a user's guide for testing organizational assumptions and molding the results into clearly articulated networks of tactical and strategic recipes for creating value in organizations.

INNOVATION STRATEGY VS. TACTICS

In many ways, organizations are just like the individuals who work for them. For instance, in order to change, both must understand where they are, where they want to go, and how to get there. That is, they both must solve problems as discussed previously. Perhaps more important, they need to know *why* they want to get there. And, just as with individuals, organizations must have a strong impetus for change—a "felt need."

Any form of change requires a plan—a strategic plan—focused on the direction and type of change. This is an interesting dilemma because organizations often take the road they think is best. However, this road may be a dead end because they haven't done their due diligence to determine if it is the right road for them at that time. Or, they haven't properly diagnosed an issue and, instead, go with an intuitive decision leading to faulty outcomes.

Ideally, the *is* (the current state) and the *should be* (the desired state) will be identical; pragmatically, there may be discrepancies between the two as well as disagreements on how to close the gap. When a gap is perceived as being closed, then a challenge has been resolved. Of course, this assumes that these perceptions are in fact correct.

One way to resolve differences in perceptions is to focus on answering the "why?" question. Organizations, as with individuals, must be able to justify changing their strategic directions. Why do they want to stay on a certain course? Why would they want to change? In organizations, however, such justifications can be acutely difficult, considering all the complexities and uncertainties involved. The answers are never easy, but there never will be answers without proper questioning.

Strategic planning at the most hypothetical and basic level is relatively simple: It is just basic problem solving involving the transformation of perceived, current situations into perceived, desired goal states. Of course, strategy is also a lot more complicated. That is one paradox of process change: simple yet complex; complex yet simple. It all depends on how you frame it.

Strategic Objectives

Creating a strategy involves identifying strategic objectives—the activities that must be undertaken to achieve the overall strategy. The specific nature of these objectives is wholly dependent on an organization's mission and vision. That is, an organization's high-level, strategic objectives must be aligned with an overarching vision. Unfortunately, some CEOs read about the latest business or management fad and tell their people to implement it without considering their missions and visions.

Some sample strategic objectives include:

- Increasing profitability and shareholder value
- Increasing return on investment and size of market share
- Meeting customer needs
- Elevating the quality of customer service
- Improving product or service quality
- Enhancing growth rates

Depending on the situation, achieving each of these may require separate processes or multiple, coordinated processes of the transformations involved in turning current states into desired states.

However, it is not always a simple matter of making progress toward objectives. Many organizations may appear to have different priorities for different objectives. (Some senior leadership also may have different priorities, thus further complicating the mix.) For instance, profitability may be seen as being more important than customer service. Moreover, one objective (for example, customer service) may be perceived as functionally subordinate—that is, secondary—to another, such as profitability. Thus, one or more subordinate objectives, such as customer service, may need to be achieved before achieving one or more superordinate—that is, primary—objectives, such as profitability.

Tactics

Strategy provides the overall direction while tactics help to ensure progress along the way. In this case, a tactic is defined as a means to achieve specific objectives. Multiple tactics may be required to achieve one objective. The tactics used to achieve this objective may be the same, similar, or different from tactics used to achieve other objectives. And, progress about a strategy can be determined by the degree to which each tactical objective is achieved.

Strategy

A strategy consists of a series of tactical actions all oriented toward obtaining a strategic objective. Each tactical action has a specific objective that when added to other tactical actions will help achieve strategic objectives. Tactics exist only in dependence with strategic objectives. That is, they are employed for the primary purpose of achieving a desired goal state. They are not independent in that they are implemented within the framework of a larger, superordinate or primary goal in mind—for example, a core strategic objective such as profitability or shareholder return.

A good strategy should provide a big-picture vision of an organization. As Austrian philosopher Ludwig Wittgenstein noted, "Don't get involved in partial problems, but always take flight to where there is a free view over the whole *single* great problem, even if this view is still not a clear one."[8] The ultimate goal is attaining one or more primary objectives. Sometimes this is done best by achieving a series of lower-priority, less abstract secondary objectives.

INITIATING STRATEGIC DECISION MAKING

Research on organizational decision making indicates that most innovation initiatives are prompted by stakeholder "activists" who call attention to challenges facing their organizations. These stakeholders draw attention to issues requiring organizational awareness. Decision makers then must decide what, if any, action might be warranted. If it is decided that some action should be taken, a decision then is made to apply either a quick fix or a more innovative approach. For instance, if it is determined that the company's stock price is declining, top management members can determine the validity of stakeholder claims and act accordingly.

Stakeholders frame their perceptions in ways to convince management that some degree of attention is warranted, if only to justify paying attention and investigating a potential challenge in more depth. As a result, how successful they are in persuading management to pay attention to a challenge will depend on *how* they frame the challenge. Moreover, these frames may dictate the action taken to deal with challenges. One frame, for instance, might result in a decision to benchmark a potential threat or opportunity; others might trigger efforts to create innovative responses. To make such distinctions, some research suggests that organizational decision makers tend to rely on networks of key stakeholders for identifying needs and how to deal with them.

Innovation Frames

Once needs are recognized, organizations are *supposed* to act based on their strategic visions and planning processes. When they decide to innovate, they create strategic innovation frames to guide the innovation process. A primary obstacle, however, is how to state innovation challenges and link together objectives so that they will produce the strategic results desired.

Many organizations have a primary objective of achieving, sustaining, or increasing profitability. Achieving this objective, however, is not as simple as asking, "How might we achieve/sustain/increase profitability?" This challenge fails to incorporate other *secondary objectives* that could (and should) be linked together to increase profitability. In this case, secondary objectives are those that must be achieved before others can be. Conversely, *primary objectives* are those at a higher level of abstraction than subordinate objectives and are attained only by reaching one or more subordinate objectives.

For instance, from reading an analysis in *Business Week* of aerospace giant Boeing Company,[9] the company's challenges might be described as:

- Restoring the company's tarnished image
- Squeezing more profit out of existing businesses
- Increasing revenue
- Improving a toxic corporate culture
- Reducing bureaucracy
- Encouraging innovation
- Increasing financial growth

Each of these challenges could function as a single corporate objective worthy of innovative solutions. However, the question is: "How should these objectives be framed and linked together in the most productive way?" This is where framing strategic innovation can help.

Consider the conceptual map presented in Figure 1-1. These relationships illustrate that strategies are complex, interrelated decisions. Most objectives are nested within hierarchies of other, related objectives and multiple goals typically must be achieved to accomplish one primary goal. Once semantic, perceptual framing is placed in the context of organizations and their strategies, things can become quite complex.

As shown in Figure 1-1, there may be clusters of objectives linked together by commonalities. These clusters can exist at the same or on different levels. Also, they might be linked with other clusters within a hierarchical level or between levels. Moreover, not all objectives in a

FIGURE 1-1. *Boeing Company hypothetical challenge map.*

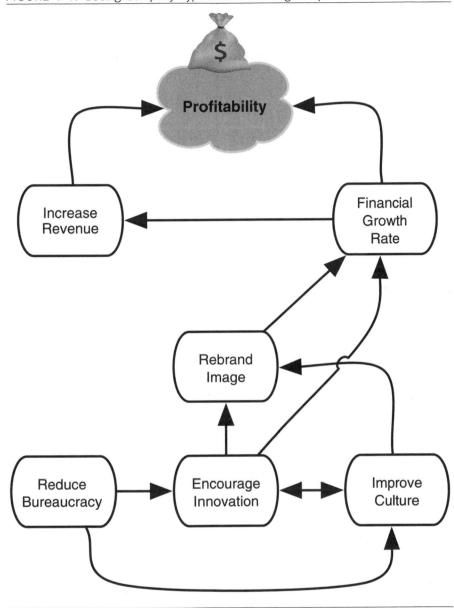

cluster may be linked across levels. For instance, Figure 1-1 shows en-couraging innovation at the fourth level linked with financial growth rate at the second level. How these objectives are linked may depend on a variety of factors, especially the competitive environment within different industries.

Conceptual Framing Maps

Visual diagrams of knowledge and organizational strategy have been around for some time, especially from the perspective of cognitive map-ping. For instance, most cognitive strategy maps draw on what is known as *personal construct theory*. It suggests that we understand our environments by organizing concepts that are relevant to a specific en-vironment. Some researchers who interviewed senior managers in the grocery store industry observed that they tended to create hierarchies of their competitive environments based on degrees of abstraction. That is, some environments are seen as broader and more encompass-ing than others. For instance, increasing profit might be viewed as more abstract than reducing employee absenteeism.

To some extent, Figure 1-1 parallels the more encompassing and elaborated strategy mapping process used with the balanced scorecard (BSC) approach of business strategy consultants Kaplan and Norton. They maintain that traditional strategic planning is based too much on historical financial data and not enough on the intangibles present in corporations. To increase performance, organizations first should create a strategy map consisting of the following four value-creating processes or perspectives:

1. Financial
2. Customer
3. Internal processes
4. Learning/growth

These maps then are used to translate an organization's vision and mission statements into effective performance. Basic strategy maps can involve thirty or more components, all of which must be aligned with each other and monitored over time.

The hypothetical Boeing objectives shown in Figure 1-1 correspond roughly with the top three BSC perspectives. Thus, "Profitability," "Increase Revenue," and "Financial Growth Rate" represent financial perspectives involving long-term shareholder value. (These also might be labeled as high-level, primary objectives.) Next is the customer perspective of rebranding the corporate image. This would be subordinate to the financial perspective because rebranding could help increase the financial growth rate. Finally, "Reduce Bureaucracy," "Encourage Innovation," and "Improve Culture" all reside at the internal process perspective. Although these three objectives obviously are quite ambitious, they still are attainable—or, at least, worthy of attention.

As appealing as the BSC approach may be, there might be situations in which it may not be as useful when compared with informal conceptual strategy mapping. For instance, it may be deemed too expensive for some organizations, too complicated, or just plain overwhelming. It also may conflict with idiosyncratic organizational barriers such as turf protection, competition for scarce resources, and resistance to broadscale change.

Weaknesses, in addition to the previous hindrances, include assumptions about rationality—shared by most behavioral/cognitive approaches—and the lack of integration opportunities within the *internal processes perspective*—for example, links between product development, operations management, and customer management. Along these lines, others argue convincingly for the adoption of *value creation maps* that incorporate interdependencies between tangible and intangible assets.

In spite of any shortcomings, BSC and strategy maps remain useful tools for strategic planning, systemwide change, and performance management enhancement. They just are not the major focus of this book. However, it is important to be aware of their existence. For instance, "Learning and Growth," the lowest-level BSC perspective, is not represented in Figure 1-1 because it is hypothetical and limited just to the topics in the article about Boeing. Other objectives also are not represented that should be in a comprehensive strategy.

Instead, the focus of this book is more on clusters of challenges that organizations perceive as salient at a specific point in time. Moreover, most of the focus is on the internal processes perspective; that is, framing that is need-driven at a particular time—and not necessarily framed in the context of more encompassing variables. Finally, this book's primary goal is to describe how to state (or frame) individual challenges and then link them together as frameworks to guide segments of innovation initiatives. Thus, the emphasis on strategy maps provides the strategic terrain needed to frame challenges productively.

FRAMING INNOVATION CHALLENGES

Even if you are not concerned with strategic innovation, the need still exists to frame challenges for productive idea generation. Innovation challenges at any organizational level should be relatively open-ended and target an explicit objective such as increasing product sales. However, there must be an appropriate, targeted focus. I once was asked to facilitate a brainstorming session faced with the following challenge: "How can we generate ideas for new floor-cleaning products?" Well, one answer is to use many idea generation techniques! Obviously, that is not the challenge. The umbrella objective may be to produce a lot of floor-cleaning products, but the means for doing this should be targeted at specific, subordinate challenges.

To illustrate, consider the floor-cleaning products example further. A common way to state challenges is to begin with the phrase, "How might we . . . ?" This provides a prompt for open-ended idea generation. It then is necessary to deconstruct the challenge into its parts, simply by asking basic questions representing potential subordinate objectives, such as the following:

- "What is involved in cleaning floors?"
- "What do people dislike about it?"
- "How often should floors be cleaned?"
- "In what ways are current floor-care products ineffective?"

The answers to these and similar questions then can be used as triggers for specific challenge questions. For instance, answers to the previous questions might lead to challenges such as:

1. "How might we make it easier to dispense floor-cleaning products?"

2. "How might we reduce the amount of effort involved in scrubbing a floor?"

3. "How might we make floor cleaning more convenient?"

4. "How might we reduce the frequency with which floors need to be cleaned?"

5. "How might we increase the sanitizing effect of floor cleaning?"

The outcome is a list of potential challenges that might be organized according to their priority and the order in which they should be dealt. In this instance, reducing the frequency with which floors need to be cleaned would help make cleaning floors more convenient. Thus, the first challenge to address might be the former. Because other factors are involved in making floor cleaning convenient, other secondary challenges also might be considered—for example, making it easier to dispense cleaning products. Based just on these limited examples, challenges #1 and #4 both might make cleaning more convenient. Although these examples certainly are not strategic issues, the basic principle of ordering challenges according to whether they are primary or secondary is the same, regardless.

NOTES

1. *Simpson's Contemporary Quotations,* compiled by James B. Simpson (Boston: Houghton Mifflin Co., 1988).

2. Christopher M. Barlow, "Deliberate Insight in Team Creativity," *Journal of Creative Behavior,* 34 (2): 113.

3. Robert M. Entman, "Framing: Toward a Clarification of a Fractured Paradigm," *Journal of Communication,* 41: 55.

4. J. Edward Russo, and Paul J. H. Schoemaker, *Winning Decisions: Getting It Right the First Time* (New York: Currency/Doubleday, 2002), p. 22.

5. "Strategy Blockers," *Training & Development Magazine,* August 2005.

6. Mark Turrell, "How to Connect Corporate Objectives and Investment in Innovation," *Innovation Tools,* 2005. Retrieved November 25, 2005, from http://www.innovationtools.com/Articles/EnterpriseDetails.asp?a=202.

7. Thomas Mucha, "How to Ask the Right Questions," interview with Peter Drucker, *Business 2.0*, December 10, 2004.

8. Ludwig Wittgenstein, *Notebooks 1914–1916,* entry for November 1, 1914. *The Columbia World of Quotations* (New York: Columbia University Press, 1996).

9. "I Like a Challenge—And I've Got One," by W. James MacNerney, Jr., president and CEO of Boeing. In "News Analysis & Commentary," *Business Week,* July 18, 2005.

TWO

Question Banks:
Understanding the Strategic Terrain

Willy Sutton, a notorious U.S. bank robber in the 1930s, supposedly was asked once why he robbed banks. His answer was simple and to the point: "Because that's where the money is!" Strategic questioning banks (or "Q-banks") are used because asking questions is "where the answers are!" Simple as that. To understand just about anything, we need to ask questions—a basic component of natural human inquisitiveness. However, systematically asking questions in organizations—no matter how valid and useful they may be—often results in dissension and resistance among organizational stakeholders.

When Nike chairman Phillip Knight announced William D. Perez as his successor as CEO of Nike, one of the first things Perez did was undertake an extensive review of the company's strategies and operations. He hired Boston Consulting Group and asked all managers to reply to a detailed questionnaire. One manager commented that most of the longtime employees never had to answer such questions and that surveys just do not fit with Nike's culture. After all, if you ask questions, you might discover some answers you really don't want to know! Nevertheless, if a company is open to such questioning, the pay-off can be dramatic. The remainder of this chapter will look at Q-banks for collecting strategic information.

QUESTION BANKS (Q-BANKS)

Before innovation challenges can be created, organizations first must research the strategic terrain in terms of opportunity areas. This chapter will discuss how to use categories of strategic questions to collect data as the basis for generating innovation challenges. A focus on innovation is critical, and it should be guided by a systematic exploration of possible tactical and strategic options. This chapter will describe how to conduct Q-banks involving such areas as core competencies, customers, the company as a brand, competitive positioning, markets, and overall goals. Finally, this chapter will provide a list of sample questions for each of these areas and others as well.

At the outset of strategic planning, organizational members often are in different perceptual locations—that is, organizational stakeholders may differ in their perceptions regarding the organization's tactical and strategic positioning with respect to a number of variables. A Q-bank is a broad process that can help an organization take a hard look at itself and increase understanding about what it does and does not do, as well as what it should do. The outcome will be a sense of potential strategic directions to pursue and the beginning of a sense of priorities.

One way to do this is to conduct a question bank, which is simply a list of questions and responses developed to help draw out information, knowledge, and perceptions of value held by key organizational stakeholders. Although a lot of this information already may exist in various documents and in the form of tacit knowledge held by organizational members, not all stakeholders may hold the same perceptions; be aligned with this information; or, even more important, be aware of some information with strategic consequences. Moreover, some information, as well as perceptions, may be outdated. A strategic, perceptual realignment, however, may help get everyone on the same page cognitively as well as psychologically. Thus, it can be quite useful to collect such data periodically.

In general, Q-banks are especially useful when an organization:

- Is trying to find its direction
- Wants to affirm all or parts of its current strategic plan
- Lacks consensus about strategy among key stakeholders
- Wants to chart a new strategic course
- Is losing market share and competitive advantage

Q-banks are not, however, a substitute for conventional strategic planning. Many organizations already have collected the information needed, but they still could benefit by involving key stakeholders or by just updating old information. Planning is a process, not an end result. Q-banks are a logical choice to use during strategic framing because the responses contain the answers needed to generate organizational challenges. (Challenge banks, or "C-banks," are discussed in Chapter 3.) Innovative ideas then are generated from responses to the challenge questions.

A STEP-BY-STEP GUIDE TO Q-BANKS

Q-bank responses eventually are used as the basis for generating potential innovation challenge questions. The basic Q-bank process is shown in Figure 2-1. A preliminary list of questions first is generated, organized into categories—for example, customer service, marketing, or branding—and sent to stakeholders for their feedback and any new questions they might want to add. The data are analyzed and summarized by categories used in the Q-bank. Any responses not falling into the presented categories are organized into affinity groups (new categories with commonalities). These data are sent to the stakeholders again for a second round of additional responses or they are sent directly to the client with no feedback. A third, final round also can be conducted if desired and time is available. (A client is any individual or group for whom the questions are generated. Clients can be internal or external to organizations. For example, an HR manager might sponsor an innovation challenge for members of the R&D division in the same company.)

FIGURE 2-1. Basic Q-bank process.

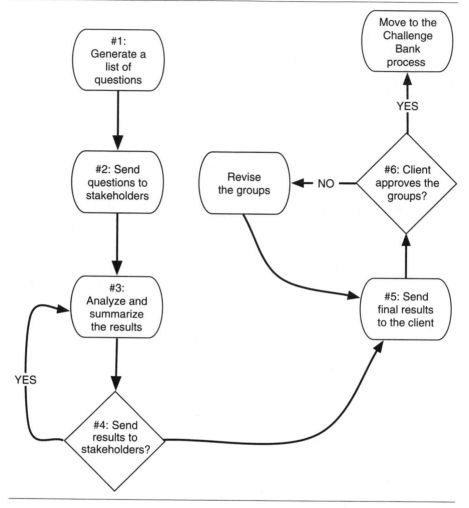

After all rounds are concluded, the results are sent to the client for approval and any suggested revisions. The list of responses then is used to generate a list of potential innovation challenge questions. Finally, this list is narrowed down to one or more challenges for ideation.

The specific Q-bank steps are as follows:

1. Generate a List of Questions

You can use all or part of the list presented next. Most organizations will not use all of the questions. Just delete those for which you already may have adequate intelligence. Make this decision judiciously, however, because it generally is better to retain questions than to delete them. Deleting one important question could make the difference between innovation success and failure. If you decide to use a relatively large number of questions, you might consider sending them out in batches with generous due dates. Advanced planning is always important in these matters.

Consider conducting a small pilot test to evaluate the quality of the questions—that is, their potential usefulness—and their readability for the intended audience. Send out a preliminary list to three or four people, including outsiders, whose opinions you respect and who would be willing to provide feedback. Ask them to do the following:

a. Make any revisions that might affect the intended meaning.

b. Suggest any additional questions that should be asked.

c. Consider the organization's priorities and select the top twenty most important questions.

Then, incorporate their suggestions as you see fit.

A typical Q-bank is implemented by sending out a list of generic questions to key stakeholders—usually around ten to thirty—although more could be used if necessary. This can be done via e-mail and might involve one or two rounds or possibly three. At the end of each round, the responses are collected, summarized (omitting duplicates), and resent to the participants for additional responses.

Of course, not all of these questions will apply to every organization. You will have to decide which ones are best for your situation. In general, you could leave out those for which you already have sufficient information (this assumes the information is valid). Also, before even starting a Q-bank, you might consider developing a preliminary list of questions and soliciting feedback from others, especially those less likely to be biased or emotionally involved in any potential issues reflected in the Q-bank. You also might want to solicit additional questions before initiating a Q-bank.

The ultimate goals of asking and answering these questions is to uncover potential areas to explore for applying creative thinking, increasing innovation, and creating value. So, the more questions asked and the more detailed the responses, the greater the likelihood that the information generated will result in the most important innovation challenge statements eventually being generated.

A Sample List of Q-Bank Questions

A list of sample questions follows. If there appears to be some duplication among the questions, that is intentional. Sometimes, phrasing a question a little differently can elicit richer, more robust responses capable of getting at core issues.[1]

Our Organization

1. What does our company do?
2. What are our core competencies?
3. What is our primary vision?
4. What is our primary mission?
5. What are our core values?
6. Who are our strategic partners? Why?

Our Customers

7. Who are our customers?
8. Whom would we like to have as customers?
9. Whom do we not want to have as customers?
10. What customer needs do we meet?
11. What customer needs should we meet that we aren't now?
12. Where are we positioned in the minds of our customers?
13. Where would we like to be positioned?
14. When should we reposition ourselves?
15. What value do our products, processes, and services provide our customers?

16. Why do our customers like us?

17. When don't our customers like us?

Our Brand

18. What is our brand?

19. What are our subbrands?

20. What values are associated with our brands?

21. How consistently do we transmit these values?

22. What is our brand equity?

23. How do we know that?

24. What are the components of our brand equity?

25. What extensions would be best for us to explore?

26. What is our aided brand awareness?

27. What is our unaided brand awareness?

28. Should we broaden or narrow our brand? Why?

Our Markets

29. What markets are we in?

30. What markets would we like to penetrate? Why?

31. What markets would we like to segment?

32. What do we know about current markets we are pursuing?

33. What do we need to know for success in these markets?

34. What markets are we overlooking?

35. What markets should we leave or reduce our presence in?

36. Are we exploiting market trends?

Our Goals

37. Where do we want to be in one, three, or five years?

38. If anything were possible, what should we do?

39. What do we want to do in the future that we aren't doing now?

40. What do we want to do differently?

41. How do we know when we achieve our goals?

42. Which goals, if any, should we change? Why?

43. How often do we revise our goals?

Our Competition

44. Who is our competition?

45. What are they doing right?

46. What are they doing that is not working?

47. What do we like about our competition?

48. What do our competitors' customers like about them?

49. What do our competitors' customers like and dislike about us?

50. Who has achieved the positive results we want?

51. How are they doing that?

52. How can we do that?

53. Who is doing something well in our industry or another?

54. What can we borrow from them (e.g., learning, tools, approaches)?

Our Innovation

55. How do we define innovation?

56. How do we measure it?

57. Do we have a strategic innovation process?

58. What is our innovation process?

59. How effective is it?

60. How do we know it is effective?

61. What are our top three to five barriers to innovation?

62. How might we overcome these barriers?

63. How do we reinforce/motivate innovation?

64. How do we reduce the motivation to innovate?

65. Do we have a way to generate and track new ideas?

66. How often do we generate new ideas?

67. What sources do we use for new ideas? Internal only? Customers? Vendors?

68. How well do we manage the ideas we generate? Why?

69. How might we manage them better?

70. At any one time, how many ideas do we have in our innovation pipeline?

71. Do we reevaluate promising ideas we once left on the shelf?

72. When do we innovate best? Why?

73. When do we innovate least well? Why?

74. How do we reward innovation?

75. How might we become more innovative?

76. What new products, processes, or services should we explore?

Our Financials

77. How is our stock valued in the market?

78. How do analysts value our stock?

79. How do we measure financial success?

80. What is our residual income?

81. How much do we invest in R&D?

82. How does our R&D investment compare with our major competitors'?

83. Should our R&D investment be smaller or larger?

84. Do we meet expected returns according to analysts' estimates?

85. What is our return on investment?

86. What are our net margins?

87. What is our market share?

88. What should be our market share?

89. What financial value do we place on our intellectual capital?

90. What are our projected revenues for the next quarter? The next year? The next five years?

Our Products

91. What products do we have that are successful?

92. Do we know why they have been successful?

93. What products do we have that are unsuccessful?

94. Do we know why they have been unsuccessful?

95. What extensions would be best for us to explore?

Our Processes

96. What are our core processes?

97. How do we measure process effectiveness and efficiency?

98. How well do we meet our goals for these processes?

99. When do our processes function best?

100. When do our processes function least well?

101. What are the greatest obstacles to internal process functioning?

102. What value do our processes add to us?

103. What value do our processes add to our shareholders?

104. What are our process inputs?

105. What are our process outputs?

106. What are our process outcomes?

107. What are our process throughputs?

108. How well do we track and manage new ideas?

109. How well do we convert new ideas into commercial innovations?

Our Shareholders

110. Who are our shareholders?

111. When are our shareholders happiest?

112. What upsets our shareholders?

113. How do we know when they are happy or upset?

114. Why are they happy or upset?

115. What value do we add to our shareholders?

2. Send Questions to Stakeholders

A stakeholder can be defined as a person with a financial, emotional, psychological, personal, or professional interest and investment in an organization and its success. This is a broader, more generic term than that of a shareholder, which typically applies to financial shareholders. Even though some shareholders also may have personal or professional stakes in an organization, all shareholders are, by definition, stakeholders. All stakeholders, however, are not necessarily shareholders since they may not have a financial stake. Stakeholders often (but not always) have a financial stake in addition to other areas of perceived ownership.

The first activity of this stage is to identify the stakeholders who should participate in a Q-bank. This can be a politically tricky decision, depending on the organization involved, a variety of environmental factors, resource availability, and the purpose of the Q-bank. In general, Q-banks should be framed in a positive light as having potential benefit for everyone, at least to some degree.

Once this list is generated, approved, and the participants agree to respond, the questions should be sent. This normally is done using e-mail, although questions can be posted on organizational Web sites, listservs, or Web sites such as www.surveymonkey.com. Another option is to use any of the numerous idea management enterprise software programs, such as www.imaginatik.com, www.jpb.com ("Jenni"), www.ideacrossing.com, or www.brainbankinc.com.

Emphasize that the focus now is only on answering the questions to use for evaluating challenges later on. Otherwise, some participants might submit challenge questions as well as ideas for resolving various challenges. If they do, analyze these data separately during the next stage.

3. Analyze and Summarize the Results

Ideally, question responses should be analyzed by two types of people: (1) the client and other internal stakeholders, and (2) external resource personnel such as subject matter experts. Two sets of eyes can help provide a more objective, yet knowledgeable interpretation of the results. So, an internal project manager might be teamed with an external consultant. However, this is not essential and might not always be practical. At a minimum, at least two internal people should review the results to ensure a more balanced, unbiased interpretation.

Duplicates should be eliminated, but ensure that a response is a true duplicate and not just similar or a variation in degree. Otherwise, potentially useful information might be discarded. This obviously can be a very subjective decision. Again, a second person could help make such decisions. If any of the responses are ambiguous, the project coordinator might contact whoever submitted the response and seek clarification.

This raises the issue of stakeholder anonymity. In general, it probably is best to present the Q-bank as being an anonymous process. You might emphasize that participants should feel free to provide their names or identifying information if they wish. Such decisions often are based on various internal political issues, regardless of the preference for anonymity. Thus, some people will want to be anonymous, fearing some form of retaliation, status differentials, or perceptions at odds with their view of what others expect them to say; other people, in contrast, may want to be identified to make a more persuasive case for some cause or issue they support. So, a decision regarding anonymity ultimately may be a political one. Nevertheless, you need to make a decision.

Sometimes, respondents may provide answers to questions not asked or they might provide solutions to various challenges not included as part of the Q-bank. If this occurs, you should organize the results into affinity groups so that there is a theme common to the responses. This can involve functional areas, strategic goals, or other aspects of commonality. If all of the responses fall within the original categories, move to the next step. If any responses do not seem to fit anywhere and represent general comments or criticisms other than the focus of the Q-bank, consider not returning them to stakeholders if you use a second or third round. Nonresponsive data are likely to create ambiguity and misunderstandings about the purpose of the Q-bank.

To illustrate the results from a typical Q-bank, consider this example from a major financial services firm. Approximately twenty upper-level managers were sent a list of thirty-six questions and asked to respond within a week. Samples of these questions and their responses are provided next. (Select responses have been altered to maintain confidentiality and only the questions with responses are repeated here.)

Our Customers

1. Who are our customers?
   a. Rich people.

2. Who[m] would we like to have as customers?
   a. Rich people.
   b. Those who would not qualify for a prime product today but could in the future.
   c. People with established credit histories.
   d. Gift card users.

3. Where are we positioned in the minds of our customers?
   a. Could be better.
   b. Brand recognition is low.
   c. Nonexistent.

4. Where would we like to be positioned?
   a. We would be the number one provider of our product in the world.
   b. We would like to be viewed as the premier financial services brand for our target niche market.

5. What value do our products, processes, and services provide our customers?
   a. They get to finance their debt through credit card use.
   b. Access to financial resources as they are needed.

6. When don't our customers like us?
   a. When we do not live up to their expectations.
   b. When we reprice our products and services.
   c. When they have to pay fees.

Our Brand

7. What values are associated with our brands?
   a. Don't know.
   b. Exceptional customer service.
   c. Good product at a fair price.

8. What is our aided brand awareness?
   a. Not very good.
   b. Nonexistent.

Our Markets

9. What do we know about current markets we are pursuing?
   a. Not enough.

10. What do we need to know for success in these markets?
    a. A lot.
    b. How do we communicate with new and "alien" segments?

Our Goals

11. If anything were possible, what should we do?
    a. Enter South America and solidify our presence in Western Europe.
    b. Design an infrastructure to understand the people to whom we are offering our services and products.
    c. Develop, test, and launch new products faster.
    d. Become a more nimble organization that can take advantage of opportunities more readily.
    e. Improve our public relations.
    f. Increase profitability for the next decade consistent with the past decade.
    g. Become the number one financial services company in the world.
    h. Achieve financial targets related to our target markets.

12. What do we want to do in the future that we aren't doing now?
    a. Increase our penetration in the Asian market.
    b. Move from a single-product marketing approach to a one-to-one marketing approach.

Our Products

13. What products do we have that are successful?
    a. Credit cards.

14. Do we know why they have been successful?
    a. People who charge have high revolving balances.
    b. People with balances often pay only a minimum and never pay off the debt.

15. Do we know why [our products] have been unsuccessful?
    a. Consumer finance.
    b. No brand equity.
    c. No consumer trust.
    d. No competitive advantage.

The value of a Q-bank can extend beyond the individual responses. What can be most telling are the questions and categories receiving responses. In this case, the category, "customers" received the most responses (15), followed by "goals" (10), "products" (7), "brand" (5), and "markets" (3). Such numbers do not necessarily indicate a priority order of concerns from a strategic perspective. It is possible that the majority are from only a few individuals. So, it is important to have a breakdown of how many people responded and the number of responses from each. If there are few respondents, then the results might not be representative of the sample of shareholders. If so, additional input should be sought.

4. Send Results to Stakeholders

This stage is a decision point in which a choice must be made about sending the results back to the stakeholders or using them to generate challenges without any feedback and sending them directly to the client. In general, results should be submitted to the participating stakeholders, unless organizational politics, time, money, or other considerations dictate otherwise. For instance, if there is an off-site retreat planned within a certain period of time and it is based on the results, there might not be enough time to solicit responses from another round of questions. Or, organizational politics could play a role if the particu-

lar situation is not supported fully by a key manager who only reluc-
tantly approved a single-round Q-bank—perhaps for reasons known
only to him or her. And, of course, time and politics combined, as well
as other variables, might play a role in this decision. Regardless, if you
decide to return the responses, send all including questions without
responses, since a second reading might prompt additional reactions.

The purpose and obvious advantage of sending the tabulated results back to stakeholders is that they might benefit from seeing others'
perceptions. This, in turn, might enhance the quality of the output so
that more realistic and appropriate innovation challenges are generated
later on. Seeing others' responses provides a larger set of stimuli that
might provoke richer perceptual sets (frames) about potential challenges. The person who generates a question response might not be
aware of its value in provoking challenges that need resolving. Others,
however, may see the value in such a response. Finally, an advantage
to seeing other responses is that the initial pool of responses may have
been limited in scope, focus, or quantity. A second, or even a third,
round increases the odds of collecting more relevant and useful information.

If the results of the first round are sent to the stakeholders, ask
them to review all the responses and try to generate additional ones.
As with Step #2, emphasize that the focus now is only on answering
the questions to use for generating challenges later on. As a rule of
thumb, conduct no more than three rounds, assuming time and other
required resources are available. If there is sufficient time, you also
might want to use the last round to solicit perceptions of priority affinity groups for the responses to each question. This could prove useful
for the client when evaluating the final results and before creating the
actual challenge statements for idea generation.

5. Send Final Results to Client

Up to this point, you should have kept the client informed about the
results of each round. Some clients request a lot of input and want to
approve the results before they are sent out for another round; others
only want to see the final results. So, try to determine such preferences
before starting the Q-bank.

To organize your final report to the client, use the original categories. If you have added any categories, note this so the client is aware
of them. Finally, ask whether the client wants to make any changes.
As shown in Figure 2-1, client approval is a decision point used to make
revisions based on client feedback. Thus, if the client does not approve
the list and suggests revisions, make them and resend the list to the
client. Then, once the Q-bank results are approved, you can move to
the next step and use the results to generate a challenge bank (C-bank).

NOTE

1. Some of these questions were contributed by Addys Sasserath of MarketQuest
    Consulting, e-mail to author, 1999.

THREE

Challenge Banks: Generating Innovation Challenge Questions

In the late 1970s, Charles Schwab dramatically altered the competitive landscape of financial brokerage houses by providing investors with discounted investments. His company also was the first to offer online investing in the late 1990s and soon became the market leader in discount brokerage services. This success was not to last, however, and the vagaries of the marketplace and his retirement as CEO (although still board chair) soon led to difficult times in the early 2000s. So, the board asked him to come back and turn around his company. A little more than a year and a half later, the Charles Schwab Company reported record quarterly and annualized earnings in excess of $1.2 trillion in client assets. The turnaround was a success.

It would have been easy to blame the previous problems on market forces and to credit the turnaround to better management. However, much more was involved. At about the same time, Schwab was interviewed by *Business 2.0* regarding how he could explain his success. Some of his answers reflected the type of results expected from using a Q-bank. In addition, some of his observations demonstrated an incisive understanding of the specific challenges he needed to overcome, much in the same way that a C-bank generates potential challenges.

His analysis indicated that the company's financial slide was caused by more than market forces. Instead, he believed that the company had lost its emotional connection with its customers and did things to alienate them, such as increasing fees and losing the personal touch in marketing its products. The company also seemed to have lost the ability to generate customer referrals that, at one time, had been a cornerstone of its success. Morale was at an all-time low and pricing in the market seemed unfocused and made it difficult to retain new customers. Finally, Schwab's cost structure became inflated, resulting in revenue paralysis.

Based on this analysis of the challenges facing the company, each challenge represents an explicit goal to help the company innovate and get back on track. For instance, by targeting specific areas, Schwab in effect created a C-bank of challenges such as:

- How might we reconnect emotionally with our customers?
- How might we reduce our fees?
- How might we increase the number of new customer referrals?
- How might we improve our pricing?
- How might we retain momentum with new customers?
- How might we retain more customers?
- How might we improve employee morale?
- How might we improve our cost structure?
- How might we streamline our cost structure?

All of these insights could have resulted from a Q-bank of stakeholders. In this case, it wasn't necessary. However, assuming you don't have this ability to hone in quickly on identifying priority challenges, there still is hope. The processes described in Chapter 2 and in this chapter provide a systematic, inclusive way—involving select stakeholders—to identify opportunities and to frame them as potential innovation challenges.

Everything done to this point, as part of a Q-bank, is designed to increase familiarity with the strategic challenges facing your organization, consider innovation obstacles and opportunities, and begin aligning key stakeholders with potential innovation targets. You now should have more clarity regarding your strategic terrain and some sense of priority with respect to areas requiring more innovative responses. Even if the results were as expected, the systematic exploration provided by the Q-bank will provide additional validation.

CHALLENGE BANKS (C-BANKS)

Once the client has approved the final list of responses from the Q-bank (Step #5, Figure 2-1 in Chapter 2), it is time to move on and conduct a C-bank of potential innovation challenge questions. The challenges are generated by using the responses to the Q-bank as stimuli. Each response is used as a potential trigger to generate an innovation challenge question, beginning with the words, "How might we . . . ?" This open-ended "invitation" to generate ideas helps to focus efforts toward a singular objective, yet encourages a diversity of responses.

C-banks can begin in one of two ways. First, a positioning statement can be presented to a group of stakeholders who are asked to use it to generate challenge statements and return them to a coordinator (Round #1). For instance, a manager might request challenges based on the following script:

> As you know, we currently face competitive threats from emerging markets such as Brazil, Russia, India, and China. As we transition from a technology product to a service-based business model, what challenges should we address? For your responses, please put them in the form of, "How might we . . . ?" For example, "How might we improve human resources functions in emergent countries?" Please e-mail your responses to me no later than the end of the week. I then will collate everything and send you the results to stimulate additional challenges. Thanks for your help with this vital project.

Figure 3-1 shows this version of a C-bank. The basic steps involved are described next.

The positioning statement helps participants understand the pa-

FIGURE 3-1. C-bank process using a positioning statement.

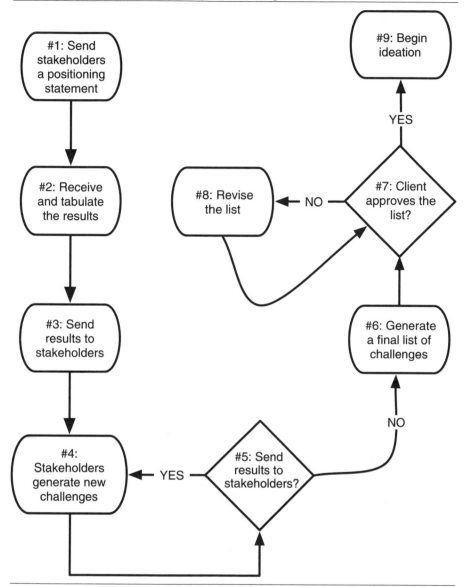

rameters involved by framing the key issues. Once stakeholders have a chance to generate additional challenges after inspecting the previous ones (Round #2), you can return the responses for a third round. The option also exists, of course, to conduct only one round without returning the results. Or, you could do only two rounds, organize those results into affinity groups, and send them to the client for approval and eventual ideation.

The second way to conduct a C-bank is to use the results from a Q-bank and generate a preliminary list of innovation challenges. You then could perform one or more rounds, each time organizing the results into affinity groups. Once the client approves the final challenge(s), ideation can begin.

This C-bank version is shown in Figure 3-2 and is described next.

1. Turn Q-Bank Responses into a C-Bank

Use responses from the Q-bank to help generate a list of challenges, grouped according to the original categories. Transforming stakeholder responses into challenges involves looking at each Q-bank question and response and using them to trigger potential challenge questions. In general, it is better to create too many challenges than too few. So, don't worry if some may overlap each other.

It also doesn't matter from which categories the challenges originate. This applies even if there is no logical connection between a Q-bank response and a C-bank challenge. For instance, consider a question from the "Products and Services" category listed in Chapter 2: "Do we know why [our products] have been unsuccessful?" One stakeholder response was, "No brand equity." The resulting challenge might be: "How might we increase our brand equity?" This challenge now could be moved to the "Branding" category since the focus is no longer on products exclusively. It now is framed for possible ideation, which is more important than the category from which it was derived.

Sample Questions

The best way to illustrate this step is to use the examples in Step #3 for the Q-bank (Chapter 2). Based on the sample responses to selected questions from the Q-bank, some possible challenge statements are presented next. (Remember, not all of them may be derived directly from the original categories.)

FIGURE 3-2. C-bank process for framing innovation challenges.

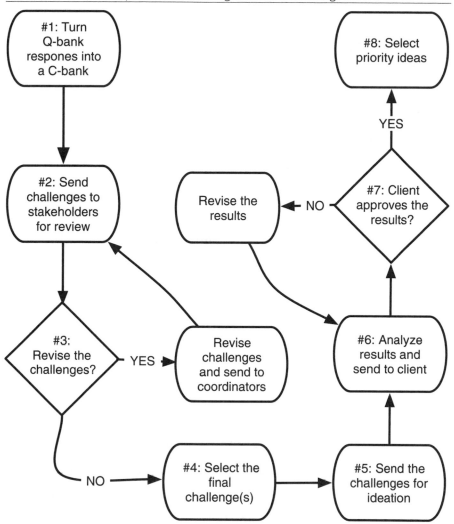

Customers

1. How might we increase the number of wealthy customers?

2. How might we help potential customers qualify for our products and services?

3. How might we increase the number of qualified customers?

4. How might we increase the number of gift card users?

5. How might we help current customers to increase their credit ratings?

6. How might we encourage customers to increase their debt?

7. How might we increase customer access to our financial services?

8. How might we better meet customer expectations?

9. How might we improve our customer service?

10. How might we better understand our customers?

Financials

11. How might we increase the transparency of our fee structure?

12. How might we reduce our fees?

13. How might we eliminate our fees?

Branding

14. How might we increase our brand recognition?

15. How might we increase our brand equity?

16. How might we increase our aided brand awareness?

17. How might we increase our unaided brand awareness?

18. How might we better position ourselves in our customers' minds?

19. How might we be perceived as the number one financial services provider in the world?

20. How might we brand ourselves as being *the* company for the _____ financial market?

Markets

21. How might we learn more about our current markets?

22. How might we learn more about new markets we want to enter?

23. How might we be more successful in our current markets?

24. How might we be successful in future markets we want to enter?

25. How might we communicate better with our markets?

26. How might we increase our competitive advantage?

27. How might we shift from single-product marketing to one-to-one marketing?

Goals

28. How might we best enter the South American market?

29. How might we solidify our presence in Western Europe?

30. How might we become more future-oriented?

Processes

31. How might we improve our infrastructure for servicing customers?

32. How might we become a more nimble organization?

33. How might we improve our public relations?

34. How might we increase our profitability for the next decade?

35. How might we become the number one financial services company in the world?

36. How might we achieve financial goals related to our target markets?

Products and Services

37. How might we better price our products and services?

38. How might we ensure high revolving balances?

39. How might we increase the perception that our products are priced fairly?

40. How might we develop new products faster?

41. How might we test new products faster?

42. How might we launch new products faster?

2. Send Challenges to Stakeholders for Review

This step is optional. If time or other resources are scarce, you might want to select the final one or two challenges from the previous list and move directly to Step #4, selecting the final challenge(s). Another reason to skip a stakeholder review might be if undue political issues are involved that might interfere with selecting priority challenges, collecting quality ideas, or otherwise disrupt the process. Thus, the project coordinators—usually internal managers and one or more external consultants—might revise the challenges using the criteria to be discussed in Chapter 4.

However, if time is available, consider sending the complete list of challenges to the stakeholders as is. Because they eventually will receive one or more challenges to use for idea generation, it can be useful to have them first review the master list of potential challenges, make revisions, and provide input on the priority challenges. A more refined and targeted product could result.

3. Do You Want to Revise the Challenges?

As noted previously, if stakeholders do not want to revise the challenges or cannot do so, or if there are other reasons not to revise (such as lack of time), move to Step #4. If the stakeholders choose to participate in revisions, ask them to evaluate the challenges by giving them the following instructions:

a. Read through all the challenges once to become familiar with them.

b. Go back through the challenges and look for ones that might be unclear or require editing or revising.

c. It is not mandatory, but try to see if any logical commonalities exist between or within the categories. If so, organize them into affinity groups that might become new categories or subgroups of existing categories.

d. Select the priority challenges and create a list of your top three to five preferences.

e. Please feel free to add any comments you might care to make.

Before starting revisions, however, emphasize that the purpose of this activity is to evaluate the challenges and *not* to generate ideas—that will be the next activity. Suggest that if they think of any ideas while revising the challenges, they should write them down and save them for Step #5, which is idea generation.

Once the stakeholders have finished revising and adding any comments about the challenges, they should return them to the coordinators. The coordinators then should review all of the changes and revise the list of challenges as deemed appropriate. Then, the coordinators should send the revisions back to the stakeholders (Step #2) for any additional revisions, based on the input from others. This input can increase the quality of the list of challenges and sometimes, more important, increase the amount of stakeholder buy-in with respect to the overall project. (Even though only one or a small number of challenges will be used, the remaining ones can be retained for later idea generation.) Finally, review the second round of revisions, make any changes, and decide if you want to use one final round or move directly to idea generation.

4. Select the Final Challenge

Depending on how well the challenges were framed, selecting the final challenge (or challenges) could be a difficult process. The first decision is to determine if the C-bank statements were relatively "clean" overall. In this case, a clean challenge is one that conforms to the seven evaluation criteria listed here (which will be discussed in more detail in Chapter 4):

1. Begins with the phrase, "How might we . . . ?
2. Singularity of objectives?
3. Absence of evaluative criteria?

4. Absence of solutions?

5. Appropriate level of abstraction?

6. Appropriate use of positioning elements?

7. Clear and unambiguous?

Next, the selection process should focus on assessing differences among any new challenges submitted. This involves looking for duplicates and possibly rewriting some challenges for clarity, if necessary. You must exercise some caution, however, to avoid deleting a challenge that is only a slight variation instead of a duplicate. Also, the same caution must be used when rewriting for clarity.

Finally, one or more client representatives may need to approve the final challenge or challenges. One way to facilitate this process is for the coordinators to create a list of priority challenges that are grouped by commonalities. In information theory, this is known as *chunking,* meaning that it is easier to evaluate a small number of clusters of alternatives than a large number of individual ones. For instance, choices might be made on a group of challenges pertaining to branding and another group to internal processes, as opposed to rating all the individual challenges within these categories. Thus, the choice becomes a simpler one of selecting from *between* rather than *within* groups or categories. Of course, this process can be as detailed or as general as desired. (This process will be discussed in Chapter 11.)

5. Send the Final List of Challenges for Ideation

People who participate in idea generation for challenges typically include some or all of the stakeholders used to generate the list of challenges. However, it is usually better to involve a broader group in idea generation. Different perspectives and knowledge bases from participants outside the organization can provide a more creative and richer set of potential challenge solutions.

When you send the challenges, always remind the recipients that they should defer all judgment when generating their ideas. This is the most important of all idea generation principles. It is probably also the most violated principle in everyday brainstorming, despite its emphasis in business literature for the past seventy years. And, more important, such behavior persists in the face of numerous empirical research studies verifying the value of deferred judgment on idea quantity during group brainstorming.

For instance, small groups on reality television shows such as *The Apprentice* typically demonstrate an alarming lack of practice in applying this principle. Instead, the teams of wannabe apprentices more often than not use a sequential process of generate-evaluate-generate-evaluate, et cetera. Each idea is given one chance to survive and then is eliminated immediately if there is not unanimous approval. People whose ideas are rejected so quickly often become disillusioned with the process and are more reluctant to suggest anything new, especially ideas that might differ from the prevailing direction of the rest of the group. The result is a negative group climate that is not conducive to innovative thinking. As Alex Osborn, the father of brainstorming, used to say, "It is much easier to tame down a wild idea than to tame up one."[1]

For readers who may not be aware of the disadvantages of failing to defer judgment, the answer is relatively simple: Ideas are the raw material of solutions. Ideas should be viewed merely as triggers to help stimulate solutions that can be applied to resolve challenges. Viewed this way, every idea at least has minimal potential to spark other ideas or modifications. Moreover, the more ideas generated (regardless of their quality), the greater the odds of coming up with at least one plausible solution; toss ideas away quickly, and you lose the power of their numbers and stimulation value. Remember, there will be an opportunity to judge all the ideas, so you can choose when that will be.

As with the Q-banks, you probably should conduct at least two rounds of idea generation. So, resend the ideas, but do not alter the wording in any way, even if they are not clear to you or contain criteria or reflect biases. Such things can be removed during the final evaluation. It is more important to preserve the original intent of the persons who generated the ideas.

6. Analyze the Results and Send to the Client

Once the rounds have been completed and the project coordinators have received the final list of ideas, their first task is to remove duplicates. Again, be careful to ensure that duplicates are just that and nothing more. Even minor differences in wording can alter semantics and how others interpret meanings. If there is any doubt at all about an idea being a duplicate, keep it on the list.

Next, look for affinity groups and organize the ideas into clusters of commonality. As discussed previously, the original categories typically provide the structure needed for such groups. However, now is the time to see if there are enough "outliers" within a category—that is, ideas that do not fit that category cleanly, but seem to have commonalities—to justify creating a new category for them. A few ideas generated across multiple categories might be better listed under a different or a new category. So be sure to scrutinize all the ideas for their appropriateness of "fit" within the categories.

You also should try to assign some priority to the ideas. There are at least three ways to do this. First, if time is available and it is important to get stakeholder buy-in, you might solicit the stakeholders' input by having them rate all the ideas on preestablished criteria (see Chapter 11). A second way is to involve only key stakeholders and/or outside people, even if they did not participate in the idea generation process. A third option is simply a combination of the first two: Involve some or all of the idea generators and also some outside personnel who originally were not part of the C-bank process.

Finally, if several challenges seem to be interrelated and dependent on each other, you might consider constructing a conceptual map to illustrate the possible connections. For instance, consider the following challenges from the previous C-bank (numbers in parentheses refer to the specific challenges listed previously):

a. How might we increase our brand awareness? (#16)

b. How might we increase the transparency of our fee structure? (#11)

c. How might we reduce our fees? (#12)

d. How might we improve our customer service? (#9)

e. How might we increase customer access to our financial services? (#7)

If more clarity is needed, a concept map, such as the one shown in Figure 3-3, also can be developed depicting how these objectives might be interrelated. Otherwise, such maps can be created after finishing a C-bank. A major advantage of these maps is their ability to help users identify priorities in terms of which challenges should be attacked first and how some might be either subordinate or superordinate to others.

That is, some relatively specific challenges should be resolved before working on broader ones; or, broader ones might be best dealt with directly if the subordinate challenges are not perceived as being in a causal relationship. For instance, in Figure 3-3, the broadest challenge is to increase profitability. In this hypothetical situation, the map suggests that reducing fees is one way to do this, presumably based on the

FIGURE 3-3. *Hypothetical interrelationships among innovation challenges.*

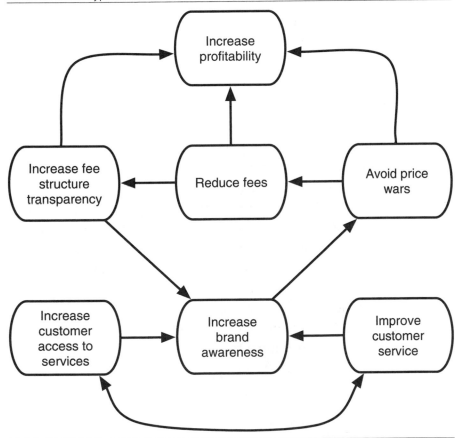

assumption that lower fees will drive higher sales volume and, hence, profit. (A more detailed description of strategy maps is provided in Chapter 5.)

Once you are satisfied with the results and have organized them satisfactorily, you may send them to the client for final approval, the next step in the C-bank process.

7. Client Approves the Results?

Sometimes, the client already has been involved in processing and analyzing the final list of ideas. This is a matter of available time and personal preference. Some managers obviously feel a greater need to "ride herd" on a project than others, depending on their perceptions of how important the project is, the risks to them if the outcome is not acceptable to higher-ups, and their idiosyncratic need to monitor all activities—or to micromanage in some cases! Of course, if the client does not approve the results, you must revise them and resubmit for approval.

8. Select the Priority Ideas

The final evaluation and selection of the C-bank ideas should be an exhaustive, systematic, inclusive, decision process involving all important stakeholders. This process is detailed further in Chapter 11, so only a few comments will be made here. Perhaps the most important consideration—especially when working with a group—is to begin with a relatively long list of explicit evaluation criteria. As with idea generation, criteria evaluation also should be a process involving deferred judgment. List all possible criteria first before starting decision making. If there is an extensive list of criteria, you can group items into common categories. Finally, if you have a lengthy list of ideas to narrow down, consider creating screens to filter ideas—that is, an idea must satisfy one or more criteria to pass to the next level.

NOTE

1.   Alex F. Osborn, *Applied Imagination,* 3rd ed. (New York: Scribner, 1963).

FOUR

How to Write and Evaluate Innovation Challenge Questions

Notables such as Aristotle ("Well begun is half done") and educator/philosopher John Dewy ("A problem well-defined is half solved") have echoed Nobel Prize–winner Herbert Simon's notion that a well-defined problem is a solved problem. The closer a problem frame approaches a desired goal, the more likely it is to become a solution or, at least, it has the potential to be turned into one.

Instances of this situation often occur when people who are brainstorming potential challenge definitions incorporate solutions within their definitions or challenge statements. Although that scenario generally should be avoided, it actually is quite appropriate when first attempting to frame a challenge. That is because you should defer judgment when generating challenges, just as you should when generating ideas. Otherwise, you risk losing the potential stimulation value of even poorly worded challenges. However, once you've generated all possible challenges, you should review them and make modifications as appropriate, based on the criteria discussed in this chapter as well as any others you think might apply. This chapter will discuss framing innovation challenges for the most productive and effective idea generation.

When a solution is included as part of a challenge, I call it a "nested" challenge. The reason is that it could stand alone as a challenge, but it is part of a broader objective within which it is nested. An example is the question: "How might we increase our sales by creating a more emotional connection with our customers?" This type of frame is fairly common, but totally inappropriate because of the ambiguity it can create. In this case, the obvious primary goal—that is, the "superordinate" goal—is increasing sales. It is obvious because the phrase that follows it implies that the goal of increasing sales can be achieved by creating a more emotional connection with customers. However, in addition to being a solution, this goal itself is a challenge objective to be achieved. As a result, it can be viewed as a secondary or "subordinate" goal. In other words, it can stand by itself *or* serve as a means to an end—in this case, the primary goal of increasing sales. Thus, the initial challenge might be deconstructed into two separate challenges as follows:

1. How might we increase sales?
2. How might we create a more emotional connection with our customers?

CRITERIA FOR EVALUATING INNOVATION CHALLENGES

All the challenge statements used previously in this book are based on the assumption that they are well-framed. In real life, however, that often is not the case. Well-framed challenges must satisfy various criteria before even considering how to link them together or determine their priority. Nested challenges, as discussed previously, are just one example of a criterion against which all challenges should be assessed—that is, whether or not they contain a nested challenge.

Evaluation criteria typically can be classified as general or specific. General criteria apply to most decisions and typically involve resources such as time, people, materials, and money. Specific criteria pertain directly to the nature of the alternatives available. Based on research and experience, I believe that the seven most important criteria required for evaluating and selecting innovation challenges are:

1. Begins with the phrase, "How might we . . . ?"

2. Singularity of objectives?

3. Absence of evaluative criteria?

4. Absence of solutions?

5. Appropriate level of abstraction?

6. Appropriate use of positioning elements?

7. Clear and unambiguous?

1. *Begins with the phrase, "How might we . . . ?"* Posing challenges as open-ended questions helps to ensure they can be used to generate specific ideas for specific challenges. Otherwise, the challenge might be better focused in another direction. For instance, the challenge "What will be the most important business performance indicators over the next fifty years?" is a question calling for conjecture about trends and predictions. As phrased, it requires idea generators to converge on a limited set of options. It is not a call for unlimited innovative ideas designed to resolve product, process, or service problems. A better statement might be "How might we increase awareness about our new line of floor-care products?" This statement is divergent and more likely to elicit a variety of possible responses.

2. *Singularity of objectives?* This means that there should be a focus on only one objective in each challenge. It is difficult enough to generate ideas for one challenge, let alone two or more at the same time. Although this may seem obvious, it occurs frequently in the real world. People have multiple tasks to achieve and their priorities may not always be well sorted out. So, it is important to evaluate every challenge for the presence of competing objectives.

Consider this example from a major produce distributor: "How might we differentiate ourselves from our competition and radically increase consumption of our produce?" There obviously are two objectives: "differentiation" and "increase consumption." They both can be used, but not at the same time. Better wording would be: "How might we differentiate ourselves from our competition?" and "How might we increase consumption of our produce?"

As will be discussed later, a decision then is needed as to which of these, if either, should be subordinate, or secondary, to the other. For instance, in this case, it might be assumed that if the company can differentiate itself effectively, then consumption will increase correspondingly. Therefore, the framers might decide to focus first on differentiation. If this challenge is resolved satisfactorily, it might not even be necessary to work on the primary challenge because it may take care of itself.

3. *Absence of evaluative criteria?* Perhaps the most common mistake in framing innovation challenges is including evaluation criteria. You might wonder why this is a mistake because criteria always are involved whenever a decision is made. The problem is that the human mind has trouble generating concepts while simultaneously trying to determine if they would satisfy all possible criteria. Juggling criteria at the same time you are attempting to generate ideas can create information overload and result in lower-quality ideas that are unlikely to satisfy the criteria. Thus, a focus on judgment during creative activity can restrict the potential of any challenge or the creativity of any idea.

Sometimes, even output viewed initially as unsatisfactory might actually be more than satisfactory when modified, combined with other challenges (as long as they don't represent multiple objectives), or used simply to trigger new ones. Numerous examples exist of this phenomenon. A focus on judgment also creates a negative thinking climate—within an individual or a group—that can detract from both the quantity and quality of creative output. So, the issue is not whether to use criteria but *when*. Whenever possible, use criteria later, after you have generated all possible challenges. There is a choice, so use it.

4. *Absence of solutions?* As discussed at the outset of this chapter, it may appear paradoxical, but there can be a fine line between challenges and solutions. One reason is that challenge objectives and criteria are often both included within a single challenge. In addition to the example used previously, here is another example from a restaurant chain: "How might we increase the number of diners in our restaurants by creating a more healthy menu?" It appears that the primary objective is to increase the number of diners. Thus, creating a healthier menu is

one potential solution for achieving that objective. Or, the challenge might be framed as, "How might we make our menu healthier?" The solution becomes a challenge based on the assumption that a healthier menu will increase the number of customers.

Moreover, the emphasis on health also could be a criterion or a positioning element. In this instance, it probably would be better to eliminate the focus on health from the challenge, but include it as a positioning element or as a separate challenge. That is, the challenge might be reframed as, "How might we increase the number of diners in our restaurant chain? Solutions may involve healthy menu items, but other approaches also should be considered." Or, a new challenge might be, "How might we make our menu healthier?" Of course, both challenges could be used separately.

5. *Appropriate level of abstraction?* This can be a difficult criterion to apply. In general, the broader the level of challenge abstraction, the better the challenge. Broad challenges encompass a greater number and diversity of potential challenges. Overly specific challenges can be limiting in scope and not contribute much from a strategic point of view.

For instance, a company might become so focused on increasing the sales of one product model that it neglects its overall strategic marketing campaign, with a resulting negative impact on profit margins. Or, in the example used regarding an absence of solutions (Criterion #4), a healthy menu could be used as a subordinate challenge to increase the number of customers (as implied in discussing Criterion #4). What is appropriate depends on values, priorities, and the efficiency with which different objectives can be achieved. To help make such decisions, challenge maps can be created consisting of visual diagrams of how different challenges might be related. These maps can illustrate more vividly the hierarchical relationships that are perceived to exist among various challenges. (This concept will be discussed in more detail in Chapter 5.)

6. *Appropriate use of positioning elements?* Positioning elements are types of criteria that help to frame the scope of the primary challenge. Although they typically are used to help select ideas after ideation, they should not be emphasized as the primary focus. For this reason, they

should not be overly specific, nor should they be included as part of the challenge statement.

Instead, positioning criteria should be more general. In the restaurant example, it could be stated that ideas for increasing restaurant customers should, in some way, emphasize health. Or, consider an executive recruitment firm using the following challenge: "How might we brand ourselves as the leader in online job placements?" The firm might position this question by noting that ideas should reflect the use of advances in digital technology. Or, a beverage company may want new beverage ideas that somehow convey a sense of physical or mental energy.

Using positioning criteria effectively can be tricky. Management often wants to ensure that people who generate ideas understand the exact objectives to be achieved. And they may feel pressured to complete an assignment exactly as they think their superiors have requested. As a result, they sometimes include too much information, either as part of a challenge or as auxiliary information. If this information is not stated clearly and distinctly from the primary objective, it may serve only to confuse idea generators, rather than to clarify management's intentions. Positioning criteria should be used sparingly and not "positioned" as separate challenges. Instead, they can be used later on as criteria for evaluating the final ideas. So, one way or another, they can be involved in a challenge. (This is especially important in political situations in which different parties may be competing for scarce resources.)

7. *Clear and unambiguous?* This criterion is rather subjective and difficult to satisfy. The degree of clarity and ambiguity in a challenge can be viewed differently by people from varying occupations. This is known as *functional myopia*, a perceptual state in which people tend to view the world from their occupational frameworks. To test this criterion, review the challenge to be sure that all of the previous criteria have been considered and that there is a clean, simple, and straightforward challenge capable of generating ideas.

Most important, before beginning any idea generation session, ask all participants if they understand the challenge. However, even if no one says anything and the challenge is not clear, this fact usually becomes obvious once ideation starts. Although it may not be intentional, an ill-framed initial challenge often becomes apparent when brainstorming participants begin generating ideas so diverse that they reflect different perceptions as to what the actual challenge is. You may have been in idea generation sessions where, after brainstorming for a while, someone says, "Now exactly what is our problem?"—*that* is the major sign that additional framing is required.

A challenge is well framed if it satisfies all the preceding criteria, because they all represent the general criteria needed to qualify a challenge as appropriate and useful for productive idea generation. As a rule of thumb, if one to three criteria are not satisfied, then the challenge in question may be considered as "semi well framed"; if more than three criteria are not satisfied, then it could be characterized as "ill framed." Any challenges not satisfying at least three criteria should be reevaluated. However, remember that this is just a rough rule of thumb. The ability to satisfy the best criteria for a given situation always has priority over the number of criteria satisfied.

Therefore, use caution in basing any challenge selection decisions on these guidelines. The specific criteria *not* satisfied also should have an impact on this decision. Perhaps the most pivotal criteria in this respect would be the inclusion of evaluative criteria and the level of challenge abstraction. Evaluative criteria within a challenge can bog down an idea generation session by considering the merits of individual ideas before all possible ones have surfaced. The level of abstraction, however, is probably more important because it can determine the order in which challenges should be used to achieve strategic objectives. A too narrow or too broad challenge can be just as detrimental, if not more so, than trying to implement a bad idea.

If there is any doubt as to whether or not a challenge satisfies a criterion, try to gather more information to increase your understanding of the challenge and/or solicit opinions from others, including experts and those who may not be as close to the topic. The Q-bank process described in Chapter 2 is an example of how to involve a diversity of stakeholders in generating and evaluating challenges.

RELATIVELY SIMPLE CHALLENGE FRAMING

To illustrate how to apply these criteria, here is an actual, relatively simple challenge from a consumer products company:

> How can the Big Bucks Company develop brand awareness for its new XYZ brand of products with little marketing or PR funds?

A quick scan of the seven criteria discussed previously suggests that this challenge contains two criteria ("little marketing" or "little PR funds") that should be removed and used as positioning elements or reserved for later use as evaluation criteria. After presenting these options to the client, the company decided to do the latter and frame the challenge as:

> How might the Big Bucks Company improve the brand awareness of its XYZ line of consumer products? Solutions ideally would not involve significant marketing or PR funds.

The primary challenge was to increase awareness, so it stands alone. In this instance, however, the positioning elements themselves might be so specific that they still could interfere with open-ended idea generation. As stated, too much focus on them could be distracting if they are viewed as criteria that must be satisfied by every idea generated. Thus, it probably would have been better to have reserved them as decision-making criteria later on.

MODERATELY COMPLEX CHALLENGE FRAMING

Consider this moderately complex challenge from an international hotel and resort chain, with the pseudonym "Beds-R-Us":

> With a diverse and creative workforce, what strategies can Beds-R-Us implement to deliver a new level of service? We want ideas that can be implemented that would also make the Beds-R-Us brand more distinctive and result in a more emotional connection with travelers.

Rather than use this presented challenge as it is, let's see how we might deconstruct it for more effective ideation. The first task is to create a single objective using the "How might we . . . ?" format. In this case, the phrase "a new level" is ambiguous. So, the challenge might be reframed as: "How might we improve customer service?"

As stated in the presented challenge, ". . . ideas that can be implemented," might be reserved as a criterion. Brand distinctiveness could be used either as a criterion or as another challenge objective. And "a closer and more emotional connection with travelers" might be posed as the following challenge: "How might Beds-R-Us create a more emotional connection with travelers?" (This was the challenge the client selected.) One potential concept map for Beds-R-Us is shown in Figure 4-1.

This diagram incorporates all the elements of the presented challenge. As displayed, the goal of improving customer service directly affects creating a more emotional connection with travelers. The emotional connection is critical to making the brand more distinctive, which, in turn, directly impacts the occupancy rate. Customer service also affects the occupancy rate directly, as do an emotional connection and making the brand more distinctive.

COMPLEX CHALLENGE FRAMING

Some presented challenges are quite complex, reflecting in-depth research and input from a variety of stakeholders. For instance, consider this presented challenge from an international mailing service organization ("Mail-Is-Us"):

> The objective for this challenge is to develop a new product/service/process or an enhancement to an existing product/service/process that will result in increased revenue for Mail-Is-Us. This can be accomplished by:
>
> 1. Developing a new product/service/process for current customers
>
> 2. Enhancing an existing product/service/process for current customers

FIGURE 4-1. Strategic objectives concept map for Beds-R-Us.

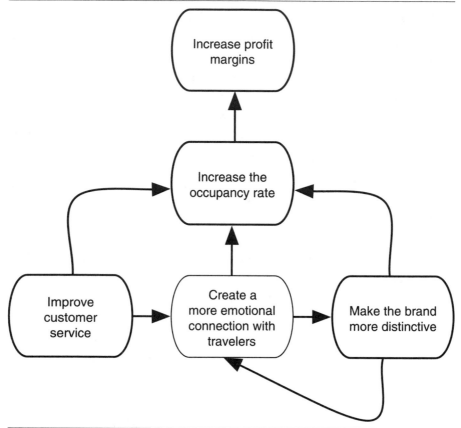

3. Developing a new product/service/process for new customers

4. Enhancing an existing product/service/process for new customers

5. And/or developing new marketing/partnership opportunities

Whew! That's a lot to take in and far too much for any productive ideation in one bite. This challenge definitely needs to be deconstructed and sorted out.

The primary objective seems to be increasing revenue, which is what management indicated was the primary goal. So this objective can be described as the core challenge, at least based on an initial analysis. (A case might better be made for profitability since revenue enhancement may or may not have an impact on the bottom line.) The remaining information serves only to increase complexity by suggesting a focus on all the possible combinations present—for example, develop a new product for new customers, enhance an existing product for new customers, or develop a new service for existing customers, ad nauseam. Clearly, the presented challenge does not have a singular focus.

Evaluating these possibilities against the decision criteria suggests that the only criteria satisfied by these challenges are an absence of evaluation criteria and including solutions. However, this is not quite accurate because the complex wording implies that there are multiple, general paths to solutions—for example, "developing a new product/service/process for current customers." Also, there are too many variables to process while simultaneously generating ideas. More important, specific objectives other than increasing revenue or profitability need to be identified.

To identify these objectives, I reviewed multiple documents from the client involving strategic issues such as the competition, markets, strengths and weaknesses, and trends—much as would be done using a Q-bank (Chapter 2). Based on this research, I then harvested twenty-one potential challenges that key stakeholders reviewed and narrowed down to nine and were approved by the client (Chapter 3).

The task then was to decide which challenges would be secondary to others—that is, which should be accomplished first to achieve the primary objective of increasing revenue? It also was important to decide how the different objectives might be interdependent—that is, linked in ways so that achieving one will help to achieve another. Because of the complexity of priorities involved with this process, I created a challenge map depicting potential relationships for the client to consider (see Figure 4-2).

For instance, Figure 4-2 indicates that two primary challenges secondary to increasing revenue are increasing access and awareness of the company's products and services. These challenges, in turn, are likely to be affected by the challenges indicated in this figure. For example,

FIGURE 4-2. Mail-Is-Us concept map.

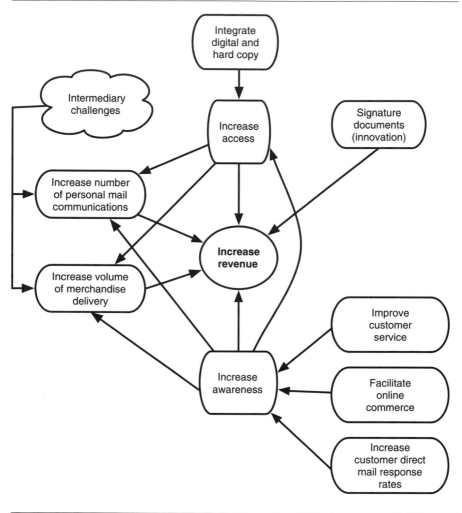

increasing awareness should increase delivery volume, which, in turn, should increase revenue directly. Finally, facilitating online commerce should increase access so that revenue also increases.

In the end, the client chose to focus on both increasing access and awareness. Of course, this does not mean that the other challenges would be abandoned. All of them could be used to facilitate these dual objectives, which, in turn, should increase revenue (with the implicit assumption that profitability also would result). Moreover, the remaining challenges can be reserved for later innovation challenge projects.

Reviewing Additional Framing Examples: Financial Services

Here are some examples, modified from an actual C-bank process used in a financial services organization (the wording has been changed in several cases to maintain confidentiality), to illustrate further how to deconstruct and clarify presented challenges. Each presented challenge is listed—that is, as submitted to the C-bank—followed by comments and suggested reframes.

PRESENTED CHALLENGE #1

> To create a process that significantly differentiates us from our competitors, delights our existing customers, and attracts new customers with value pricing and convenience.

Comments

The first action is to determine the primary objective. This can be somewhat tricky because differentiation from competitors and attracting new customers both could be objectives. In this case, it appears that differentiation would be the primary objective for two reasons: (1) it was mentioned first; and (2) achieving differentiation could help achieve the objective of attracting new customers—most likely the umbrella or superordinate objective in this situation. However, both could be used for ideation, so both should be included, either in priority order or jointly as dual objectives to be worked on.

The phrase "with value pricing and convenience" initially seems to represent two criteria that ideas for either of the objectives might need to satisfy. However, because of the wording, "*with* [italics added] value pricing and convenience," they probably would best be classified as solutions, even though that may not have been the intent. Thus, they should be removed from the challenge statement. Nevertheless, solutions also can be used as criteria—

when stated in the context used—so that possibility should be considered. For instance, offering value pricing and convenience together might attract new customers or they might be used to evaluate solutions for differentiating the organization from its competitors. (Other criteria, of course, can be used, but pricing and convenience are mentioned only because they were contained within the presented challenge.)

Suggested Reframe #1

- How might our process differentiate us from our competitors?

Evaluation Criteria

Solutions should be likely to improve customer satisfaction, to attract new customers with value pricing, and to increase convenience.

Suggested Reframe #2

- How might our process attract new customers?

Evaluation Criteria

Solutions should be likely to improve customer satisfaction, to attract new customers with value pricing, and to increase convenience.

PRESENTED CHALLENGE #2

How can we exceed customer expectations, deliver a premier product in such a manner that our clients want to refer us business, provide value-added functionality, be the most effective and efficient at what we do by utilizing resources and technology to its fullest, all at a competitive, fair price?

Comments

This is a fairly complex presented challenge in that it contains multiple objectives, solutions, and criteria, plus parts are relatively ambiguous with inappropriate levels of abstraction. So, let's break it down:

Potential objectives include exceeding customer expectations, an implied, superordinate objective of increasing customer satisfaction (derived from the intention to exceed expectations); increasing customer referrals; and becoming more effective and efficient—the latter two would have to be defined operationally so that outcomes could be measured. The nested potential solution involves using resources and technology in optimal ways (to redefine "fullest" slightly more specifically). Finally, providing "value-added functionality" (an ambiguous quality) and "at a competitive, fair price" clearly are evaluation criteria and should not be included in a challenge.

Suggested Reframes

- How might we exceed customer expectations?
- How might we increase customer satisfaction?
- How might we increase client referrals?
- How might we improve product quality?

Evaluation Criteria

Solutions should be likely to provide value-added functionality, to use resources and technology efficiently and effectively, and to involve a competitive, fair price.

However, as stated, these criteria should be operationalized and made more specific. For instance, *value-added functionality* might be defined as "the ability to reduce errors or eliminate steps in a process." Efficiency and effectiveness should also be defined specifically.

PRESENTED CHALLENGE #3

I would require everything, regardless of where it is in the workflow process, to be checked, not only to ensure quality but to ensure that the customer and the [company] understands what the customer is asking for and what the customer will be receiving.

Comments

This is a solution and not a challenge. Therefore, it cannot be used as an innovation challenge as presented. Solutions, however, typically contain implicit challenges, so wording in the presented challenge could be used to suggest challenges that would satisfy the criteria. In addition, it can be set aside as a solution or used to create criteria such as "likely to meet customer expectations," which also could be used as a reframe, as shown next.

Suggested Reframes

- How might we improve the work-flow process?
- How might we better monitor all aspects of the work-flow process?
- How might we improve the quality of process outcomes?
- How might we better understand customer expectations?

PRESENTED CHALLENGE #4

How can we cut in half the time it takes to process customers while significantly increasing accuracy and overall customer satisfaction and still double the revenue we generate from these services?

Comments

The primary objective of this challenge appears to be reducing processing time, while the remaining parts are either spin-off objectives *or* evaluation criteria. In this instance, spin-off objectives are linked in some way to one or more different objectives. Thus, ideas for reducing processing time might suggest or be in some way related to increasing accuracy, achieving higher customer service, and generating twice the revenue. So, all of these goals, plus the reduction of processing time, could be set up as separate challenges. A case might be made that the primary objective is reducing processing time in half, although it usually is better to save such constraints as criteria. Otherwise, idea generators might focus too much on how likely it is that their ideas would result in a 50 percent reduction. So, the primary objective should focus on reducing processing time.

Suggested Reframe

- How might we reduce the time involved in processing customer orders?

Evaluation Criteria

Solutions should be likely to increase accuracy, improve customer satisfaction, and increase revenue.

If the implied criteria are used as objectives, they might be framed as follows:

- How might we increase processing accuracy?
- How might we improve the quality of our processing service?
- How might we double our revenue?
- How might we improve customer satisfaction?

Just these four challenges alone demonstrate the close relationship between challenges and solutions and how challenges are interrelated in terms of priority. For instance, increasing processing accuracy would be one solution for improving the quality of processing, which, in turn, could improve customer service.

To illustrate the overall interrelationship among the challenges, a concept map might show how increasing processing accuracy would contribute to processing quality, which might increase—either in tandem or sequentially—customer satisfaction and/or revenue. That is, increasing customer satisfaction could directly affect revenue enhancement or it may not be a causal relationship and just occur at the same time as an increase in revenue. (For more information on concept maps, see Chapter 5.)

PRESENTED CHALLENGE #5

One of the things that could help retain our retail Category 1 customers centers on developing reasonable expectations for the customers before using the "Schmelkin process" [a fictional process]. We need to give the day-to-day operations personnel a tour of the Schmelkin process facilities before we go live. We need to explain our reports, terms, and processes so that they can have reasonable expectations of outcomes. I feel that many times the decision makers are aware of the changes, but the rank and file don't fully understand them.

Comments

This is another instance of a proposed solution, but with a bit of emotional, persuasive rhetoric thrown in. The contributor appears to feel rather strongly about his or her prescriptions to improve things. However, any emotional reactions—whether in agreement or disagreement—should be cast aside. The focus, instead, should be on generating challenges from their input. The presented challenge leads with the notion of retaining customers, so that is a logical first challenge. The other challenges then can be extracted by sifting through the remainder of the statement, as shown in the following reframes:

Suggested Reframes

- How might we retain our retail Category 1 customers?
- How might we improve the Schmelkin process?
- How might we better clarify customer expectations?
- How might we increase understanding of the rank and file with regard to process changes?
- How might we communicate better with rank-and-file employees?

Writing the Challenge Briefing Document

Once you have reframed potential challenges and selected one or more for idea generation, the next activity is to create a briefing document ("brief") for the *ideators* (people who will be generating the ideas who may or may not always be stakeholders). This document is second in importance to selecting a final challenge because it is designed to frame the challenge so that it is positioned correctly in the minds of the ideators. It aids in placing the challenge in the intended perspective with respect to the objective and desired scope of the challenge. If possible, the document should be aligned clearly with organizational strategy and vision.

In general, most briefing documents address positioning criteria as discussed previously regarding challenge evaluation criteria. These documents may vary considerably from one challenge to another, but most contain three major parts:

1. Background information

2. Desired scope of the challenge (what is wanted and what is not wanted as the focus)

3. Other considerations that might be included but are not mandatory

Background information can vary depending on the knowledge and experience level of the ideators, plus how much information is available or can be made available, given constraints such as time, access, and confidentiality. If a specific market segment is targeted, some general background on it should be provided. Some challenges are relatively broad in scope, such as, "How might we better market our line of consumer appliances?" Other challenges can be more focused, such as, "How might we market our appliances to create an emotional connection with millennials?" In this instance, two more data points are added: "emotional connection" and "millennials." This probably should be the extent of the challenge's content. Although creating an "emotional connection" could be used as a criterion, it also could be an objective. If the intention is to limit the challenge objective to a specific line of appliances—for example, portable beverage appliances—that should be noted as well, but as a positioning element in the brief. Finally, a brief might hint at some *wishes* as opposed to *needs*. For example, it could be mentioned that the focus is on millennials in North America and South America, but not countries in other continents.

To illustrate a brief, I will use the previous challenge: "How might we market our appliances to create an emotional connection with millennials?" A sample brief for this challenge might be written as follows:

Millennials (aka NextGen, GenY, echo boomers, C generation) are part of the Friendster, MySpace, and YouTube generation. Although there isn't complete agreement on their age range, most sources cite people born between 1980 and 2001. In the United States, they represent a potential market of roughly 80 million individuals, closely approximating the number of baby boomers now heading into retirement. The oldest millennials are beginning to become established in their careers and are estimated by some to have a purchasing power base of over $1 billion (although well short that of baby boomers). As a group, they tend to be leading the "wired," digital revolution by embracing electronic gadgets such as cell phones, iPods, computers, and especially being online as part of numerous social and peer-to-peer networks of e-mails, instant- and text-messaging, blogs, photos, videos, and music. Self-expression characterizes this generation, which thrives on being connected 24/7. They may not be technically savvy, but they do know how to use technology "under the hood" to stay connected. They can be impatient multitaskers who expect their products to be customizable.

CHALLENGE FOR THIS PROJECT

How might we market our appliances to create an emotional connection with millennials?

We are not interested in any particular segment of the millennials market and your focus primarily should be on small kitchen appliances in both North and South America, but no other continents. We have a special interest in beverage appliances, but you are not limited to them.

PREFRAMED GENERIC CHALLENGES

Wouldn't it be nice if you didn't have to generate your own challenges and then hope they satisfied all the criteria discussed in this chapter? Or, at least not have to bother with evaluating them? If so, you might be interested in reviewing the challenges in this section and the next one.

The list immediately following represents a compilation of fairly general challenge questions that can be applied across a variety of industrial, educational, and governmental sectors. I have organized them into the same broad categories used in previous chapters. This organization should make it easier to find challenges most appropriate for your needs. In some cases, only slight changes in wording are required. For instance, if you were a director of admissions at a higher-education institution, instead of using the word *customer,* you might modify challenges by substituting the word *student* for customer. (A frame of students as customers, however, also might provoke more unique ideas.)

This list and the one that follows (based on case studies) are by no means exhaustive. However, just as any idea—regardless of its apparent merit on first seeing it—can spark newer, more productive ideas, all of the challenges in this list have the potential to trigger new ways to frame challenges.

Customers

1. How might we acquire new customers?
2. How might we reacquire old customers?
3. How might we improve our customer service?
4. How might we reduce the time to process customer orders?
5. How might we increase the transparency of our customer policies?
6. How might we increase customer access to our products or services?
7. How might we make it easier for customers to _____?
8. How might we better anticipate customer needs?

9. How might we create a more emotional connection with our customers?

10. How might we increase our customer retention rate?

11. How might we reduce the costs of acquiring new customers?

12. How might we better identify our customers?

13. How might we reward our customers?

14. How might we better deal with customer complaints?

15. How might we reduce the time to resolve customer complaints?

16. How might we reduce the number of customer complaints?

17. How might we better assess the validity of customer feedback?

18. How might we better determine why our customers like our products or services?

19. How might we better determine why our customers do not like our products or services?

20. How might we learn more about our customers?

21. How might we better use media to reach our customers?

22. How might we better evaluate our customer service?

23. How might we ensure management commitment to customer service?

24. How might we discover what our customers don't know they want?

25. How might we make it more convenient for customers to place orders?

26. How might we better communicate with our customers?

27. How might we increase customer satisfaction?

28. How might we reduce customer dissatisfaction?

29. How might we involve customers in product development?

30. How might we encourage customers and suppliers to collaborate?

31. How might we convert customers into corporate promoters?

32. How might we increase the number of wealthy customers?

33. How might we help potential customers qualify for our products and services?

34. How might we increase the number of qualified customers?

35. How might we increase the number of gift card users?

36. How might we help current customers increase their credit ratings?

37. How might we encourage customers to increase their debt?

38. How might we increase customer access to financial services?

39. How might we better meet customer expectations?

40. How might we improve our customer service?

41. How might we better understand our customers?

Products or Services

42. How might we increase access to our products or services?

43. How might we create products or services to _____?

44. How might we reduce the product development cycle time?

45. How might we increase consumption of our products?

46. How might we improve our products or services?

47. How might we make it easier to assemble our products?

48. How might we make it easier to use our products or services?

49. How might we provide R&D with more freedom?

50. How might we increase our new product success rate?

51. How might we reduce the time to launch new products?

52. How might we communicate better with design and engineering when developing new products?

53. How might we increase internal commitment to new products?

54. How might we persuade sales personnel to market new products?

55. How might we better differentiate our products from competitors'?

56. How might we improve our service infrastructure?

57. How might we make it easier to contact service specialists?

58. How might we add value to our products or services?

59. How might we better position our products or services in customers' minds?

60. How might we better identify new product opportunity areas?

61. How might we increase the number of our product extensions?

62. How might we reduce perceived risk of the "fuzzy front end?"

63. How might we improve our new product screening and evaluation process?

64. How might we better communicate new product/service features and benefits?

65. How might we improve the new product prototype development process?

66. How might we increase the number of products in our pipeline?

67. How might we improve the interface between new product development and marketing?

68. How might we better meet production deadlines?

69. How might we increase the number of patents we generate?

Branding/Marketing

70. How might we become better known as the _____ company?

71. How might we penetrate the _____ market?

72. How might we acquire more customers at point of sale?

73. How might we differentiate ourselves from our competition?

74. How might we increase market share?

75. How might we reduce sales training costs?

76. How might we increase our aided brand awareness?

77. How might we increase our unaided brand awareness?

78. How might we increase awareness of specific brand attributes?

79. How might we better monitor consumer perceptions of our brand?

80. How might we use branding to contribute more directly to long-term business development?

81. How might we increase our brand equity?

82. How might we use our brand to differentiate ourselves from our competitors?

83. How might we strengthen our brand with business-to-business companies?

84. How might we better identify our brand values?

85. How might we increase the perceived reliability of our brand?

86. How might we ensure that we don't overlook important communication channels?

87. How might we better position ourselves in our customers' minds?

88. How might we be perceived as the number one financial services provider in the world?

89. How might we brand ourselves as being *the* company for the _____ market?

Processes

90. How might we reduce the costs of _____?

91. How might we improve communication between _____?

92. How might we reduce waste?

93. How might we increase the number of employee suggestions?

94. How might we improve our supply chain?

95. How might we reduce regulatory restrictions?

96. How might we improve product or service quality?

97. How might we reduce bureaucratic procedures?

98. How might we improve our infrastructure for servicing customers?

99. How might we become a more nimble organization?

100. How might we improve our public relations?

101. How might we become the number one _____ company in the world?

102. How might we achieve financial targets related to our target markets?

103. How might we reduce equipment idle time?

104. How might we improve the fit in corporate mergers?

105. How might we better execute our strategy?

106. How might we improve our strategic planning process?

107. How might we better merge our corporate acquisitions?

108. How might we reduce managerial decision-making time?

Human Resources

109. How might we recruit more employees?

110. How might we train employees more efficiently?

111. How might we acquire more employee tacit knowledge?

112. How might we better use employee knowledge?

113. How might we reduce employee turnover?

114. How might we reduce conflict in _____?

115. How might we streamline our hiring process?

116. How might we improve our existing interview process?

Financials

117. How might we better capitalize our R&D?

118. How might we ensure ethical accounting procedures?

119. How might we improve our accounting procedures?

120. How might we increase our cash flow?

121. How might we improve our financial reporting?

122. How might we reduce production costs?

123. How might we increase profits?

124. How might we reduce debt?

125. How might we increase earnings per share?

126. How might we improve our asset turnover?

127. How might we increase our sales per dollar of assets?

128. How might we increase our book value?

129. How might we increase bond yield?

130. How might we reduce the time to convert accounts receivable into cash?

131. How might we reduce our debt-to-capital ratio?

132. How might we improve our efficiency ratio (overhead burden)?

133. How might we increase investor confidence?

134. How might we increase R&D-generated revenues?

Constructing Conceptual Maps for Innovation Challenges

While working with a client on a complex set of potential innovation challenges, I was asked to provide a rationale for the final list of challenge statements I would present to management. As I evaluated the challenges the client submitted, it occurred to me that I was limited by the processing capacity of my brain. Specifically, I had to deal with my cognitive abilities to juggle—somewhat simultaneously—multiple concepts, the meanings of those concepts, how these "clusters of meaning" might fit together to make sense for client objectives and align with them, the various ways these clusters might fit together, and the order of priority among the clusters. All of that is a pretty tall order!

Even if I could do all that juggling, however, there was no guarantee that the client would understand what I was trying to communicate. This is not necessarily due to any intellectual limitations the client might have. We all have different cognitive maps that we construct to represent our separate realities of cause and effect and conceptual relationships among variables. Because our experiences differ in many ways, we are likely to perceive and understand concepts and their inter-relationships differently. I also may communicate in writing or verbally in ways that some may not understand, just because our communication styles may differ.

If the previous assumptions and observations are valid, it probably is even more important that *I* understand what I am conceptualizing! If I can't understand or make sense out of a web of concepts, then it will be even more difficult for me to communicate my understanding to others. After struggling quite a while attempting to write a narrative description of my thought processes, I decided it would be easier to create a visual diagram.

I first reviewed all the challenges and organized them into affinity groups, based on commonalities such as challenges involving processes, financials, customers, and branding. I next thought about ways to create a hierarchy among the groups, so that one might be an ultimate or primary objective that would require resolving by first addressing more subordinate objectives. Finally, I took out a sheet of paper and started writing down keywords representing the essence of the concept groups—for example, *increase revenue* and *improve customer service.* I then drew circles around each concept and experimented with connecting the concepts by drawing lines with arrows on the ends. Once I was satisfied that my drawing made sense in terms of how the clusters were connected, I transferred my pencil drawing to a computer using the Macintosh-only software program OmniGraffle (a Windows equivalent is Visio).

An example of my final map would be similar to Figure 4-2 in Chapter 4. Once I represented my rough drawing on the computer, I began to elaborate and make it more detailed, including indications of possible interrelationships and depicting how some objectives would have to be achieved before others. After experimenting with different configurations, the nature and priority of the challenges began to emerge more clearly. I now had the degree of basic understanding I sought. I included this drawing with my rationale and the client indicated a better understanding of the complex network of challenges the organization faced and how to go about resolving them. One conclusion to draw from this incident is the old saw that one picture is worth a thousand words.

MIND MAPS, CONCEPT MAPS, AND STRATEGY MAPS

Visual diagrams traditionally have been used as part of project and knowledge management because of their ability to portray complex processes and relationships. They can introduce order and structure to help simplify what often is ambiguous.

If innovation challenge concept maps sound familiar, it may be because you already know about mind maps and strategy maps. The former have been a popular tool for recording information in a nonlinear way; the latter have been used for systemwide planning and evaluation in a variety of organizations. Although there are similarities between them, there are some distinct differences as well.

Mind Maps

As developed by brain learning author and speaker Tony Buzan, mind maps are used to collect information and organize it by using branches of associations. Visually, they might appear as branches of a tree. Mind maps begin with a central concept or word. You then add lines to other words associated with that central concept and write words or concepts to describe each preceding word. Each of these secondary words or concepts may have lines radiating out from them, which, in turn, may have additional lines and concepts until you have exhausted all categories or space. An example of a mind map with three major nodes is shown in Figure 5-1. In this case, the mind map is used to convey information about mind maps and not to describe relationships that might exist among variables, as would be the case with concept or strategy maps. Software available includes MindJet MindManager, MindMapper, FreeMind, ConceptDraw, MINDMAP, VisualMind, Mind-Genius, BrainMind, MyMind, and Inspiration (for education)—and these are just a few.

Concept Maps

Concept maps generally are believed to have originated with Professor Joseph D. Novak (now emeritus) of Cornell University in the 1960s. He based his work on that of American psychologist David Ausubel, who emphasized the need to draw on previous knowledge when learning something new. This process involves organizing new concepts into current *cognitive structures*. According to Novak and Canas, now researchers at the Florida Institute for Human and Machine Cognition,

FIGURE 5-1. Sample mind map.

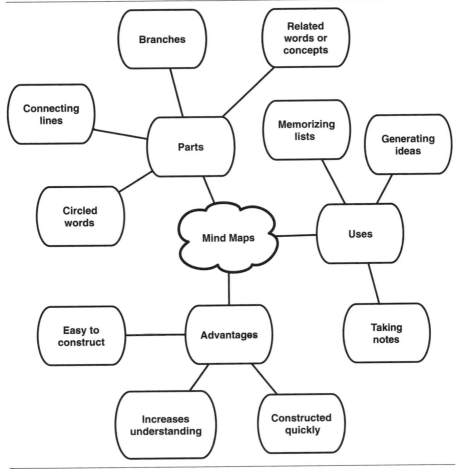

concept maps are graphical tools that help to organize and represent knowledge while showing how different concepts are related.

This book views concept maps as being different from mind maps in that concept maps typically help to clarify relationships among hierarchically ordered, interrelated innovation challenge objectives. That is, each node of a concept map represents an objective used to achieve other objectives (subordinate, or secondary) or is the goal of other objectives (superordinate, or primary). For instance, an innovation challenge concept map might illustrate how an objective of improving customer service must be achieved before an objective of improving customer satisfaction.

Another key difference is that there usually is more than one central concept in concept maps. Related concepts might radiate out from these multiple concepts and connect with others so that the resulting diagram represents more of a network than tree branches. Concept maps typically require more thought, reflection, and time than mind maps, which often are characterized by free, associative thinking—one word leads to another, which leads to another, and so on. Concept maps are not necessarily better or more useful than mind maps. It all depends on the context and purposes you want to achieve: If you want a natural way to generate and record ideas quickly without concern about a logical or hierarchical order, then mind maps would be useful; if you want to depict hierarchical relationships among variables, concept maps would be more valuable. Examples of innovation challenge concept maps were presented in previous chapters and will be discussed in more detail later on in this chapter.

Strategy Maps

A special type of a concept map is a *strategy map*. A variety of such maps have been used over the years, some more formal and complex than others. Perhaps the most notable use of strategy maps in recent years has been based on the work of Robert Kaplan and David Norton, developers of the balanced scorecard (BSC) approach to management strategy. They make the important distinction between *strategies* and *objectives*. An objective would be something like, "We want to be the number one pharmaceutical company in North America." A strategy, in contrast, is how to achieve that objective.

According to Kaplan and Norton, strategy maps are visual representations of how organizations can create value for their shareholders. What is known as the BSC approach to strategy is based on four levels. At the top level is long-term shareholder growth and value, typically expressed in financial terms. Below that level is the customers' value proposition. The third level involves major organizational processes used to meet customers' objectives. This might include developing new products to satisfy consumer needs, for example. The lowest level (learning and growth) represents the foundation of an organization's strategy and includes intangible assets such as organizational climate, skills, ability to learn, and technologies to support processes. An example of this type of a map was described in Figure 1-1 (minus the lowest level) in Chapter 1.

Cam Scholey, president of Advanced Management Initiatives and author of *A Practical Guide to the Balanced Scorecard*, provides the following steps for constructing BSC strategy maps, most of which parallel those of concept maps:

1. *Choose the overriding objective.* An organization should select the single objective it wants to achieve. This typically is a financial goal in for-profit enterprises and can be a more general objective in nonprofits. For instance, a consumer-goods manufacturer might have the objective of growing shareholder wealth; a nonprofit, branding itself as the leading health-care service provider in its market.

2. *Select the appropriate value proposition.* The goal of this step is to consider how your company creates value for your markets. According to Treacy and Wiersema, three primary value propositions are operational excellence, product leadership, and customer intimacy.[1] One example of the latter would be the standard of service offered by Ritz-Carlton hotels. When room attendants notice a soft drink can in a room, they might note it so that guests have the same type of drink waiting for them during their next stay, no matter which property.

3. *Determine general financial strategies to follow.* All organizations must decide on an optimal combination of revenue growth, productivity, and asset use. Deciding on the composition of this blend will depend on the value proposition chosen. If you concentrate on improving internal processes, you probably should stress productivity and asset use. That is, if you can reduce costs by emphasizing these latter two objectives, you can become a price leader with corresponding revenue growth. Wal-Mart is an example of a company with this strategy.

4. *Determine customer-focused strategies.* Organizations must decide what and how much to offer their customers in terms of value. Two common examples are price and how a product might benefit customers in some way—for example, save them time or effort. Some compa-

nies might choose to emphasize price over functionality whereas others choose the opposite. For those deciding to stress price and functionally, they would be pursuing a strategy of optimal customer relationships. The outcome of these decisions will impact an organization's brand image.

5. *Decide how internal processes will support execution of strategies chosen.* This stage is geared toward all the processes required to support the value proposition. Companies perceived as being innovative usually excel here due to their innovative internal processes. They might achieve excellence in creative ways to engage customers in improving operational procedures. For example, a bank involved in retail remittance might engage its customers—such as electrical utilities—in devising innovative ways to scan bills.

6. *Implement the skills/capabilities and employee programs required to achieve strategy.* All of the previous stages will make it evident how well a strategy is being implemented and what objectives still need to be achieved. Organizations must make key, strategic decisions with respect to the priority with which various conceptual gaps should be closed. Thus, organizations with a focus on products might implement strategies with an emphasis on R&D; companies with a focus on creating more emotional connections with customers might concentrate on programs likely to cultivate stronger customer relationships.

To illustrate how these stages can be used to create a strategy map, Scholey creates objectives for each of the four BSC perspectives. For instance, the financial perspective for a hypothetical transportation company might involve objectives such as cost reduction, increasing revenue per transportation unit, and improving cash flow. Customer objectives could include increasing customer satisfaction, solutions tailored to customer needs, and around-the-clock customer service access. For the third level of internal processes, objectives might be improved technology maintenance, better supply chain management, and more efficient fleet management. Finally, objectives at the lowest level, which is people, could involve attracting more competent workers, providing more professional training and development, and encouraging more employee loyalty.

A strategy map showing some possible relationships among these objectives is shown in Figure 5-2. In this example, customer satisfaction is depicted as the primary input to financial objectives. (Remember, this is not intended to be a complete portrayal of a strategy map.) Next, customer satisfaction is presented as being driven by efficient fleet management, which, in turn, is influenced by competent employees. One conclusion to be drawn from such a relatively simple schematic is that a fair amount of attention should be given to people and internal processes. This is because of the numerous hypothetical relationships assumed to exist within and between these two perspectives. For instance, employee training and development is seen as directly impacting improved maintenance within the process perspective and indirectly affecting more efficient fleet management in the same per-

FIGURE 5-2. Sample BSC strategy map for a transportation company.

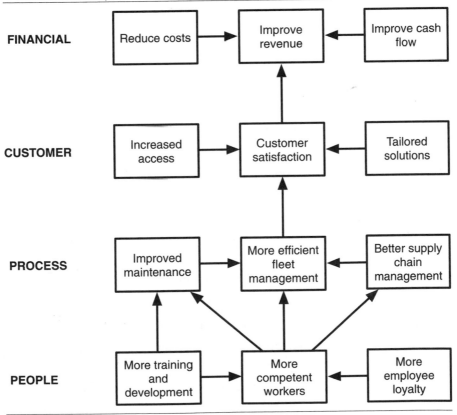

spective because it affects more competent workers directly within the people perspective. (Note that if you read this paragraph as is *without* referring to the strategy map, it is much more difficult to understand the relationships among the objectives.)

The following sections will discuss concept maps created in different areas based on varying amounts and types of background information. This reflects how such maps typically are created in real life. We don't always have access to all the information needed or there isn't the time necessary to collect and analyze the information.

The first example is based on rather extensive information provided from the community services branch of a health-care organization. As described, the challenges are rather broad and more difficult to visualize. The context of a nonprofit organization also provides a perspective different from what is normally found in for-profit organizations.

The second example involves a for-profit organization (Sony) and was drawn from third-party perspectives solely for the purpose of illustrating how to create concept maps from a limited amount of information. Thus, it represents an alternate way to create a concept map without direct client input. It is not recommended that client input be excluded, of course, but external input can create unique perspectives that can be useful as supplemental data.

Example number three involves a map created with a client's list of potential challenges from the client's perspective. These are true presented challenges that require some editing using the criteria discussed in Chapter 4 on writing challenges. What distinguishes these challenges from some others is that they were created from more of a tactical than a strategic perspective.

Example #1: A Concept Map in the Nonprofit Sector

The emphasis of the preceding section was on constructing BSC-influenced strategy maps that are viewed in this book as similar to—but not the same as—innovation challenge concept maps. One difference between the two is that strategy maps are more intensive and encompassing than innovation challenge maps. By definition, strategy maps are oriented toward broad organizational strategies involving all major elements involved in achieving missions and visions; innovation challenge concept maps are designed with a specific focus on creating value through innovation with a more targeted, narrow focus.

Innovation challenge processes, whether competitive or not, always occur in the context of systemwide challenges; however, they may not be driven exclusively by formal or informal strategic plans. Thus, they might focus on internal processes, for example, and only indirectly pertain to customer or financial perspectives. This is not to say that those perspectives are unimportant. They are, of course, very important; they just may not be the focus for one specific innovation challenge conducted as single-event innovation. Over a period of time, multiple concept maps might be linked together in a more encompassing way (and probably should be).

To illustrate how a concept map might be created, consider the case of nonprofit hospitals and their impact on local communities. In this instance, the client's presented challenge was how to persuade others that it deserved a tax-exempt status. Nonprofit hospitals are affected by the perceptions of various stakeholders beyond the local community, including legislators, regulators, consumer groups, and government enforcement agencies. The client was concerned that there was not enough awareness as to the role it played in contributing to the health-care system. For instance, many people may not be aware that nonprofit hospitals contribute a disproportionate share to the uninsured and underinsured, and frequently have trouble with reimbursement from payers. So, the client believes that major stakeholders must be educated on the issues involved.

To create an innovation challenge concept map from this document, I used the following steps:

1. Ask about the client's perception of the primary, overall challenge. In this case, it was as previously described—convincing others of the need for the community service health-care facility to retain its tax-exempt status.

2. Read the entire document.

3. Read the document again, but note possible challenge objectives. If in doubt as to whether or not something is an objective, always err on the side of caution and include it.

4. Starting from the beginning, write challenges beginning with the words, "How might we . . . ?"

5. List all the challenges and organize them into affinity groups. To do this, note which challenges seem similar in some way. There is bound to be some overlap, so just do the best you can. (Consultants should seek input from their clients in the event of uncertainty.) An example is shown in Figure 5-3 on page 98.

6. Read each group and look for internal consistency. In other words, do the groups seem to hang together based on their commonalities? Do all the challenge objectives seem related in some logical way? If not, reorganize the challenges as needed.

7. Compare the groups to assess whether each group is relatively independent and does not overlap excessively with another. In the example, two of the groups are organized with an emphasis on community benefit. One has a focus on increasing understanding about the community benefit of nonprofit health services and the other on persuading others as to the degree of community benefit provided. This suggests the need to determine any type of priority or causality involved. That is, does persuading others about community benefit help to achieve understanding, does achieving understanding persuade others, or are both required? Finally, because of the overlap across groups, I decided to create a list of the three core challenges. It is at this point that a visual concept might help sort out relationships among the challenge objectives.

8. Review all of the groups again, and draw a preliminary concept map. To do this, I selected achieving tax-exempt status as the primary, ultimate objective. I decided to place it at the top of a concept map and work backward, first to the stakeholders who hold direct or indirect ability to influence those who could de-

termine tax status, then to the challenge of persuasion, then to improving understanding of the community benefit, followed by branding and building awareness. A concept map for these challenges is also shown in Figure 5-3.

Here is a list of sample challenges for Community Healthcare Services, organized by the following categories:

Increase Understanding of Our Community Benefit

1. How might we increase public understanding of our community benefit role?
2. How might we increase regulator understanding of our community benefit role?
3. How might we increase understanding among consumer advocacy groups of our community benefit role?
4. How might we increase understanding of government agencies of our community benefit role?
5. How might we increase understanding of the IRS of our community benefit role?

Better Persuade Others of Our Need for Tax-Exempt Status

6. How might we better persuade the public of our need for tax-exempt status?
7. How might we better persuade regulators of our need for tax-exempt status?
8. How might we better persuade consumer advocacy groups of our need for tax-exempt status?
9. How might we better persuade government agencies of our need for a tax exemption?
10. How might we better persuade the IRS of our need for a tax exemption?

Better Persuade Others of the Community Benefit Role We Play

11. How might we better persuade the public of our community benefit role?

FIGURE 5-3. Nonprofit health-care organization challenges.

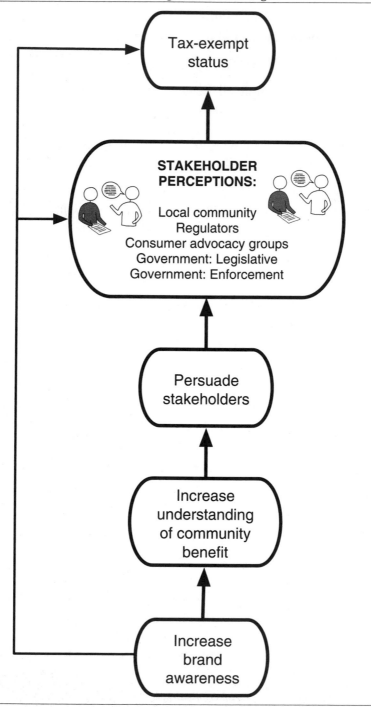

12. How might we better persuade regulators of our community benefit role?

13. How might we better persuade consumer advocacy groups of our community benefit role?

14. How might we better persuade government agencies of our community benefit role?

15. How might we better persuade the IRS of our community benefit role?

Communicate Better with Stakeholders and the Public

16. How might we communicate our mission better to the public?

17. How might we communicate our mission better to legislative bodies?

18. How might we communicate better our community health offerings?

Processes

19. How might we improve community needs assessments?

20. How might we improve our existing health-care services?

21. How might we increase program effectiveness?

22. How might we increase program effectiveness?

23. How might we better evaluate our programs?

24. How might we increase team effectiveness?

Access

25. How might we increase access to preventive care?

26. How might we increase access to remedial care?

27. How might we collaborate more with community groups?

Administrative/Financial

28. How might we reduce administrative costs?

29. How might we increase the reimbursement rate of health-care services?

30. How might we reduce the complexity of health-care delivery?

Consolidated Primary Core Challenges

31. How might we increase stakeholder understanding about our community benefit role?

32. How might we better persuade stakeholders about the need for our tax-exempt status?

33. How might we better persuade stakeholders about the need of our community benefit role?

As shown in Figure 5-3, achieving tax-exempt status might originate with a plan to build brand awareness of the facility's services and the impact it has on people's lives. One way to do this would be to create a strategic communications plan for increasing awareness regarding community benefit. This even could be the only challenge needed to achieve tax-exempt status. The logic then would follow that once understanding about community benefit is established (in terms of a "brand" known for its positive outcomes), key stakeholders can be persuaded as to the validity and importance of the benefit. With the stakeholders persuaded, tax-exempt status then should be attainable. The map also shows that tax-exempt status, once created with strong brand equity, will reinforce stakeholder perceptions and brand awareness.

In spite of this analysis of these challenges, there is nothing to "prove" that it correctly describes how the challenges are or should be related. This is a relatively subjective process. As with any other concept map, it is intended to help stakeholders better understand the challenges they face and how to act on them. To illustrate further how to construct concept maps, next is another business example with a less-strategic but more-limited focus that can be seen as more evident by using a diagram.

Example #2: A Concept Map from External Sources

In fall 2005, the CEO of Sony Corporation, Howard Stringer, faced a challenge of how to appease shareholders in the face of news that Microsoft and Intel had decided to support Toshiba's next-generation DVD technology known as HD DVD. Sony's competing product, Blu-ray, was seen as technologically superior. Although business analysts applauded Stringer's decision to eliminate several thousand employees and reorganize management to engender more internal collaboration, they still were disappointed by the company's ability to generate innovative consumer products.

According to an October 10, 2005, article in *Business Week*,[2] Sony might do well to emulate Samsung Electronics, in spite of its differing technical capabilities. *Business Week's* depiction of Sony's situation provides fertile ground for generating a concept map to understand better what Sony is facing. Here is a summary of how *Business Week* views Sony's challenges:

First, Samsung seems to have improved its ability to collaborate better with its partners and listen to its consumers' needs. Sony, in contrast, tends to emphasize innovations it can brainstorm internally and then sell at sometimes inflated prices. *Business Week* cites the company's decision to cling to its Trinitron television platform, well after flat-panel televisions were dominating the market. In addition, some of its products tend to favor the tastes of Japanese customers who desire more bells and whistles than the West may want.

One reason for this mind-set may be the factionalism that rules at Sony. Different business divisions such as music, movies, and electronics all may have conflicting visions and resist cooperating with one another. A noted example is when Sony's music division prevented the consumer electronics area from making digital music players because of a concern about piracy. As *Business Week* stated, "Hello iPod; goodbye Walkman."[3]

Another reason for some of Sony's troubles may be the company's inability to link up with strategic partners. For instance, it took some prodding, but Samsung eventually was able to persuade Apple to use Samsung's flash memory chips in its music players. The result was the iPod Nano. Sony could do the same by licensing some of its technology. To accomplish such objectives, major cultural changes may need to occur inside Sony. New CEO Stringer now is taking steps to shake things up and may be able to overcome many of these challenges.

Based on this description, a concept map of Sony's challenges can be developed as shown in Figure 5-4. As with all such maps, it is based

FIGURE 5-4. *Hypothetical Sony Corporation concept map.*

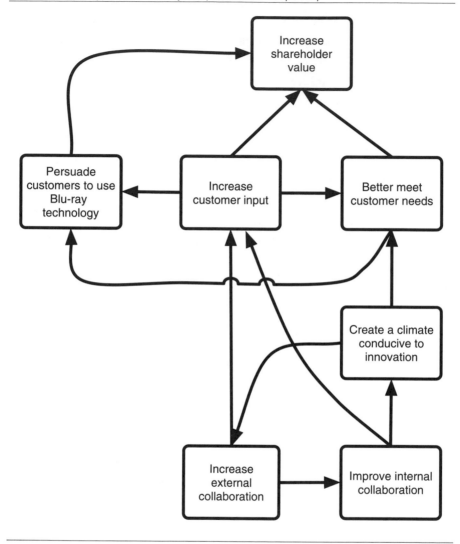

on a set of assumptions about objectives to achieve, their relationship to one another, and their priority. The ultimate objective is to increase shareholder value. Since this, technically, is not a strategic map, it is not required to include any financials, but at least one end state in this area helps to provide some closure. The bottom of the figure shows two key objectives discussed in the article: increasing external collaboration and improving internal collaboration to overcome nonproductive factionalism. (It can be argued that minimal factionalism sometimes can be positive in spurring healthy competition.)

If internal collaboration is improved, then the organizational culture conducive to creativity—shown in Figure 5-4—also might be attained. A more conducive internal climate then could help increase the company's ability to collaborate with externals such as partners and customers. If external collaboration is increased, it might help drive improved internal collaboration that would cycle through the process as indicated—that is, internal collaboration improving a conducive climate, which increases external collaboration *and* helps better meet customer needs while also reinforcing external collaboration, which, in turn, increases internal collaboration, et cetera.

One thing a little different about this concept map is that not all of the objectives have the same level of abstraction. Improving collaboration in two areas is relatively the same in terms of abstraction and specificity, and so are increasing customer input and better meeting customer needs. They both focus on customers in general. Persuading customers to use Blu-ray technology, in contrast, is a more focused objective with a very specific and measurable outcome. So, it could be argued that it shouldn't be included in the map. However, if that is a priority objective, then it should be included, even if it varies in focus or abstraction.

In this instance, it is estimated that increasing input from customers is one potential way to persuade customers to use the technology. If research indicates that significant market share can be gained from successful sales of Blu-ray technology, shareholder value would increase, thus justifying its inclusion. Figure 5-4 also shows that increasing input from customers would better meet customer needs and possibly persuade them to use Blu-ray technology as would better meeting customer needs in general. That is, if Sony brands itself in terms of meeting customer needs in general, then it increases its ability to persuade first adopters to use new technology. (The addition of first adopters as a market target suggests using them as a positioning criterion to better frame customer challenges.)

Example #3: Constructing Tactical Concept Maps

Sometimes organizations conceive of challenges from more tactical perspectives, rather than strategic ones. Tactical approaches, of course, should be presented in the context of clearly articulated strategies, but it is not always feasible or possible to do so. It often is more expedient to address a challenge less abstractly to extinguish a crisis situation, even though it may be short term in its effect. Certain forces may dictate that these challenges be addressed first and then reengineered to fit into what is often an ever-changing strategic direction.

The next case is used to illustrate the conversion of presented challenges into reframed ones, accompanied by conceptual maps. The following is an edited, shortened list of the challenges the client, an automotive manufacturer, originally presented:

Original Presented Challenges

1. How do our brands become relevant to millennials?

2. What should our role be on community Internet sites (e.g., MySpace) and how should we market through those communities?

3. How do we market the use of alternative fuels?

4. When does it make sense to market a brand versus a vehicle nameplate?

5. What kind of pricing strategies should be pursued?

6. How will aging affect the baby boomer generation's auto-buying behavior?

7. How to build a brand from scratch?

8. What is the market potential of increasing the appeal of small pickup trucks for women?

Then the client was asked to divide the challenges into high- and medium-priority groups:

High-Priority List of Original Presented Challenges

1. How do we market the use of alternative fuels?

2. When does it make sense to market a brand versus a vehicle nameplate?

3. What is the market potential of increasing the appeal of small pickup trucks for women?

4. How to build a brand from scratch?

Medium-Priority List of Original Presented Challenges

1. What kind of pricing strategies should be pursued?

2. How will aging affect the baby boomer generation's auto-buying behavior?

3. How do our brands become relevant to millennials?

4. What should our role be in community Internet sites (e.g., MySpace) and how should we market through those communities?

Only the high-priority challenges will be addressed next, with an evaluation of the quality of the statements, suggested reframes, and then some potential conceptual maps.

Before attempting to construct a concept map of these challenges, it first is necessary to review the presented challenges and determine if they should be reframed. For this task, I will assume you already are familiar with the challenge criteria presented in Chapter 4, so they will not be repeated here.

1. *How do we market the use of alternative fuels?* The first high-priority challenge is stated a little too broadly, so its abstraction level probably is a little too high for effective ideation. It might be answered by listing different marketing media and selecting the most appropriate ones with the highest likelihood of reaching the target market. So, the answer might be to advertise in certain urban newspapers and magazines such as *Fast Company*, *Wired*, and *Business 2.0*. Or, an answer could be

to conduct focus groups. Neither of these is especially innovative, so some reframes might be considered. For instance, a simple change in wording might be more beneficial, such as:

- How might we better market alternative fuels?
- How might we increase the brand equity of alternative fuels?

2. *When does it make sense to market a brand versus a vehicle name-plate?* One obvious concern with this challenge is the phrase, "When does it make sense." This is a little ambiguous. However, it might have been stated in the context of some tacit knowledge possessed by the stakeholders. In the past, they may have used similar wording with explicit situations involving explicit criteria. For instance, previously they might have dealt with decision-making situations regarding when to introduce a new brand or line extension. The answer may have been something like, "The best time to introduce our new brand is when the marketing environment is characterized by factors such as disposable income and high unemployment." By default, those factors then would make sense to those individuals in that situation. However, that is con-jecture and should not be used as an excuse to avoid reframing the challenge.

Perhaps more important is that the presented challenge is offered as a decision choice situation rather than a problem-solving challenge created for open-ended ideation. To do this requires making some as-sumptions about the intentions of the client when the challenge was written. So, one option is to just ask the client. However, that doesn't always yield positive results if the client has trouble articulating inten-tions, isn't aware of them, or when you are the client. An alternative is simply to ask, "Why do we want to market a brand versus a name-plate?" In this case, responses might include, "Because our brand equity is so strong," "Because we want to differentiate ourselves from our competitors?" and "We are uncertain about the reliability of our aided or unaided brand awareness."

What may be most important here, however, is to recognize the difference between brand image and brand identity. Brand image con-sists of all those attributes with which consumers associate a particular brand; it is a current perception that implies an expected promise to be delivered on a number of variables—for example, value, performance, or reliability. Brand identity, in contrast, can be viewed as a desired state of consumer perceptions about a product and thus is more strategic. (In the context of this book, this distinction between image and identity represents the perceived gap denoting a problem, which was discussed previously.)

Brand image is established when consumers perceive specific, intended associations. One way to achieve those associations is by concentrating on brand. The first step to that would be increasing aided brand awareness that should result in unaided awareness. Once the later state of perceptions is reached (brand identity), the desired brand image should exist. Of course, this assumes that the process should start with a focus on aided brand awareness. It may be that unaided awareness should be addressed first, if aided awareness is deemed adequate.

With respect to the issue of marketing a brand versus a vehicle nameplate, the previous discussion suggests a focus on branding the nameplate and generating brand-positioning statements to enhance brand identity to the point where the desired brand image is created. With this strategy, reframed challenges, such as the following, can be created that provide the basis for a conceptual map:

- How might we increase aided brand awareness of our vehicle nameplates?
- How might we increase unaided brand awareness of our vehicle nameplates?
- How might we increase the brand identity of our vehicle nameplates?

Figure 5-5 shows a simple, linear, sequential, tactical concept map that starts with increasing aided nameplate awareness that should develop into unaided awareness that then creates the desired amount of brand identity and eventually leads to the nameplate image wanted for that particular vehicle. Again, this process is based on assumptions as to the amount of awareness that currently exists.

3. *What is the market potential of increasing the appeal of small pickup trucks for women?* This challenge has the appearance of being a task for

FIGURE 5-5. *Concept map for marketing a brand vs. a nameplate.*

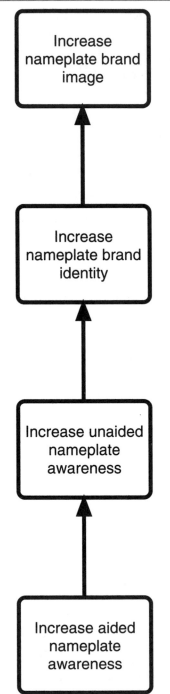

conventional market research. And that just may be because it appears to be exactly that! So, one response might be to segment the female market for trucks, conduct focus groups, and use the results to determine if the market has the potential to explore further. The results then could be used to generate challenges because, as stated, the challenge seems to imply that the client wants to converge on a single result, rather than to diverge, as typically is the process for innovation challenges.

Another reading on this challenge, however, would be that the primary objective is to increase the appeal of the company's trucks for women. It then becomes a conventional marketing innovation challenge in which divergent ideas can be created. As with the previous priority challenge, it probably would be a good idea to seek clarification. Without clarification, you possibly could increase your understanding by again asking, "Why . . . ?" So, in this case, "Why do you want to learn the market potential?" and "Why do you want to increase the appeal of these cars to women?" Answers to these and similar questions might help to create such reframes as:

- How might we better market medium-size pickup trucks to women?

- How might we increase the appeal of medium-size pickup trucks to women?

- How might we persuade more women to purchase medium-size pickup trucks?

- How might we increase sales of medium-size pickup trucks to women?

- How might we increase market share of medium-size pickup trucks to women?

Although several of these challenges might be similar, minor wording changes sometimes help to spark the best reframes and, especially, the best ideas.

4. *How to build a brand from scratch?* This obviously is an incomplete sentence. In this case, the client wanted to brand a new product. The process here is similar to that suggested for priority challenge #2

discussed previously: Increase aided brand awareness, then aided awareness that should lead to brand identity. In addition to this rather staid approach, some other challenge reframes might be used to create some of the "attitude" often needed for creative thinking. For instance:

- How might we create aided brand awareness of our new product?

- How might we create unaided brand awareness of our new product?

- How might we increase the brand identity of our new product?

- How might we make potential customers "lust" after our new product?

A concept map for these challenges would be virtually identical to Figure 5-5 with the exception of adding one for the "lusting" challenge. This particular outcome logically would be an outgrowth of increasing brand identity and/or image.

NOTES

1. Michael Treacy and Fred Wiersema, *The Discipline of Market Leaders: Choose Your Customers* (Cambridge, Mass.: Perseus Books, 1995).

2. "The Lessons for Sony at Samsung" from "News Analysis & Commentary," *Business Week,* October 10, 2005.

3. Ibid.

SIX

How to Conduct Innovation Challenges

As discussed in Chapter 4, the general structure of innovation challenges is based on assumptions about subjectively perceived current and desired states of performance. In other words, how we perceive the challenges facing our organizations determines how we try to close the perceived gaps. Based on these assumptions, to reframe a challenge is to alter one or more of these three ingredients: the perceived *is*, the *should be*, or *how to close the gap*. Most organizations are fairly good at defining where they are and where they want to be. That is within the sphere of strategic planning—assuming, of course, adequate resources and ability. They may be less effective, however, at generating ideas with the potential to close challenge gaps. This is where innovation challenge events can help. Organizations can set up idea-capturing processes in which they focus their resources on resolving challenges creatively.

Although the basic technology has been available for many years, only recently have organizations begun conducting innovation challenges systematically to generate a stream of ideas for their innovation pipelines. Most of these challenges represent single-event innovation in which just one focused target is dealt with at a time. They can be conducted any number of times based on need and available resources and need not be integrated tightly with existing innovation change processes. The nature and scope of such challenges, however, should be congruent with clearly articulated strategic visions.

THE TYPES OF INNOVATION CHALLENGES

There are at least two distinct types of idea campaigns used for innovation challenges: *competitive* and *noncompetitive*. Competitive challenges frequently offer specific incentives for participants; noncompetitive ones typically involve an organization's employees and/or key stakeholders without specific incentives, although that is not always the case. No research yet exists to draw conclusions as to which approach is better in terms of organizational outcomes. Some anecdotal evidence, however, suggests that competitive challenges have the potential for a greater quality of ideas.

There is no reason, obviously, why a project to capture ideas without rewards cannot be changed to a competitive one by offering incentives. The primary considerations in making that decision lie in the experience level of program managers who design and oversee competitive challenges. The real issue may revolve around the definitions of incentives. Awarding a small prize—such as dinner coupons—to whoever submits the best idea is likely to result in a less-competitive spirit than a cash award or a small vacation. The inherent competitive nature of many people may be more motivating. During online brainstorming sessions with which I've been associated, participants typically are paid a set fee for a given number of ideas. In many cases, they will exceed this quota once they get started.

Competitive Challenges

The most well-known international competitive innovation challenge is The Global Innovation Challenge (www.innovationchallenge.com) run by Los Angeles–based Idea Crossing and hosted by a major business school from a U.S. university. Every year, more than three hundred teams of MBA students from about one hundred universities representing around twenty countries, compete for prizes worth $50,000. The teams generate creative ideas and make a business case for dealing with pressing real-world challenges provided by such corporate sponsors as IBM, Sprint, DaimlerChrysler, the U.S. Postal Service, and Hilton Hotels & Resorts. The process and software ("Challenge Accelerator") used for these challenges also have been used for internal organizational challenges along with cash incentives or other rewards. Examples of companies using competitive challenges include Illy Expresso's annual competition for young designers, Peugot Concurs Design competition, DuPont, Grainger, and various nanotechnology competitive events.

According to Idea Crossing, successful competitive challenges are marked by the following eight characteristics:

1. *Framed Questions.* Open-ended, yet carefully bounded challenges that help to spark imaginative solutions targeted at a core issue.

2. *Distributed Access.* The ability of all participants (contestants, judges, sponsors and event organizers) to perform their roles regardless of geographical location.

3. *Structured Submissions.* Use of a standardized concept plan outline and framework for idea submissions.

4. *Transparency.* All participants receive timely and explicit reminders regarding due dates, event process, and other information to ensure everyone involved has up-to-date information.

5. *Scorecard Metrics.* All participants, but especially judges, are provided with explicit evaluation criteria so that uniform standards are used to rate all ideas.

6. *Judge Selection and Management.* The selection of competition judges should be managed carefully. An efficient and flexible system also should be devised to monitor judge's progress and keep the evaluation process flowing smoothly.

7. *Scalability.* Idea competitions can vary considerably in the range and number of participants and idea submissions. Hundreds or even thousands of ideas may be involved. It is essential that a robust and proven system be used to minimize administrative burdens.

8. *Delightful Experience.* Participants in most innovation competitions are energized by the challenging and competitive nature of the

experience. The event should be characterized by a smooth submission process, an easy-to-use software interface, and effective technical and human support.

Another example of a competitive challenge is Toolkits for Idea Competitions (TIC). They have been used in Germany at the sporting goods company Adidas Salomon AG to investigate the viability of customer and user participation to supplement its new product development (NPD) process. Although many customer ideas tend to be more incremental than unique, "lead" consumer users appear to have the ability to suggest innovative ideas. This probably is due to their tendency to encounter marketplace needs sooner than other consumers and their ability to benefit from their needs. That is, they tend to be trendsetters, early adopters, and typically communicate product experiences within their social networks. This, along with their above-average product knowledge, makes them ideal candidates for generating product improvement ideas as well as entirely new product lines or categories.

Noncompetitive Challenges

According to Imaginatik.com, one of the pioneers (since 1999) of systematic, single-event, primarily noncompetitive innovation challenges, the success of idea management projects depends on a number of human problems in addition to more technical and procedural ones. For instance, managers should be supportive and responsive to new ideas submitted by employees and employees must have the courage to suggest ideas they otherwise might be afraid to submit.

In support of the single-event approach to organization-wide innovation challenges, Imaginatik cites an instance in which a large consumer products company used its software ("Idea Central") to generate 5,500 ideas from 30 different events. Of about 250 ideas selected for further development or implementation, 90 percent came from the single events, while only a few came from more traditional, random idea-capturing approaches.

All challenges should assign an innovation manager to oversee and manage the idea-capturing process and be familiar with all software and processes used. Such managers also should work with sponsors who can be internal or external to the organization. An internal sponsor can be someone who provides the administrative and financial backing for a project as well as frames the challenge statement. External sponsors might be used to provide financial support for nonprofit organizations or even competitive events such as the Global Innovation Challenge.

According to Imaginatik.com, there are twelve essential elements of single-event challenges:

1. *Management Commitment.* As with any organizational change project, senior management should support the process as well as commit and follow up with idea implementation.

2. *Right Tool for the Job.* Idea generation can occur in numerous situations involving different amounts of people. For large numbers of people, it may be best to use idea management software to process ideas more efficiently; for smaller numbers, small groups who meet in person might be best. If large-scale idea generation is to take place, idea management software would be a logical choice.

3. *Problem Framing.* Given the topic of this book, it should be evident that how a challenge is framed may determine an ideation project's success. Higher-quality ideas are more likely if broader challenges are used. For instance, instead of thinking of what promotional giveaways to use, challenge the participants to generate ways to sell more products.

4. *Establish Targets.* Before beginning any challenge, think of desired targets such as rates of participation or number of high-quality ideas. Such goals can help structure the planning process, validate the challenge, and provide guidance for future projects.

5. *Motivate People.* Most challenges work best if participants receive small prizes for the best ideas or "loyalty points" for how much they contributed to a project.

6. *Participant Selection.* Who participates in a challenge is a crucial decision. Research suggests that the most creative, novel ideas come from diverse groups of participants. However, if an event involves a relatively narrow focus, then less diverse groups might be best. As a

rule of thumb, once you have selected the ideal people to participate, add another 50 percent from outside the scope of the project.

7. *Tell Them About It.* Challenges are more likely to succeed if they are marketed internally via e-mails. Marketing plans for ideation projects should contain information about the challenge, the target audience, the idea submission channels, and the appropriate time to send messages about the project.

8. *The Right Review Team.* All generated ideas must be reviewed by a designated review team, typically appointed by a project's sponsor. It is important to include reviewers with experience from other projects and experts external to the core review team also might be included. Such experts can be valuable when judging specialized topics such as technical feasibility. Review teams also should be well versed in the evaluation criteria.

9. *Keep Your Eyes Open.* The innovation project manager should monitor the process to evaluate the contributions and the degree of collaboration among participants. It is especially important to assess the degree of participation and to encourage more submissions if the number appears to be decreasing below preestablished targets.

10. *People Need Closure.* Following an innovation event, provide the participants with feedback regarding the project's outcome and thank them for their contributions. Also, if you are not able to review all the ideas, indicate so to the participants. Honesty is vital in such situations.

11. *Path to Implementation.* Once the review team has chosen the best two to five ideas, the sponsor should initiate an implementation plan, including the order in which ideas should be implemented. The sponsor also should mobilize any resources needed for successful implementation.

12. *Plan for the Next Event.* Single-event innovation challenges may appear to outsiders as just that: one event directed at one target. In fact, that is accurate. Innovation challenges are directed at one target at a time. Instead, they should be viewed as supporting systemwide, sustained innovation initiatives. Thus, multiple events should be planned at least a year in advance along with details as to how each

event will fit with the next and the organization's overall strategic plan.

PREPARING FOR INNOVATION CHALLENGES

Innovation challenges are more likely to be successful when senior management aligns itself with an innovation vision and seeks to communicate it to all stakeholders to obtain their buy-in. As with any major endeavor, preparation is the key to success. Everything needs to be in place before ideas are collected. One of the first tasks is to create—as much as feasible, given limited resources—an organizational climate conducive to innovation. This, of course, assumes you are not interested just in a single event. If, instead, your focus is more on integrating innovation challenges with existing process change innovations (highly recommended!), then you must focus on how to create an innovative climate—a subject for another book, however.

Jeffrey Baumgartner, a Belgian innovation consultant and developer of Jenni idea management software, proposes that all organizations create an "innovation manifesto" to prepare for innovation initiatives. He suggests something like the following:[1]

In view of the fast changing marketplace, continuous introductions of new technologies and our competitors' relentless growth, our company declares that innovation shall rule our products, operations and actions. Henceforth:

1. Top management shall embrace, encourage and nurture innovation at all times. Every decision they make will take into consideration how that decision shall affect the innovativeness of the organisation.

2. Top management themselves shall adopt more creative behaviour—via training if need be—and demonstrate their creativity to employees, clients and shareholders.

3. The company shall communicate in every possible way the importance of innovation, the innovations we have performed and our future innovation goals. Such communications shall be both internal and external and target employees, customers, shareholders and the general public.

4. We shall establish a reasonable budget for implementing radically innovative ideas. The return on investment of implementation of those ideas shall take into consideration not only income, but also learning value. There will be no [negative] consequences for implementations that are not financially successful.

5. Managers shall ensure that . . . team members [have] time to be creative and understand that being creative, which leads to innovation, is a critical component of [their] job responsibilities.

6. Realising that innovation is our future, we shall all learn to greet new ideas with open arms and consider the innovative potential of those ideas. Rather than criticise ideas, as we have done in the past, we shall challenge those who propose ideas to improve their ideas and make them more innovative.

7. Creative thinking skills shall become a priority in our internal training programmes.

8. Employees shall be rewarded for their innovative ideas, even if those ideas are not implemented or are not profitable.

9. No employee shall ever be reprimanded for sharing an idea to others in the firm, even if the idea seems preposterous. We understand that one employee being scolded for sharing a silly idea can do irreparable damage to our firm's innovativeness.

10. We shall adopt an idea management process and system in order to encourage, capture and evaluate innovative ideas from our employees.

11. Project teams shall be filled with a variety of people from various divisions in order to ensure breadth of creative thought and innovative solutions in all our projects.

12. We shall take great pride in our innovativeness and strive to improve it daily.

Other elements involved in preparation include making decisions such as who should participate; how they should participate; how to reward participants; how to process ideas; and what, if any, idea management software program to use.

CONDUCTING INNOVATION CHALLENGES

Once an innovation vision and mandate for strategic change have been established, management must begin the work of collecting ideas to resolve innovation challenges. Historically, this has been done in-house; within corporate R&D departments; via consultations with vendors; and by scouring a variety of market research reports and, sometimes, soliciting consumer ideas for new products. Unfortunately, some research suggests that consumer-based market research often isn't accurate enough to identify more than general trends.

New product processes in particular also seem to be characterized by an internal or "closed" focus. The "Not Invented Here" syndrome still appears to thrive within some organizations. Such a focus, of course, limits the pool of potential innovative solutions. In its place, many practitioners and researchers such as Eric von Hippel, author of *Democratizing Innovation,* now are calling for more open source or "distributive" innovation in which ideas are sought outside traditional organizational networks. "Crowdsourcing" and similar means of collaborating with broad bases of consumers are becoming more common wells of innovation from which organizations can draw. The Idea Crossing approach described previously was dubbed "Crowdcasting" by *Business 2.0* magazine.[2]

For the most part, internal or external sources have tended to be formal initiatives for new products and processes to the exclusion of other aspects of organizational life. Idea generation for improving organizational challenges such as customer service, the interface between marketing and R&D, communication between departments, or brand awareness all seem to receive much less attention and emphasis. In the past, this might be excusable to some degree, given limited resources to mobilize idea campaigns on topics other than core innovation issues such as new products. However, the current availability of knowledge experts, unarticulated consumer insights, ethnographic research methods, and idea management software removes most excuses for not engaging in targeted and deliberate idea generation for a variety of innovation challenges.

WORKING THROUGH THE STAGES OF
INNOVATION CHALLENGES

One way to increase external participation in idea generation and to take advantage of technological advancements is to conduct formal idea campaigns or competitions. In the past several years, increasing numbers of organizations in all sectors have been turning to software solutions that go beyond the simple suggestion programs of the last couple hundred years. Software now is used regularly to collect and process vast quantities of ideas from employees, even those who are geographically dispersed. And, market research increasingly is being conducted on the Internet using virtual focus groups of consumer panels to both generate and evaluate new ideas. Some of these are collected from internal employees whose contributions are considered to be part of their jobs; other times, organizations are conducting competitive innovation challenges in which participants compete for various incentives. Moreover, the participants increasingly are externals such as consumers and creative professionals.

Most enterprise idea campaign software is available for hosting on an organization's intranet or by an idea management consulting firm on its servers. The majority of enterprise innovation software is designed for idea management campaigns in which employees submit ideas that then are evaluated by review teams for later implementation. As mentioned previously, idea management software involves participation by externals such as subject matter experts, consumers, or creativity professionals. The second form of enterprise idea software is designed to conduct idea competitions in which diverse groups of participants (sometimes working as teams) submit ideas and receive various types of incentives for the quality of ideas they submit in comparison with those of others.

Although not all innovation challenges may be competitive, the basic process stages are fairly similar and parallel generic problem-solving stages: Define and frame a challenge, solicit and collect ideas, evaluate and select the best ideas, transform ideas into workable solutions if necessary, and implement the ideas. Such stages provide a structure that ensures a successful project outcome. Nevertheless, the ultimate key to quality innovation challenges lies in the details of conducting the process—just as with any complex process—and in the essential elements needed to conduct idea campaigns. The stages of three firms that conduct innovation challenges are discussed next.

Idea Crossing's Process

Idea Crossing emphasizes the importance of executing competitive innovation challenges by thinking through an entire event before setting it in motion. Once deadlines are communicated, they must be upheld. Missing deadlines can shatter participants' confidence in the event and its outcomes. It is therefore critical to follow a very well thought-out and tested process. Although the one described next is certainly not the only recipe for conducting a successful competition, it is one Idea Crossing has used and refined over the years of running these events. The organization calls it the Three P Three E process and its stages are:

1. *Preparation.* This is the most important of all stages. The aim is to define the strategic goal(s) of the competition, as well as to define target participant base, and to decide on a time line, judging methodology, and prizes. Setting the strategic objective of the event outcome is often time-consuming, and it should involve the highest levels of an organization. The most-common objectives (beyond the generation of ideas themselves) include engaging an organization in a creative exercise; finding new talent (e.g., from within the pool of top MBA candidates); or extending a brand's position as an innovative, forward-thinking, and consumer-engaged company.

The most essential activity, however, is properly framing the challenge question. Idea Crossing spends a significant period of time with clients framing the core challenge questions, the subject of this book. The company brings in experts in the field and works closely with senior client executives to ensure challenge questions direct participants to consider issues core to the strategic objectives of the event, as discussed in other chapters. A properly framed challenge question is part art, part science—and can make or break the event. And, a well-articulated question helps to ensure participants generate innovative solutions to clients' most-pressing business challenges.

One final aspect of the preparation phase involves assembling background material for contestants. This includes a concise packet of information, referred to as a *challenge brief*. This document allows the organization to provide its current thinking and background data on the problem at hand to participants. It also helps guarantee contributors will not duplicate client efforts or generate off-topic ideas.

2. *Promotion.* One of the key decisions in the preparation phase is the target contestant base. Depending on this decision, the promotion phase can involve a large-scale public marketing and PR campaign; take the form of more targeted communications (such as inviting students from the top one hundred global business schools to compete); or may simply be an internal, corporate, e-mail campaign. Whether the ideal participant group is based on geography, age, gender, or other demographic metrics, corporations should design and launch a targeted, yet viral marketing campaign aimed at generating significant buzz among the identified pool of contestants.

Converting educated and interested individuals into registered contestants requires clear communication. Describing the benefits of participation in a compelling and succinct manner is critical to attracting registrations. Equally important, clearly articulating the submission criteria, event time line, and judging methodology reduces the volume of questions from potential registrants (and the administrative support burden of event organizers).

3. *Participation.* The first step of the participation phase is to broadcast the challenge question, along with the challenge brief, to participants. Different challenge questions are given to different groups of participants, according to their topic preferences or areas of expertise. This introduces some complexity to the assignment process because the preferences of participants must be balanced with the need for a uniform distribution across all topics.

Organizations often decide to expand on the question and challenge brief with a global conference call to discuss the question in real time with contestants. These calls frequently elicit useful information as the central question is discussed and the current business strategy around it is reviewed.

Participants then are given a discrete period of time in which to

generate and submit their concept. It is important that the event organizers define a standard submission structure before the event begins.
This helps to standardize all ideas so that they can be judged on a level
playing field. Often, idea submission structures can include criteria
areas such as feasibility, value proposition, competitive advantage, and
bottom-line results. The final list will depend on the target audience.

Finally, when in the participation phase, organizations may wish to
provide creativity and brainstorming tools. Although there are myriad
techniques and exercises found online, many organizations have their
favorites and may wish to include these. Several examples are also provided in Chapters 8 and 9.

4. *Identification.* The key to effective idea evaluation rests on identifying a qualified judging panel and providing it with an understanding
of what constitutes a winning concept. Organizations should define a
standardized judging scorecard, with both quantitative and qualitative
metrics. This scorecard should not be kept secret from contestants. In
fact, it should be widely distributed and understood by participants as
they generate concepts. Judges should be familiar with not only each
evaluation criterion but also the relative weighting of each.

Some competitions should employ a two-phased judging methodology, especially if the event seeks to identify a small percentage of
concepts for further exploration. If necessary, organizations should
work to define first- and second-cut judging panels and scoring criteria,
guaranteeing only the best ideas are bubbled up for review in the second cut.

5. *Extraction.* Organizations should extract only the most promising ideas for further review or pilot. This phase allows clients to invite
contestants in for face-to-face presentations of fleshed-out concepts. To
do this, Idea Crossing recommends that clients conduct an exciting and
high-energy final round event. This event can crown the first-, second-,
and third-place ideas and may be used to determine pilot funding or
project go-ahead publicly. The importance of concluding the event
with a high-visibility final round cannot be overstated. It is an obvious
and very public show of support for the challenge, the participants, and
the ideas generated.

6. *Exploration.* The final phase provides an opportunity to conduct
a 360-degree review of the competition, including key learnings and

opportunities for system or process enhancement. Such an exhaustive review can help organizations prepare for subsequent innovation competitions. In addition, organizations should provide access to all ideas for authorized employees, searchable by scores, keywords, topic areas, et cetera. During this final phase of the competition, talk usually begins around the next event. Idea Crossing suggests that companies make innovation challenges an annual part of their business calendars. Not only can additional competitions build off previous ones and resolve new challenges; they also can contribute to a more innovative corporate culture.

Imaginatik's Process

Imaginatik.com's idea management approach is based on four major components, each of which contains several defined activities: requirements and decisions prior to launch, preparations for launch, during the event, and closing the event.

1. Requirements and decisions prior to launch
   a. Gain executive support and commitment.
   b. Define objectives and measures of success.
   c. Define desired types of input.
   d. Define audience.
   e. Define intellectual property.
   f. Define reward approach.
   g. Define approach to idea implementation.
   h. Define review team approach.
   i. Identify required technical resources.
   j. Define communications approach.
2. Preparations for launch
   k. Collect challenges from executives.
   l. Select and prepare review team.
   m. Prepare communications and feedback.
   n. Configure the application.
3. During the event
   o. Launch internal marketing campaign.

    p. Launch event.

    q. Manage the audience.

    r. Manage the review process.

    s. Manage executives.

4. Closing the event

    t. Finish reviews and conclusions.

    u. Present results to executives.

    v. Distribute rewards.

    w. Define plans for implementations.

    x. Evaluate the performance and establish potential improvements.

    y. Send closure communications.

Jenni Idea Management's Process

Jenni software captures ideas using a four-step process:

1. *The challenge is defined.* These statements typically begin with, "How might we . . . ? or "In what ways might we . . . ? Once the challenge is selected, the campaign is promoted to participants who, ideally, will represent a diverse mixture of individuals in order to increase the creativity of the ideas. (The Jenni program, as well as Imaginatik and others, makes it possible for managers to initiate idea campaigns themselves so that an entire organization always does not have to be involved.)

2. *Open, collaborative idea generation is begun.* A space is provided where ideas can be submitted and viewed by others for possible "builds." Such openness, also characterized by ideas from people who may not know each other, helps to foster a spirit of collaboration. Moreover, the transparency of the process helps prevent people from submitting duplicate ideas.

3. *Peer reviews of ideas are conducted.* One way to do this is to use five key criteria. For instance, for a project involving new product ideas, reviewers might ask questions such as: "How profitable is this product likely to be?" and "How well does this product integrate with our existing product line?"

4. *Ideas and criteria are sent to experts for additional or final evaluation.* Once ideas are evaluated, a list of overall scores can be created such as listing the ideas from lowest to highest scores.

As incentives to participants, they can receive recognition for the best ideas, personal notes of thanks from key managers, small gifts, work-related privileges such as attending a conference, a higher class of flying, or time off. Regardless of what rewards are used, mention them at the outset of the conference. Finally, Baumgartner notes that the end of one idea campaign can be the beginning of another. Thus, the solution to one challenge might prove to be the challenge for another idea campaign. For instance, one new product idea might be used in a new project to stimulate ways to improve or launch that product.

In summary, Internet technology now makes it possible to bypass conventional methods of collecting ideas and to gather large numbers of ideas from large numbers of participants. Internal idea competitions truly have merit and should be researched further. Some elements of competitive approaches may not always translate, however, for consumer/marketing research. One problem with soliciting ideas from consumers is using incentive systems such as cash awards. The ideas submitted might reflect a self-selected sample that responds more to financial rewards than the need to solve a problem or the joy of creating. Of course, there is nothing inherently wrong with cash incentives and there is no reliable way to determine participant motivations. I strongly recommend that using consumers to generate ideas online be supplemented by creative-type professionals working in the creativity and innovation areas and/or creative professions such as in the arts, design, and architecture.

NOTES

1. Excerpted from online newsletter *Report 103,* "Your Innovation Manifesto," Tuesday April 4, 2006, Issue 79, available at http://www.jpb.com/report103/archive.php?issue_no=20060404. Retrieved January 25, 2007. Published by Jeffrey Baumgartner, Bwiti bvba, a jpb.com company, Brussels, Belgium.

2. Melanie Haikon, "Want Fresh Ideas? Try 'Crowdcasting,'" *Business 2.0,* November 21, 2006.

PART II

After the Game

In one sense, the chapters in this part are supplemental to the broader innovation challenge process—at least with respect to generating ideas. The primary focus of Part I was on planning, setting up, and conducting competitive and noncompetitive idea challenges. However, once ideas are captured and organized, they still need to be evaluated and turned into viable solutions for resolving innovation challenge objectives. Part II begins with a description of major idea management software programs designed specifically to structure and facilitate the capturing and processing of large quantities of ideas (Chapter 7). This chapter also includes brief descriptions of software programs for generating ideas by individuals or groups. The remaining chapters focus on more traditional idea generation methods, some basics of designing and facilitating traditional brainstorming retreats. (Yes, face-to-face idea generation still has advantages over computer-assisted innovation!) The last two chapters deal with some basic guidelines and techniques for smoothing out the evaluation, selection (Chapter 11) and implementation of ideas (Chapter 12).

SEVEN

Idea Management and Creativity Software

Numerous software programs have been developed to facilitate conducting innovation challenges. The majority of these programs can be described as *idea management software* and are intended for use by relatively large numbers of participants. Other programs exist to assist with idea generation or more comprehensive creative problem solving. This chapter will present some examples of both types, but it is not intended as a comprehensive review of all existing software programs on the subject. New programs are continually being created, so you may want to do some Internet searches. One excellent resource is www.innovationtools.com.

THE EVOLUTION OF IDEA MANAGEMENT SYSTEMS

How organizational leaders frame innovation challenges for the rest of the organization is essential for enduring change. Many researchers maintain that management framing creates a social architecture in which people's views lend validity to the need for change. More recently, the focus in innovation has been on what Tim O'Reilly, CEO of O'Reilly Media, Inc., has referred to as the "architecture of participation."[1] Collaboration among all organizational stakeholders has emerged as a current focus on how to solicit innovation input from a diversity of sources. Numerous enterprise idea management and Web-based software programs now provide a variety of options for gathering and delivering input on resolving organizational innovation challenges.

However, before these digital devices descended on the corporate world, they were preceded by employee suggestion systems. According to Mark Turrell, the CEO of Imaginatik.com, formal suggestion projects began in the late 1700s in the British navy. About one hundred years later, a Scottish shipbuilder created an actual physical box into which employees could place their ideas. His reward system was supposedly one of the first to reward employees for workable ideas. The first U.S. organization to use company-wide employee suggestion efforts was NCR, whose CEO, John Patterson, promoted what he termed, the "hundred-headed brain." During the industrial boom years during and after World War II, suggestion boxes spread widely and eventually were integrated within various quality improvement programs. Of course, with the advent of the Internet and e-mail, virtual suggestion boxes now are more prevalent. Unfortunately, most suggestion programs were not implemented properly and failed to contribute significantly to the corporate bottom line.

The precursor to today's idea management software probably was solicitation and acquisition of ideas using e-mail. An e-mail message is sent to a select group of participants who are asked to reply with ideas to some challenge defined by senior management. Sometimes, participants chat with each other in real time (*synchronous communication*) and build on each other's ideas as generated; more commonly, however, participants respond to e-mails according to their own schedules based on when they have time available (*asynchronous communication*). Although e-mail idea management is an economical and simple way to collect ideas, it also has its downsides. Even if the challenge is framed well, the process lacks the structure needed for productive idea generation. Even worse, there can be an overwhelming amount of data to process and make sense of—suggesting a clear-cut need to manage the idea management process.

One way to manage ideas productively is to use idea management software, either as enterprise software (installed within a company's existing computer network) or as a Web-based system (hosted via external servers). One unique relative of Web-based software programs is Idea Crossing's Challenge Accelerator, which is similar to idea management software, but was designed exclusively for conducting scalable idea competitions using different types of participants. In this respect, Challenge Accelerator serves as a turnkey program for idea competitions, much as more conventional idea management programs do for noncompetitive idea-capturing campaigns.

Companies such as Masterfoods USA, Bristol-Myers, Coca-Cola, Georgia-Pacific, Bayer, Kraft, Hilton Hotels, Merck, and Hallmark all have used such software in different ways to enhance their innovation initiatives. Cingular Wireless, for instance, uses software that captures and routes ideas during monthly online chat sessions. Perhaps most important, idea management software has become known as the savior for knowledge management initiatives that did not always have the support of management without hard, statistically verifiable results. In 2001, Imaginatik.com and the Baroudi Group estimated that global spending on idea management software and related services approached $3 million; that figure was expected to rise to $14 million in 2002.

A lot of the information for this chapter was based on Chuck Frey's summaries of idea management software programs found on his Web site: http://www.innovationtools.com. In an overview of a number of these programs, Frey notes that most systems can be described as having the following:[2]

- Singular focus on specific idea campaigns
- Customizable idea capture forms
- Customizable evaluation criteria
- Focus on collaboration and idea sharing

Singular Focus on Specific Idea Campaigns

As a subset of knowledge management, idea management programs can be created to address specific challenges such as new product ideas, cost reductions, and many other types of challenges, such as those detailed in Chapter 4. These single-event projects can be fruitful if structured sufficiently and accompanied by results-driven implementation, including detailed action plans, time frames, and assigned responsibilities.

Customizable Idea Capture Forms

One advantage idea management software has over e-mails or the most basic, generic idea capture programs is the ability to tailor response options for a specific project. For instance, some programs allow users to comment on ideas they submit by noting the estimates of potential risks involved or the likelihood of consumer acceptance. This information may not be useful or applicable for other projects, however. Thus, a project to generate ideas for new beverages may request comments about the novelty of ideas in relation to competing projects; a project on how to create brand awareness, in contrast, may ask the submitters to note how their ideas are likely to affect awareness in different market segments.

Customizable Evaluation Criteria

Once all ideas have been generated, participants may be given the opportunity to review all ideas and rate them using numerical scales. Although such scales use subjective perceptions, they possess a degree of objectivity that can be useful for quantifiable, global comparisons. That is, they are better than using purely subjective choices using implicit criteria and relying solely on intuition. Rating scales have the advantage of using at least a set of shared, explicit criteria.

Collaboration and Idea Sharing

As noted previously, systemwide innovation challenges help to involve organizational stakeholders in organizational processes that can impact organizational outcomes directly. Employees are more likely to support ideas they suggest and participating in a collaborative venture creates a sense of identity with the larger organization (given a perception of positive incentives). More important, being able to view others' ideas can help trigger new ideas and involve people no matter where they are located.

Frey goes on to note the following advantages of idea management systems:[3]

- They focus employees' creative efforts around specific organizational goals and objectives.

- They encourage employees to capture all their ideas.

- They collect ideas from all areas of the organization.

- By placing ideas in a shared repository, idea management systems promote greater transparency.

- They help companies share best practices.

- They help companies increase their speed to market.

- They can be used in many types of common corporate applications.

IDEA MANAGEMENT SOFTWARE PROGRAMS

A variety of software programs now exist for soliciting and processing ideas—as previously noted, as either enterprise or Web-based services. A number of these idea management programs are discussed next in alphabetical order. They are followed by a brief list of idea generation software programs. The difference between the two is that the former are intended for relatively large-scale idea capturing and can involve several thousand participants. Most idea generation software, in contrast, is designed for individuals or small groups who are presented with a variety of idea stimuli and sometimes—depending on the software—guided through a series of problem-solving steps. Finally, no claim is made that this chapter presents all available idea management or idea generation software programs. In fact, by the time this book is published, there also may be a number of new ones.

BrainBank

BrainBank (www.brainbankinc.com) offers two programs that might be of interest for idea management campaigns: Ideaswarm and Idealink. Ideaswarm is designed to facilitate collaboration with varying degrees of participation. It is designed especially to capture concept input from both internal and external participants who can be organized into ad hoc teams to generate ideas and to build on them progressively. Idealink helps to capture and convert ideas into workable concepts. It contains three integrated modules. The first, Idealink Employee, helps to streamline employee suggestion processes. Idealink Customer Idea Management is for tapping the vast intellectual capital residing within customers. Finally, Idealink Supplier is intended to "enhance your value chain by transforming your vendors into idea team partners."[4]

So far, BrainBank appears similar to other idea management programs. However, it also has quite a variety of diverse features, including:

- Contextual tutorials
- Voting management
- Online training
- Notification engine
- Motivational quote engine
- Configurable workflow
- Customizable profile
- Single sign-on
- Security management
- Online simulations
- Staging site
- Online survey
- Talent referral
- Video integration
- Light PLM management
- TRIZ integration
- Six Sigma integration
- Telephone submission

- Podcast review
- PDA and mobile integration

Brainline

Creativity consultant Peter Lloyd has created an online idea management program that users access on his Web site. Lloyd notes that *brainlining* can help to promote cross-pollination of ideas and provides a jump start for live brainstorming sessions. Unlike some other sites, Brainline provides a variety of stimuli for brainliners to use as idea triggers. A project can be up and running in as little time as two hours and can last from a few hours to several weeks. As with other sites, brainliners can include external creative types from around the world to help spark ideas in others and increase the pool of ideas. Groups of such external contributors are called *Brain Gangs*. Client users can specify the composition of these gangs such as national origin and professional backgrounds.

Brainline contains three linked Web pages titled Challenge, Ideas, and Stimulation. The Challenge page details the Brainline's objectives, scope, and any general background information. The Ideas page is used to capture ideas and to browse those submitted by others. Every time users enter the Ideas page, add a new idea, or refresh the page, they are provided with a new prompt for sparking ideas. The bottom of the Ideas window contains a HINT button that, when clicked on, triggers a random combination of specially chosen stimulus words. Finally, the Stimulation page consists of links to other Web pages chosen specifically for a project. The pages with these links provide a suite of online reference tools for providing additional stimulation. For a sample Brainline, go to http://www.gocreate.com/Brainline/samplename/chal.htm. There you will find a sample challenge involving ideas for naming a new coffee. It contains links to coffee-related Web sites plus other sites containing varied stimuli, such as inspiration from advertising slogans (www.sloganeeze.com) and word resources such as www.onelook.com and www.wordgizmo.com. It also provides some sample ideas.

Brainline is an extremely easy-to-use, cost-effective approach to generating numerous ideas in a relatively short time. It may not have all the bells and whistles of some higher-end programs, but you don't have to buy and administer any software. As described previously, it can be implemented literally within a few hours and produce ideas a few hours after that. Finally, one advantage it may have over competing approaches is the database of Brain Gangs available for generating diverse ideas with little advanced notice. Too many projects are limited by working with the same people on the same challenges. The result often is the same old ideas.

BrightIdea.com

This program was designed for small- and medium-size companies that do not want to deal with a relatively expensive system cobbled into their own internal network. There are six modules provided as a Web service approach:

1. *Research.* This module provides an opportunity for internal collaborative communications regarding a variety of topics such as progress on a particular project, what the competition has been doing, new technological developments, and any comments and perspectives that participants might want to share with others. Such postings can serve as a fertile ground for seed ideas to germinate later as innovative concepts or projects. One important feature of this module is the ability to rate the importance of all the postings. This way, new participants can become informed quickly about a project or spend time learning just about the projects rated as most significant by others.

2. *Ideas.* Any authorized user can initiate an ideation project based on needs such as specific work-flow elements. Participants submit ideas into a window that others can access for review and comments. Users also can search for ideas, review research, view the most recent entries, and consult ideas from monthly archives.

3. *Projects.* Customer feedback led to the inclusion of this module because users indicated a need to track projects at high levels of an organization and to note achievement of milestones. It is not intended to compete with conventional, more complex project management

software. Instead, it can help managers track overall progress. Thus, it can be especially useful for managing strategic innovation projects.

4. *Experts.* Most idea management projects involve idea review teams that assess the value of ideas generated. Sometimes these teams are not available when needed. To overcome this obstacle, BrightIdea .com provides a search function that allows organizations to locate other resource personnel who might help provide input. Users can screen these experts based on their skills, comments they have made in the past, and previous ideas they might have generated. External participants also can be involved. Frey notes that bringing in outside experts can be an advantage of externally hosted Web sites because no access is needed to a corporate network.

5. *Rewards and Recognition.* This set of tools allows the host to provide incentives to those generating and evaluating ideas by making it possible to see who is submitting specific ideas. Team leaders then can provide points or other incentives to those who are judged as having submitted the best ideas.

6. *Analytics/Financial Tracking.* One of the most useful features of any idea management program is the ability to provide metrics with respect to project outcomes. BrightIdea.com is not an exception. Managers can use an extensive array of utilities to assess progress and detect any bottlenecks in the process. It even uses a financial engine to monitor financial savings assumed to have resulted from submitted ideas. These metrics can be geared toward time, labor, materials, and many other resources. The "bottom line" on this module, then, is that managers can use it to help track their bottom lines!

Challenge Accelerator

Challenge Accelerator is Idea Crossing's Web-based program for facilitating large-scale idea competitions among employees, external partners, customers, or any other group. It started out as the software engine for The Global Innovation Challenge, an international innovation competition for teams of MBA students and now has been used more broadly for internal, corporate competitions as well as several statewide competitions. Competition participants typically include the contestants (idea generators), judges, administrators, and sponsors (internal or external). One advantage of a streamlined interface for competitions is having more engaged and energized participants.

As noted previously, Challenge Accelerator represents a separate class of idea management software in that it is designed solely for idea competitions and not just capturing and processing ideas. Many idea campaigns can be relatively labor intensive in that considerable resources are needed to collect registrations, answer support questions, deal with submissions from different media, distribute judging assignments, and aggregate and tabulate results. Some webmasters can introduce constraints by creating a nontransparent communication bottleneck. Challenge Accelerator can automate these and many other tasks involved in competitions and thus eliminate most communication obstacles.

Major features include:

- Customizable formats to accommodate differing submission formats, judging phases, and scoring methodologies
- Streamlined administration to oversee reporting, manage contestants, validate and assign judges, assign challenge questions to teams, assign judges to submissions, and manage scoring and results
- A user-friendly work space for both contestants and judges
- A transparent competitive environment in which it is easy to anticipate and respond to user needs and to accommodate real-time information flow and content management
- The ability to involve thousands of contestants
- The ability to quickly set up and administer subsequent competitions due to a flatter learning curve

Goldfire Innovator

There are three modules for this program developed by Invention Machines: The Optimizer, The Researcher, and Innovation Trend Analysis. All of these modules were designed to help facilitate new product and process innovation and to help maintain a full pipeline of new ideas. The program should be especially useful for R&D and engineering professionals because of its ability to evaluate, research, generate and validate new and existing products and production processes.

1. *The Optimizer*. This module has a foundation based in value engineering and TRIZ problem-solving methods. Thus, a heavy emphasis is placed on both defining and evaluating challenges. It provides a set of templates useful for improving work flows involving new systems or technologies, benchmarking utilities, and guidance on how to integrate them into existing company systems. It also can be used without the templates if users want to create their own approaches. One notable feature of The Evaluator is its ability to create visual representations of system processes, including indicators of functions and effects. The user also can enter multiple values for more detailed analyses. The result should be a better understanding of how to improve system efficiency and cost savings. Thus, the program can help to identify the best opportunities for targeting R&D resources.

2. *The Researcher*. When the problem is defined satisfactorily, the next activity involves conducting semantic searches to explore potential solutions that can be converted into new product concepts. The program provides the ability to search:

    a. General knowledge bases (in addition to corporate ones)
    b. International patents
    c. Invention Machine's proprietary database of thousands of scientific effects from multiple disciplines
    d. A pictorial database of TRIZ principles and rules for resolving design problems and how they might be applied to the target problem

The Researcher also helps the user access a variety of cross-disciplinary scientific and technical Web sites, many of which are not available via traditional search engines. One key feature is the ability to extract key concepts from lengthy, complicated patents and present summaries within limited time.

3. *Innovation Trend Analysis*. The third module can help perform competitive and intellectual property analyses. It does this by providing the following:

    a. Detailed innovation profiles of other companies (including their patented technologies)

    b. Side-by-side comparison of the innovation profiles of up to five companies (including the ability to detect possible patent infringements)

    c. Ability to anticipate significant technology trends

    d. Simultaneous assessment of groups of related patents

Although Goldfire Innovator obviously is geared toward the technical aspects of new product development, it still has the ability to be used as a more generic tool, especially in collaborative problem-solving knowledge sharing. Nevertheless, it may be more complicated and provide more tools than are necessary for broader, more traditional innovation challenges.

i-Bank

Idea Champions (www.ideachampions.com) and e-Change (www .e-change.com) developed i-Bank (not to be confused with "iBank" financial software) as a full-service enterprise idea management software program for generating, capturing, developing, and evaluating ideas. One feature not present in other applications is a variety of ways to help prompt ideas. Major parts include The Idea Greenhouse, The iBank Depository (of course!), The My Idea Status Page, and a variety of idea generation tools.

- *The Idea Greenhouse*. This component is used for entering ideas using a set of forty questions to help participants think through ideas more deliberately and to build a business case for each idea. Sample questions include "How will this concept save costs?" and "What problems do you see that could block this idea?" Answering these types of questions presumably will result in more refined ideas. Ideas also are more likely to receive a fair evaluation by the review team if they are more fine-tuned. Others also can be invited to refine any idea, although specific individuals can be denied access if desired. Highly detailed or complex ideas can be saved as drafts for later embellishments or other revisions. Finally, The Idea Greenhouse allows the ability to attach files and documents to each idea as it is submitted.

• *The iBank Depository.* Just as money is stored in a bank, submitted ideas are stored in a database known as the iBank Depository. As each idea is submitted, an e-mail automatically is mailed to the review team so its members will know it is available for evaluation. Every idea reviewed is followed by notification to the submitter. This communication helps to maintain employee involvement and can enhance collaboration since multiple employees then can work together to improve already improved ideas. There is a discussion thread tool to facilitate this type of collaboration.

• *The My Idea Status Page.* It sometimes can be challenging to keep employees focused on and involved with idea campaigns. To overcome this concern, i-Bank provides an area where participants can review their submitted ideas, make changes, consider comments made by others, and see how well their ideas scored.

• *Idea Generation Tools.* One such tool is The Idea Lottery. It is based on matrix analysis (aka *morphological analysis*) and helps to trigger ideas by dividing a challenge into its parts and arranging them in a grid. Different combinations of challenge parts then are combined and used to stimulate novel ideas. Another tool is Jump Start, which is used when there may be a lull in idea generation and the participants could use a boost. Free the Genie is designed as a set of four fun brainstorming exercises to use for creative inspiration. The idea generation tools area also contains an extensive library of articles on a variety of topics. They can function as an e-learning resource or be used to trigger new perspectives for a project.

In addition to facilitating an idea campaign, i-Bank can be used at the fuzzy front end of the innovation process by providing a means to solicit questions concerning an organization's vision or competitive strategy. Such insights then can be used for background research with future idea campaigns.

As with similar programs, i-Bank is a powerful tool that can greatly improve the odds of creating successful idea management projects and help to create a collaborative organizational atmosphere. It also contains some features not available in similar programs (although Idea-Central4.0 also contains resource papers) and could be useful depending on the features an organization might find worth purchasing.

Ideabox

Free! Free! Free! Yes, that's right, at the time of this writing, PhpOut sourcing.com's Ideabox software program can be downloaded for free from the company's Web site and used as is or modified (features can be added for a fee), or on a company intranet. It is a relatively simple program that functions as a virtual suggestion box for collecting and posting employee ideas. Although it has few major features, those it does have can be quite useful. For instance, Ideabox:

- Is easy to install and maintain
- Has fast administrative functions as well as page generation
- Can notify a project coordinator via e-mail when an idea has been submitted
- Creates different lists of ideas
- Controls access to ideas based on status, creator, deadlines, responsible parties, and so forth
- Indicates ideas with missed deadlines
- Allows any user to add comments to ideas accessible to them
- Provides user profiles

The lack of certain features, however, might render Ideabox as less cost-effective than more fully featured programs that typically involve more participants working on more complex challenges.

IdeaCentral4.0

·Imaginatik.com's enterprise idea management software program is a highly robust application that can be configured in multiple ways to meet the needs of almost any single-event idea campaign. Unlike idea management projects without deadlines, single-event campaigns are more likely to result in higher participation rates as well as produce larger quantities of higher-quality ideas. Moreover, IdeaCentral4.0 helps facilitate collaboration for the entire innovation process, in contrast to suggestion box systems that primarily collect and track ideas. (In 2003, it won the Basex Excellence Award for Collaborative Systems.) Space does not permit an adequate description here of all the features available, but more information can be found on Imaginatik's Web site, which also has numerous white papers by Imaginatik CEO Mark Turrell and his associates, Boris Pluskowski and Matt Chapman.

To use IdeaCentral4.0, users log on and read a definition of the challenge, which includes a link to more background information. It is important to note, especially for this book, that Imaginatik recognizes the importance of correctly framing the challenge. Input fields for ideas are self-explanatory and involve no training to use. The fields can be used to input different types of ideas and there are separate boxes for users to comment on such topics as an idea's risk, likely return on investment, areas of applicability, or marketability obstacles. (Answers to these questions can help review teams evaluate the ideas at a later time.) Icons provide links to additional information for each field and often involve drawings and spreadsheets as well as text files. Users can comment on the ideas of others as well as build on them to suggest modifications or variations.

One strength of IdeaCentral4.0 is that most of its features are based on metrics collected and analyzed by Imaginatik's research arm. Special attention has been given to how people naturally tend to interact with software programs. For instance, users have options such as showing or hiding their names to avoid political or sensitive situations. There even is an option to begin submitting ideas anonymously and then identify yourself later on during the review process. Research Imaginatik has collected suggestions that anonymous ideas are 67 percent more likely to be implemented; higher-quality ideas also are more likely to result when anonymity exists.

Features specific to IdeaCentral4.0 include the following:

- *Idea Minder.* When someone submits an idea, he or she receives an e-mail if someone comments on it. This eliminates the need to log on to check on comments and can be used to browse through ideas.

- *Draft Saver.* Users have the choice of saving ideas as drafts before they submit them formally. A major advantage of this feature is that it encourages spontaneous idea generation. You may not be completely satisfied with an idea as you first thought of it, so you have the chance to revise it and add detail before others can see it. The program also scans the idea database near the end of an idea project and reminds submitters that they have one or more draft ideas.

- *Idea Forwarding.* After each idea is submitted, the user receives a thank-you screen, which provides the ability to e-mail the idea link to others using the program. This is a useful feature since it alerts others as to when an idea has been submitted so they can add comments or suggest improvements. Thus, it serves as another way to enhance collaboration.

- *Controlled Access.* The system administrator can specify who can view and comment on ideas so that highly proprietary or sensitive ideas will not be divulged without intent. *Idea embargos* also are possible whereby recently submitted ideas are concealed for a specified length of time. This can be especially useful for situations involving invention disclosure and trade secrets.

- *Automated Expert Reviews.* Organizations often are interested in the opinions of internal and external experts. If a reviewer decides that additional input is needed to assess adequately an idea, he or she can fill out a form with relevant information and IdeaCentral4.0 will generate an e-mail request automatically and send response reminders at set intervals. Reviewers also receive automatic e-mails notifying them when an expert has responded.

- *Systematic Review Tools.* One of the most indispensable elements of any decision process is the use of weighted, decision criteria—standards of varying degrees of importance used to help select from multiple alternatives. IdeaCentral4.0 includes this capability in offering the use of up to ten weighted criteria. A review form incorporates pop-up explanations of the numerical values of different criteria. The idea-screening process also can be staggered so that one group of reviewers conducts a more superficial review followed by more in-depth assessments. Statistical reports can be generated as well as paper forms for users who prefer to review ideas using hard-copy versions.

IdeaCentral4.0 is a well-seasoned and tested idea management system with a lot of built-in functionality and customizability for almost any type of innovation challenge. Different configurations can be created easily so that different phases of the innovation process can be accommodated. There also is an impressive research base on the efficacy and utility of idea management campaigns using IdeaCentral4.0.

Innovator

With Innovator (www.us-mindmatters.com), MindMatters Technologies, Inc., has developed an enterprise idea management program that also is as rich in features as some of its competition. Innovator contains four major components: Analyze Report; Manage Project; Collaborate, Review, Validate; and Capture Stimulate. It was designed with new product innovation in mind, but the program can be adapted for more general purposes as well. It contains discrete modules that can be incorporated as needed and is scalable to accommodate differing numbers of participants. Major features include the following:

• *Idea Capture.* The Web forms used to collect ideas can be customized for different types of ideas and users. Idea submitters are provided with information about the overall process and receive feedback on the process as needed. The program also can be set up to include only one segment or department of an organization. This can be helpful when it is important to maintain confidentiality.

• *Challenges.* Users can define the type of idea campaign they want to have, including the need to include specific features or how much time to allow for the campaign. There are Web-based modules that make it easy to set up ideation portals based on departments, foreign languages, types of ideas, and customer profiles. Such portals then can be adjusted to align with varying work-flow processes, security requirements, and types of input. All of these functions and features can be performed and monitored by a single administrator.

• *Review and Work Flow*. One key to successful idea campaigns is the ability to conduct reviews in a timely way. Innovator provides a number of functions for idea review committees. A special work-flow engine allows administrators to manage multiple processes such as linear, hierarchical, or combinations. Rules can be applied to expedite moving ideas between committees. A dashboard provides reviewers with an easy way to monitor task progress, comments, attachments, and results of evaluations. All of this information can be viewed on a single page, which helps streamline the process as well as allow for virtual reviews.

• *Intellectual Property (IP) Management*. Capable management of IP is especially important for new product development professionals. Innovator has built-in capabilities for monitoring all patent-pending projects. The IP module makes it easier to manage new product portfolios by providing access to experts, incorporating external information research, and maintaining confidentiality throughout the process. As a result, corporate risk liability can be reduced. MindMatters even retains attorneys who are available for consultations. The functionality of this module is evidenced by Innovator's ability to safeguard snapshots of ideas as they move toward patent status, providing certified records of a project's products, patent searches, and defensive publication to automatically and proactively block competitors from *IP overreaching*.

• *Portfolio Management*. Organizations involved in creating sustainable innovation processes ultimately have to face the reality of deciding how many resources to invest in a project. They must assess the costs and benefits of one project relative to another. The portfolio management module makes it easier to conduct such evaluations by providing the ability to compare, visually, one project to another with respect to technical, marketing, and financial constraints, just to name a few.

• *Decision Support*. Innovation processes require that different questions be asked for different projects. The same decisions typically will not be made consistently and different people often must be questioned, based on their expertise. Innovator makes it relatively easy to question experts by setting up specific rules built around user-specified parameters such as the type of innovation, departmental affiliation, and explicit criteria. This attention to detail ensures that the right people use the right criteria for a given project. Over time, such processes will become more streamlined with experience as a knowledge base is created to help gauge the relative impact of different variables.

• *Collaboration and Language Support.* With the increasing globalization of business, it is important that enterprise idea management software be able to adapt to an international environment. Although it gets a lot of lip service, collaboration is not executed as well as it might be, especially across political and trade barriers. Different forms of collaboration and collaboration-enhancing features are built into Innovator's features throughout the innovation process. Users are provided home pages on which they are reminded of "hot" innovations and asked to comment on those submitted by others. One unique feature is the use of search agents to minimize submissions of duplicate ideas. Users can view departments with the most frequently implemented innovations and provide feedback. Special collaboration agents also can be set up to remind users of new innovations and people with expertise in their interest areas. To further enable international collaboration, current versions of the software include language support for Asia and Europe.

• *Incentive and Recognition.* It is important to maintain a high level of employee motivation and morale during innovation campaigns. One way to do this is to use Innovator's capabilities that make it possible to customize point systems, offer prizes and gifts, administer employee point programs in which points can be exchanged for prizes, and maintain detailed records of incentive results. MindMatters, Inc. touts the ability of Innovator to manage point totals and rewards just as frequent flyer programs operate. It even notifies managers when incentive milestones are reached.

• *Profiles.* It is widely accepted that employees are an organization's most valuable resource. Acknowledging this is not sufficient, however. There has to be some way to tap these resources. For example, it might be useful to know who has been rewarded the most for innovation, won the most incentives, or has the most expertise in a field. The answers to these and similar questions can be obtained easily by using the Profiles module. Innovator tries to document as much user information as possible and keep it up-to-date as well. Employee turnover can make such accounting a difficult task, not to mention the frustration of knowing how the expertise level in other departments may have changed over time. To keep abreast of such changes, there is a "find expert" search capability designed around a set of tools intended to keep the process user friendly.

Jenni

Jenni (www.jpb.com) is the brainchild of Belgian creativity and innovation consultant Jeffrey Baumgartner. It is a quite serviceable idea management program for externally hosted, Internet idea collection campaigns that can be used without installing a system on a corporate intranet. Instead, it is hosted on jpb.com's internal servers. It can be customized to feature corporate logos and colors as well as configured for a variety of idea collection projects.

There are three levels of access: "idea masters," managers, and participants. Idea masters have full access to all settings and features; managers can initiate and supervise idea collection campaigns; and regular users can submit, browse, and collaborate on ideas. As with similar programs, Jenni is designed to be used for single-event innovation challenges involving limited time frames. Major features are organized around basic problem-solving steps and include the following:

- *Submitting Ideas.* Ideas are submitted online and users are notified if others build on their ideas. A useful feature (as with other programs) is the ability to enter ideas anonymously and then reveal the originator after implementation. This can be valuable when sensitive ideas are involved and participants wish a greater level of comfort. It also is possible to attach to each idea up to three documents along with captioned pictures, if desired.

- *Browsing Ideas.* This is a separate screen that displays all submitted ideas in a variety of ways including order submitted, most recently submitted ideas, or by rating scores. (Such open viewing can also help to avoid duplication.) Users can build on other ideas, add their own, assign a peer-rating symbol, or subscribe to any idea by requesting e-mail notification of any future additions. Offline viewing of ideas also is possible. Finally, there is a Genius Directory, which is a directory of all users of Jenni. It contains contact information, personal descriptions, photos, and all ideas submitted by each user. This makes it easy to construct informal innovation networks.

- *Evaluating Ideas.* To evaluate submitted ideas, managers can select a default set of five criteria or create their own criteria sets. As with some other programs, the criteria also can be weighted—a vital feature for any important decision making. Once idea evaluators are selected, they receive automatically generated e-mails containing links to the evaluation Web page. Criteria can be saved and reused to avoid generating new ones for each idea project. Once all ideas have been evaluated, Jenni generates a report for later review.

- *Testing Ideas.* Users can choose from among a number of types such as business cases, market research, or prototyping. The implementation tool also can track project dates and their frequency as well as generate e-mail reminders about due dates. This ability makes it easy for senior managers to track projects and provides an archive for research at a later time.

Jenni is a feature-rich application that can be customized easily for a number of idea campaign situations. It can be hosted for both internal and external participants and provides an intuitive interface with a relatively small learning curve.

NextNet 3.0

Brightidea.com's idea management program is similar to several of the others previously described. It is a relatively cost-effective, easy-to-use application designed to streamline the process of collecting and evaluating ideas. Three types of users form the program's structure: submitters, evaluators, and coordinators. The program presents different screen views for each type.

- *Submitter's View*. People who submit ideas see several boxes for submitting ideas plus various links. The links allow users to enter new ideas, review previously submitted and draft ideas (viewable only by the submitter), plus edit personal profiles. The main page contains a number of features such as a promotion center that includes messages from project coordinators, a "goal thermometer" displaying progress toward the project's goal in terms of ideas submitted, and an employee spotlight featuring individuals currently supporting the project or contributing in other important ways. In addition to the ability to submit draft ideas, this view allows users to attach files (e.g., documents, photos, spreadsheets) that can help idea reviewers make decisions.

- *Evaluator's Views*. This page also contains links relevant to idea assessment, such as "my action items," that show ideas assigned to a submitter that will be evaluated soon. To facilitate idea evaluation, NextNet 3.0 provides color-coded icons pertaining to the status of an idea. When using this view, participants can evaluate an idea, edit it (the original and edited versions are saved), or request opinions or information from experts, all by sending an e-mail with a link to the idea involved. To speed up the evaluation process, distributed evaluations provide idea descriptions in HTML e-mails to which multiple evaluators can reply without the need to log in to judge ideas. This also makes it relatively easy to evaluate large numbers of ideas. The software then automatically collects all responses and can send to a review team, all participants, or just those receiving threshold scores, as well as schedule meeting times.

- *Coordinator's Views*. NextNet 3.0 includes a number of administrative tools to smooth the monitoring process for different types of idea campaigns. For instance, managers can configure projects to provide information on the number of ideas submitted at different times, change the types of evaluation criteria used, set goals for idea quantities, limit the time available for evaluation, and send e-mail reminders regarding pending deadlines for submissions and evaluations.

As with several other programs, NextNet 3.0 can be a cost-effective time-saver for most idea campaigns. The evaluation feature is especially useful for processing large numbers of ideas in a relatively short time.

Spark and Incubator

These two programs by OVO Innovation are designed to be used together as an integrated approach to large-scale idea management initiatives involving geographically dispersed participants. It uses state-of-the-art technology and provides unique features to manage even the most complex innovation challenges. OVO Innovation's creators plan to extend the capabilities of their software to encompass all phases of a product's life cycle.

Spark was designed for *distributed brainstorming*, much as were other idea management programs. For setting up a brainstorming session, it can incorporate user lists from Exchange Server's active directory or any LDAP-compliant server. Thus, it is easy to set up an online ideation session from employee e-mail servers. Users can be invited to participate automatically by using electronic calendars and can be provided with background information as e-mail attachments.

To generate ideas, Spark provides a tabbed interface to make its many features more convenient and less confusing. Tabs can be set to add, connect, remove, vote on, and display ideas. The ability to connect ideas is especially useful for eliminating ideas and evaluating clusters of ideas with some commonality.

The voting feature is quite flexible and provides a number of options such as regular voting (one vote per idea), preset voting in which each voter is given a number of votes or points to distribute as he or she wishes, and priority voting in which the project director assigns one or more priority votes to each participant. These votes are weighted as being more important than regular votes. Results of voting can be screened prior to sharing them with participants so that, for example, only a certain number of votes are shown. Finally, voting can be set up for multiple rounds.

In addition to the idea management software discussed in this chapter, there are a number of programs designed for general creative thinking and problem solving. Many were created for individuals, but most can be adapted for group use. Among these programs are Creator Studio 2002, eXpertSystem (formerly Idea Fisher), FlashBrainer, IdeaCue, Idea Manager (Accolade), Innovation Toolbox, MindLink Problem Solver, and ThoughtPath.

NOTES

1. Tim O'Reilly, "The Architecture of Participation." Retrieved January 17, 2007, from http://www.oreillynet.com/pub/a/oreilly/tim/articles/architecture_of_parti cipation.html.

2. Chuck Frey, "An Overview of Idea Management Systems." Retrieved January 19, 2007, from http://www.innovationtools.com/Resources/ideamgmt-details.asp?a =80.

3. Ibid.

4. Retrieved January 19, 2007, from http://www.brainbankinc.com/productservice .html.

A Crash Course in Generating Creative Ideas: Individual Methods

In the late 1970s and early 1980s, there were relatively few books on idea generation techniques. When I was interviewed by *Dun's Review* in 1979 for a cover article on creativity, the editors had trouble finding people to interview. Today, there may be almost as many creativity experts as there are companies to use them! The last several decades have seen a proliferation of books and Internet Web sites on how to generate ideas. Now the problem is deciding how to know which technique to use for the type of challenge involved.

IDEA GENERATION TECHNIQUES

There are a number of ways to classify formal techniques designed to generate ideas. (The use of the word *formal* means that the techniques were created with the intention of generating ideas.) Because I have written a number of books on this topic, I will use the classification scheme I have used previously. Such typologies often differ only in the labels used to describe similar components and processes, so I will not bother describing them here.

Individuals vs. Groups

The first way to classify techniques is to divide techniques into those designed for individuals and those designed for groups. The primary difference between the two is that *some* group methods also can be used by individuals. I say "some," because *some* group methods were not developed just for groups, but just happened to be. Their developers created them with groups in mind but did not have to use groups to generate ideas. For instance, one method created for groups involves group members looking at a photograph and using what they see as stimuli to trigger ideas. However, individuals obviously could do the same. Conversely, techniques originally developed for individuals also can be used by groups.

What is important to note, however, is that *all individual methods can be used by groups, but not all group methods can be used by individuals.* The reason is due to how people interact while generating ideas. For instance, some group methods require individuals to write down ideas on sticky notes and pass them to other group members. Obviously, it would not make sense to do this as an individual (unless you wanted to role-play). On the other hand, any method designed for individuals can be adapted easily for use by more than one person. Only individual approaches are presented in this chapter; group methods are described in Chapter 9.

Related vs. Unrelated Stimuli

One of the most important elements of idea generation techniques in general is their use of related or unrelated challenge stimuli, or both. In this case, stimuli are the triggers we use to help prompt ideas. For instance, if I am trying to think of ways to improve a computer laptop, I first might focus on the different parts and functions and use them as the starting points for ideas. Thus, I might consider ways to make the screen adjust automatically to ambient lighting, becoming brighter as environmental lighting decreases.

Although trying to improve existing attributes of a challenge can be fruitful, it may not always produce the desired level of creativity. Some challenges require an external source of stimulation to provoke novel ideas. These unrelated stimuli are found almost anywhere. Most exist as unrelated words, pictures, or objects. To use the example of improving a computer laptop, the stimuli used for ideation might come from anything not related to the challenge. In fact, the more unrelated the stimuli, the better. Thus, to improve a laptop, I might use a car key for possible stimulation. For instance, I observe the car key and notice several electronic buttons on it. I then might think of a button to push whenever I might leave my computer alone in a public place. Pushing the button activates a motion detector that sounds an alarm if the laptop is moved before using a thumbprint keypad.

According to some research, unrelated stimuli may be more likely to yield novel ideas than related stimuli. This is because unrelated stimuli help force us divert our attention from what we already know and, most important, from what we may think we know about a challenge. The so-called truth, however, probably lies somewhere in between. Both related and unrelated stimuli can be valuable because any form of stimulus has the potential to spark novelty. So, a combination may be optimal.

Free Association vs. Forced Relationships

Another way to classify idea generation methods is in terms of how related and unrelated stimuli are used. Basic free association is the process we use to generate ideas by ourselves and with others. Specifically, we or someone else offers an idea and then we use it as a stimulus to trigger other ideas that, in turn, might help provoke even more ideas. This represents quite a natural way that our brains work for thinking of ideas: One word leads to another that leads to another, and so forth.

In contrast, the process of forced relationships involves the deliberate use of one stimulus with one or more others to provoke something new. In the laptop example used previously, the laptop is a stimulus that then is connected with a key, symbolically "forcing" or linking together both stimuli to produce a new idea—the security button feature. This idea then can be used for free association or combined with another stimulus to help create a new idea. For instance, the security button might trigger an idea for a button that automatically lowers and raises the screen. In this example, the laptop represents a related stimulus while the car key is an unrelated stimulus. Two related or two unrelated stimuli also could be used.

The techniques presented next are organized as individual and group methods. Within each of these categories, the techniques are classified as using related or unrelated stimuli and then these are listed in alphabetical order. Remember: *All individual methods can be used by groups, but not all group methods can be used by individuals.* The distinction between individual and group methods sometimes is a rather artificial one and should not be used literally in all cases. Specifically, if you plan to generate ideas in a group, you also should consider methods classified for individuals; sometimes, the reverse would apply, depending on whether or not a technique classified for groups requires sharing ideas with others. All of the challenge questions will be stated beginning with the phrase, "How might we . . . ?" (This phrase will be abbreviated as HMW.)

INDIVIDUAL TECHNIQUES USING RELATED STIMULI

All of these techniques are based on stimuli that somehow are related to the problem for which ideas are being generated.

Assumption Reversals

Creativity consultant Steve Grossman developed this technique to overcome a difficulty involved in dealing with logical paradoxes. This occurs when you see a contradiction between an existing and a desired problem state. For instance, a logical paradox exists if you are told to reduce your expenditures by 15 percent but increase your output by 20 percent. To overcome this paradox, you could try reversing the problem assumptions involved.

Steps

1. Write down all major problem assumptions.

2. Reverse each assumption in any way possible (don't worry about the "correctness" of your reversals).

3. Use the reversed assumptions as stimuli and generate any ideas suggested.

Sample Problem: HMW Improve a Refrigerator?

1. Write down all major problem assumptions.

   - "A refrigerator keeps food cold."

   - "Opening the door lets out cold air."

   - "A refrigerator requires electricity to operate."

   - "A refrigerator is capable of freezing some foods."

2. Reverse each assumption in any way possible (don't worry about the "correctness" of your reversals).

   - "A refrigerator heats food."

   - "Opening the door helps retain cold air inside."

   - "A refrigerator requires no electricity."

   - "Frozen foods always melt in a freezer."

3. Use the reversed assumptions as stimuli and generate any ideas suggested.

   - Build in a small microwave oven. ("A refrigerator heats food.")

   - Opening the door triggers a burst of cold air until the door is again closed. ("Opening the door helps retain cold air inside.")

   - Have a battery-powered backup in case of brief power failures. ("A refrigerator requires no electricity.")

   - Install a timed, automatic defroster. ("Frozen foods always melt in a freezer.")

Attribute Association Chains

I developed this technique as a modification of *attribute analogy chains* (described in the next section on individual techniques using unrelated stimuli). The major difference is that attribute association chains use free associations to stimulate ideas whereas attribute analogy chains use analogies.

Steps

1. List all major problem components and their subcomponents.

2. Read one of the subcomponents and write down the first word that pops into your mind (word association). This word may be entirely unrelated to the previous word.

3. Use this word association as a stimulus and think of another word that pops into your mind. Write down this word. Continue this process until you have listed a total of four or five word associations.

4. Use the word associations as stimuli and generate any ideas suggested.

Sample Problem: HMW Encourage Employees to Stop Throwing Litter on Company Property?

1. List all major problem components and subcomponents.

   - *People*: wage and salaried employees, supervisors and nonsupervisors

   - *Litter*: paper, glass, metal, wood

   - *Activities*: walking, driving, sitting, standing

   - *Company property*: streets, driveways, sidewalks, buildings, parking lots

2. Read one of the subcomponents and free-associate, with one word triggering the next one (only a few words will be used for this example).

   - *Supervisors*: leaders, followers, people, workers, players, games

   - *Paper*: scissors, stones, rocks, streams, water, cold, ice

   - *Walking*: running, shoes, socks, sweat, equity

   - *Streets*: pavement, asphalt, black, white, snow, ski

3. Use the word associations as stimuli and generate any ideas suggested.

- Create competitive games among departments, challenging them to pick up litter (from "games").

- Have employees take walks for exercise and carry air blowers to blow trash into special receptacles (from "streams").

- Pay employees for picking up trash (from "sweat" and "equity").

- Place trash receptacles several inches into asphalt pavement to prevent them from being knocked over (from "asphalt").

- Send employees of the most trash-free area on a ski vacation (from "ski").

Exaggerated Objectives

Several idea-generation techniques generate ideas by using different problem perspectives. Although evaluation criteria generally should not be introduced until all ideas have been generated, there is at least one method that can use such criteria to an advantage. Exaggerated Objectives is such a technique. It uses criteria to help create new perspectives by "stretching" or exaggerating problem criteria.

Steps

As described by psychologist Robert Olson, the steps for this technique are:

1. List major problem criteria (objectives) that a solution should satisfy.
2. Exaggerate or stretch each criterion (there is no "correct" way to do this).
3. Use each exaggerated criterion as a stimulus to generate ideas.

Sample Problem: HMW Encourage Employees to Submit Ideas to Improve Our Company?

1. List major problem criteria (objectives) that a solution should satisfy.

- "Will cost less than $1,000 per year to administer"

- "Will result in a continual flow of ideas"
- "Will involve many personnel"

2. Exaggerate or stretch each criterion (there is no "correct" way to do this).

   - "Costs less than $1,000"—exaggeration: costs over $1 billion
   - "Continual flow of ideas"—exaggeration: produces no ideas
   - "Involve many personnel"—exaggeration: requires no people

3. Use each exaggerated criterion as a stimulus to generate ideas.

   - Costs over $1 billion—pay a bonus to people who submit a certain number of ideas, regardless of the value of the ideas.

   - Produces no ideas—make raises contingent upon submitting ideas; no ideas submitted, no raise.

   - Requires no people—start a company-wide public relations campaign to advertise the suggestion program.

Relational Algorithms

The relational algorithms method, developed by educator H. F Crovitz, generates ideas with unusual combinations of problem elements and relational words (prepositions). The idea is based on the creative thinking principle of forced relationships. Two parts of a problem concept are "forced" together with one or more relational words to produce unusual associations. The associations then are used to stimulate new ideas. Supposedly, these unusual combinations provoke unique problem perspectives. Crovitz suggests the following as relational words:

about	at	for	of	round	to
across	because	from	off	so	under
after	before	if	on	still	up
against	between	in	opposite	then	when
among	but	near	or	though	where
and	by	not	out	through	while
as	down	now	over	till	with

I have added the following words to the list:

above	below	except	toward
along	beneath	into	upon
amid	beside	past	within
around	beyond	since	without
behind	during	throughout	

Steps

1. Select two major problem elements.
2. Select a relational word and insert it between the two problem elements.
3. Examine the combination and write down any ideas suggested.
4. Repeat steps 2 and 3.

Sample Problem: HMW Improve a Portable Radio?

1. Select two major problem elements.
   - Radio
   - Listener
2. Select a relational word and insert it between the two problem elements.
   - Radio above a listener
3. Examine the combination and write down any ideas suggested.
   - Put a radio inside a hat.
4. Repeat steps 2 and 3.
   - Radio after a listener—A "fanny pack" radio.
   - Radio off a listener—Put a radio inside a ball, which is tossed at another person.
   - Radio under a listener—Put a radio inside the soles of jogging shoes.
   - Radio where a listener—Install portable radio vending machines where joggers run.

Reversals

One often becomes so familiar with a problem that creative solutions are elusive. Reversing the direction of a problem statement frequently can provide new perspectives and suggest new ideas. Many people probably have used reversals to generate ideas and not known it. For instance, consider police sting operations in which they send invitations to known criminals for a party. Once the criminals arrive, the police arrest them. This reverses the typical approach to law enforcement: Instead of police going out to capture the criminals, they try to get the criminals to come to them.

Steps

1. Reverse the problem statement in any way possible—that is, change the subject, verb, or object.

2. Use the reversed definition to stimulate a practical solution. Although there may not be a logical connection, write down whatever practical solutions come to mind.

3. Repeat steps 1 and 2 until enough ideas are generated.

Sample Problem: HMW Encourage Managers to Attend a Management Development Seminar?

1. Reverse the problem statement in any way possible—that is, change the subject, verb, or object.

   • Discourage employees from attending the seminar.

2. Use the reversed definition to stimulate a practical solution.

   • Cut pay for nonattendance.

   • Tell them they won't be promoted if they don't attend.

   • Offer them the option of taking the seminar as a videoconference.

Two Words

We sometimes have trouble generating ideas because of the choice of words in the problem statement. Simple changes in key words, however, can alter the meaning enough to suggest more ideas. The two words technique helps overcome this obstacle by providing alternate words to consider. Thus, it provides different problem perspectives.

Steps

1. Generate a list of words similar in meaning to the main verb and object in the problem statement (a thesaurus will make this task easier).

2. Select a word from the first list, combine it with a word from the second list, and use this combination to generate ideas.

3. Repeat step 2 until you have examined a number of word combinations.

Sample Problem: HMW Reduce Conflict Between Two Departments?

Depreciate	Discord
Diminish	Fight
Lessen	Dispute
Downgrade	Friction
Dilute	Contention
Discount	Disharmony

1. Select a word from the first list, combine it with a word from the second list, and use this combination to generate ideas.

   - *Dilute-Discord*: Reduce the number of interactions between the departments.

2. Repeat step 2 until you have examined a number of word combinations. For instance:

   - *Downgrade-Discord*: Downgrade departmental performance ratings until the conflict diminishes.

   - *Depreciate-Dispute*: Assess fines to departmental members every time they have a public argument.

   - *Discount-Disharmony*: Ignore the conflict and hope the department members can resolve it themselves.

Word Diamond

This technique, which I developed many years ago, is a distant cousin of the two words approach to idea generation. Instead of using different word meanings, however, the word diamond uses different combinations of words or phrases in the problem statement. At least four problem words are required, although it also will work with three words. (In this case, the technique might more suitably be called the word triangle.)

Steps

1. Choose four words or major phrases from the problem statement.

2. Place the words in a diamond shape so that each point has a word or phrase.

3. Combine one of the words or phrases with another word or phrase and write down any ideas prompted by the combination.

4. Combine the word initially selected in step 3 with the remaining two. Use these combinations to suggest additional ideas.

5. Repeat steps 3 and 4 until all possible combinations have been examined and all ideas recorded.

Sample Problem: HMW Encourage Employees to Clean Up Their Work Areas?

1. Choose four words or major phrases from the problem statement.

   - Encourage
   - Work areas
   - Employees
   - Clean up

2. Place the words in a diamond shape so that each point has a word or phrase. (See Figure 8-1.)

3. Combine one of the words or phrases with another word or phrase and write down any ideas prompted by the combination.

   - *Encourage-Work areas*: Make the environment more pleasant by increasing the accessibility of trash receptacles.

FIGURE 8-1. Example of the word diamond technique.

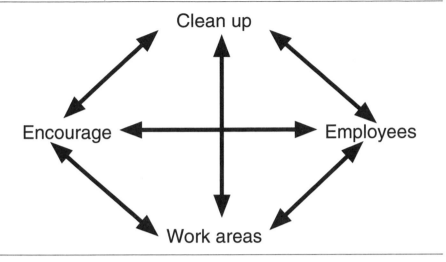

4. Combine the word initially selected in step 3 with the remaining two. Use these combinations to suggest additional ideas.

- *Encourage-Employees*: Financially reward cooperative employees.

- *Encourage-Clean up*: Pay employees a piece rate based on how much scrap waste they dispose of.

5. Repeat steps 3 and 4 until all possible combinations have been examined and all ideas recorded.

- *Employees-Work* areas: Create a sense of ownership so employees will be less likely to litter in their own work areas.

- *Employees-Encourage*: Form quality circle discussion groups.

- *Employees-Clean up*: Conduct a contest, and award prizes for the department with the cleanest work area.

INDIVIDUAL TECHNIQUES USING
UNRELATED STIMULI

The following techniques rely on stimuli other than those related to the problem of interest.

Analogies

An analogy is a comparison of similarities between like things. In creative problem solving, analogies help to provide new perspectives by forcing the user to break away from conventional viewpoints. Analogies often are borrowed from nature. For instance, a new marketing strategy might be likened to the way bees collect honey. A company might devise a marketing campaign involving *viral* (word-of-mouth) marketing in much the same way that bees fly around pollinating flowers and bring the results back to the hive. Because analogies symbolically produce unusual perspectives, they often help to generate unique ideas.

Although you could generate ideas simply by thinking of things similar to your problem and borrowing concepts, a more systematic procedure is likely to work better.

Steps

1. Decide on the major principle represented by your problem.

2. Generate a list of things (analogies) that represent the major principle. Generally, if your problem involves people, you should think of "nonpeople" analogies; if your problem involves things, think of analogies involving people.

3. Select one of the analogies. The best analogies frequently are the most unusual or violate some cultural taboo.

4. Describe the analogy in detail, elaborating with action-oriented phrases as much as possible.

5. Use the descriptions to suggest ideas.

Sample Problem: HMW Reduce the Number of Employees Who Leave Our Organization?

1. Decide on the major principle.

   - In this case, the major problem principle is retention.

2. Generate a list of analogies. For this example, generate a list of things in life that involve retention. Generate your list by

phrasing your problem in the following way: Retaining employees in an organization is like . . .

- Building a dam to retain water.
- Going to the dentist to keep your teeth.
- Trying various "magical" hair tonics to retain your hair.
- Building a wall to retain dirt.
- Sealing food in a plastic bag to retain freshness.
- Fertilizing your lawn to retain the grass.
- Keeping the gate closed on a bucking bronco.

3. Select one of the analogies.

- For instance, you might select the hair tonic analogy.

4. Describe the analogy in detail. Trying various "magical" hair tonics to retain your hair involves:

- Checking out the reputation of the manufacturer.
- Asking about research studies documenting effectiveness.
- Finding out where to purchase the hair tonic.
- Traveling to the store (or ordering by mail) to make the purchase.
- Reading the instructions on how to use the tonic.
- Applying the tonic regularly.
- Checking in the mirror to evaluate results.
- Writing to the manufacturer to complain about the lack of results.

5. Use the descriptions to suggest ideas. The final step is to examine each descriptor to see if it suggests any ideas for the problem of employee retention. For example:

- Improve the organization's reputation so employees will feel proud to work there (from "checking out the reputation").
- Conduct exit interviews to determine why employees leave (from "asking about research studies").

- Allow employees to purchase stock or merchandise and services at reduced rates (from "finding out where to purchase").

- Give free local vacations to employees who remain a certain number of years (from "traveling to the store").

- Offer in-house education programs that, when completed, lead to raises (from "reading the instructions").

- Make sure bosses meet with their workers on a regular basis (from "applying the tonic regularly").

- Conduct employee attitude surveys to highlight major concerns and anticipate future problems (from "checking in the mirror").

- Start an employee suggestion program for ideas to retain employees (from "writing to the manufacturer").

Attribute Analogy Chains

This technique was developed by educators Don Koberg and Jim Bagnall. It actually is a combination of two techniques: *attribute listing* and *analogies*. In contrast to analogies, which is based solely on unrelated problem stimuli, this method also uses related stimuli. Thus, people who may be uncomfortable with unrelated stimuli alone may find this approach appealing.

Sample Problem: HMW Improve a Filing Cabinet?

1. List problem components.

   - Name, material, function, form, parts

2. List subcomponents of each component.

   - *Name*: filing cabinet

   - *Material*: steel, aluminum, plastic

   - *Function*: storing paper documents

- *Form*: rectangular box
- *Parts*: drawers, rollers, handles

3. List analogy descriptors for each subcomponent:
   - *Name*: paper retainer
   - *Material*: hard as a diamond (steel), flexible as a wet noodle (aluminum), moldable as gelatin (plastic)
   - *Function*: a battery storing energy
   - *Form*: a coffin
   - *Parts*: train cars (drawers), roller skate wheels (rollers), lawn mower pull cord (handles)

4. Use analogies to stimulate ideas.
   - Build in a paper dispenser ("paper retainer").
   - Design one drawer as a security drawer for valuables ("hard as a diamond").
   - Attach a flexible neck lamp that can be removed when desired ("flexible as a wet noodle").
   - Design cabinet shapes using different themes or to reflect different products ("moldable as gelatin").
   - Drawers open and close electronically ("battery").
   - Hinged top ("coffin").
   - Modular cabinet units ("train cars").
   - Wheels on cabinet bottoms ("roller skate wheels").
   - Handle pulls recessed into drawer fronts ("lawn mower pull cord").

Modifier Noun Associations

I developed this technique to generate new product ideas. It helps you generate these ideas by combining a noun and a modifier and then free-associating using these combinations.

Steps

1. Generate a list of nouns and modifiers. Try to include some unusual combinations (e.g., glowing apples).

2. Select one combination and free-associate additional modifier-noun combinations from the original combination.

3. Use all the combinations as stimuli and to generate ideas.

Sample Problem: HMW Improve a Portable Radio?

1. Generate a list of nouns and modifiers.

   - Glowing apples, heavy lightbulbs, corrosive bedsheets, wicked pickles

2. Select one combination and free-associate additional modifier-noun combinations from the original combination.

   - Glowing apples
   - Radiant peaches
   - Fuzzy elephants
   - Hairy trunks
   - Fat swimmers
   - Flying boats

3. Use all the combinations as stimuli and to generate ideas.

   - Glow-in-the-dark radio (from "glowing apples")
   - Insulated storage compartment for fruit and other snacks (from "radiant peaches")
   - Radio that makes animal sounds for children (from "fuzzy elephants")
   - Novelty radio that grows hair—the louder music is played, the faster the hair grows (from "hairy trunks")
   - Radio that floats in water (from "fat swimmers")
   - Remote-controlled model ship radio (from "flying boats")

Product Improvement CheckList

I developed the Product Improvement CheckList (PICL) as an aid for generating new product ideas. It also has proved useful for generating ideas for a variety of less tangible problems—for example, marketing and customer service problems. It consists of a poster-size worksheet with 576 idea stimulators organized into four categories: Try to, Make It, Think of, and Take Away or Add. (A different version of PICL exists as Circles of Creativity. The stimulator words are arranged as overlapping circles that rotate, allowing comparisons across categories.)

Some examples of stimulators in each category are:

- *Try to*: sketch it, wipe it, tighten it, twist it, build it up backward, whip it, inflate it
- *Make it*: soft, transparent, magnetic, portable, disposable, late, zigzag, adjustable
- *Think of*: escalators, Sir Lancelot, oatmeal, stethoscopes, time bombs, eggshells, disappearing ink
- *Take away or add*: layers, sex appeal, friction, rhythm, sand, turbulence, energy, anticipation

Steps

There are a number of ways to use PICL. Here is the most basic:

1. Select one of the four categories and scan the list words or phrases.
2. Arbitrarily choose one of the words and use it to stimulate an idea. That is, mentally experiment with the word and see what concept, principle, or action it represents that might be used to prompt an idea.
3. Write down any ideas suggested.
4. Repeat steps 1 through 3.

Sample Problem: HMW Improve a Flashlight?

1. Select one of the four categories and scan the list words or phrases.
   - *Try to*: twist it.
2. Arbitrarily choose one of the words and use it to stimulate an idea.

- "Twist it" suggests ways a flashlight is or could be used.

3. Write down any ideas suggested.

   - *Twist it*: Make the flashlight handle out of rubber so it can be twisted into different shapes (Note: this idea was published in my *Idea Power* book prior to similar products now on the market.)

4. Repeat steps 1 through 3.

   - *Try to inflate it*: This makes me think of blowing up something like a balloon. Make the flashlight buoyant in case it falls into water.

   - *Make it transparent*: This word causes me to visualize seeing through a flashlight. Make the flashlight transparent as a novelty, much like transparent telephones.

   - *Make it disposable*: This is almost too obvious. Make disposable flashlights!

   - *Think of Sir Lancelot*: A knight often used a lance as a weapon. For law enforcement officers, build in a knife or single-shot gun.

   - *Think of time bombs*: This makes me think of time ticking away. Include a timer so that the flashlight will turn itself off automatically after a certain time period.

   - *Take away or add layers*: Layers cause me to think of something that can be laid on top of something else and possibly removed. Include a variety of interchangeable light filters for the lens.

   - *Take away or add anticipation*: The word *anticipation* makes me consider thinking of something before it happens—for instance, thinking of the flashlight turning on before I even touch the switch. Have the flashlight turn on by pressure on the handle.

NINE

A Crash Course in Generating Creative Ideas: Group Methods

In general, a group of people will produce more ideas than a single individual. Thus, you should consider using group methods whenever possible. Group methods are indicated when the problem is important, you have sufficient time, and the participation of individuals is needed to increase acceptance of solutions and problem ownership.

Of the group techniques described in this chapter, four also can be used by individuals: the *KJ method, picture stimulation, semantic intuition*, and *object stimulation*. However, this flexibility does not necessarily mean they will produce better ideas. The real measure of an idea generation technique is the creative capacity of the people who use it.

The descriptions that follow are presented in a format similar to that used in Chapter 8:

1. Relevant background information and comments

2. Step-by-step description

3. Sample problem

However, no sample problems are provided in instances where pure brainstorming is used. Some techniques rely on only verbal idea generation from group members, whereas others also manipulate various problem elements—for example, the use of related and unrelated problem stimuli. As a result, any sample ideas would have to reflect ideas of hypothetical individuals rather than the mechanics of a technique.

The techniques are presented alphabetically within the two broad categories of brainstorming and brainwriting. *Brainstorming* is a term familiar to most people, although it typically is used as a substitute word for "idea generation." As conceived originally by advertising executive Alex Osborn, brainstorming is applied more properly as a process used to define (frame) problems and to generate, evaluate, and implement ideas. *Brainwriting* probably is less well known and refers to the silent, written generation of ideas in a group. In general, brainwriting methods will result in a greater quantity of ideas than brainstorming methods.

BRAINSTORMING TECHNIQUES

Brainstorming techniques refer to methods in which the primary idea generation method is verbal interaction among group members. The most productive brainstorming groups are those in which group members conform to the principle of deferred judgment—that is, effective brainstorming groups separate idea generation from evaluation. The assumption is that the greater the quantity of ideas generated, the greater the probability that one will be found capable of resolving the challenge.

Force-Fit Game

This method, developed by German engineer Helmut Schlicksupp, is based on the principle of forced relationships in which stimuli are combined to provoke ideas.

Steps

1. Form two groups (A and B) of three to eight people each.
2. Assign one person (not a member of either group) to function as a referee and recorder.
3. The game begins when a member of Group A suggests an idea remote from the problem (or an impractical idea).

4. Group B has two minutes to develop a practical solution to this idea.

5. The referee writes down each solution as it is proposed.

6. The referee awards Group B one point if he or she judges the group was successful in developing a practical solution; if he or she determines the group was unsuccessful, Group A receives the point.

7. Group B next suggests a remote or impractical idea and Group A has two minutes to develop a practical solution to this idea. The referee writes down the solution and awards Group A one point if it is successful in developing a practical idea or Group B one point if Group A was unsuccessful.

8. The game continues for thirty to forty minutes and the group with the most points is declared the winner.

Gordon/Little Technique

Although it may seem contradictory, awareness of a problem can hinder idea generation. Information about a problem obviously is required to achieve a solution; however, it also can cause people to focus on obvious solutions—perhaps because of a human tendency to stereotype problems and solutions. To counter this tendency to focus on the obvious, creativity consultant William Gordon developed this brainstorming variation, which temporarily suspends information from the problem solvers. Although originally intended for problems known only to group facilitators, I have found that it still can be used successfully if group members are told to forget the problem temporarily and participate in a creative-thinking exercise. (Yes, this is somewhat manipulative, but so are all idea generation methods!)

Steps

1. The leader describes an abstract definition of the problem and asks the group to generate solutions.

2. After the group generates solutions for several minutes, the leader introduces a slightly less abstract definition of the problem and the group generates solutions to it.

3. The leader reveals the original problem to the group and asks the group to review the solutions to the two previous problems.

4. The group members use these solutions as stimuli to generate solutions to the original problem.

Sample Problem: HMW Improve a Portable Radio?

1. The leader describes an abstract definition of the problem and asks the group to generate solutions. Problem: Think of ways to improve something. Ideas:

   - Make it larger.

   - Polish it.

   - Add more features.

   - Use more expensive parts.

   - Make it smaller.

   - Make it more flexible.

   - Make it interchangeable.

2. After the group generates solutions for several minutes, the leader introduces a slightly less abstract definition of the problem and the group generates solutions to it. Problem: Think of ways to improve something portable. Ideas:

   - Put wheels on it.

   - Make it lighter in weight.

   - Make it easy to open and close.

   - Have lots of pockets for accessories.

   - Make it a convenient shape to store in different places.

   - Make it easy to pick up.

   - Remove features or parts.

   - Simplify its operation.

3. The leader reveals the original problem to the group and asks the group to review the solutions to the two previous problems.

4. The group members use these solutions as stimuli to generate solutions to the original problem. Problem: HMW improve a portable radio?

- Make it out of stainless steel (from "Polish it").

- Add a spotlight and compass (from "Add more features").

- Make a novelty radio out of rubber so it will bend (from "Make it more flexible").

- Design the portable radio to function as a component with a larger stereo system (from "Make it interchangeable").

- Add storage compartments for extra batteries (from "Have lots of pockets for accessories").

Object Stimulation

Earlier versions of this method are *stimulus analysis* and the *focused-object technique*. However, object stimulation is a blend of these methods, plus it also uses the same basic idea generation principle of unrelated stimuli. The purpose of such stimuli is to present different problem perspectives. In this instance, the unrelated stimuli are objects with no apparent relation to the problem.

Steps

1. Generate a list of concrete objects unrelated to the problem.
2. Select one of the objects and describe it in detail.
3. Use each description as a stimulus to generate ideas.
4. Write down all ideas generated.
5. Select another object and repeat steps 3 and 4.
6. Repeat step 5 until all the objects have been used.

Sample Problem: HMW Reduce the Number of Employees Who Leave Our Organization?

1. Generate a list of concrete objects unrelated to the problem.

- Telephone
- Television

- Bicycle
- Automobile
- Microwave oven

2. Select one of the objects and describe it in detail. Television:
    - Tunes in to many channels
    - Can have different size screens
    - Can use a remote control
    - Can have a sleep timer
    - Can be portable
    - Has a variety of programs
    - Has volume control

3. Use each description as a stimulus to generate ideas. Write down all ideas generated.
    - Have weekly videoconferences with management to air problems (from "tunes in to many channels").
    - Offer a sliding-scale incentive program to retain employees (from "different size screens").
    - Have higher management meet periodically with employees from "remote" areas of the company (from "can use a remote control").
    - Allow employees to take naps during the day (from "sleep timer").
    - Allow employees to work at home (from "portable").

4. Select another object and repeat step 3.

5. Repeat steps 2 and 3 until all the objects have been used or time expires.

Picture Stimulation

Variations of this method have been referred to as *visual synectics* and *Battelle-Bildmappen-brainwriting*. However, picture stimulation is virtually identical to object stimulation except that pictures are used as the unrelated stimuli. You can either give each group member a folder containing pictures or show a picture on an overhead projector.

One advantage of this method over object stimulation is that members are confronted with visual stimuli instead of having to imagine an object. (Of course, there would not be a disadvantage if an object is present.)

You should select pictures that contain a variety of stimuli. Don't use pictures containing a lot of people or close-ups of people. Instead, look for pictures of cities, factories, and country scenes. *National Geographic* is a good magazine source. Of course, there also are many sources of pictures on the Internet as well as clip art software.

When you describe the pictures, try to include as much detail as possible. Don't include only physical references such as "tree," "car," or "grass." Instead, also include many action-oriented statements, such as "The river creates erosion in the earth."

Steps

1. Select five to ten pictures that are unrelated to the problem.
2. Select one of the pictures and describe it in detail.
3. Use each description as a stimulus to generate ideas.
4. Write down all ideas generated.
5. Select another picture and repeat steps 3 and 4.
6. Repeat step 5 until all the pictures have been used.

Sample Problem: HMW Sell More Floor-Care Products?

1. Select five to ten pictures that are unrelated to the problem (one picture will be used for this example).
2. Select one of the pictures and describe it in detail. Picture: a horseshoe magnet.
   - Attracts metal
   - Is made of metal
   - Is shaped like a horseshoe
   - Has two sides

3. Use each description as a stimulus to generate ideas.

4. Write down all ideas generated.

- *Attracts metal.* Put metallic flakes on the package to attract customers.

- *Is made of metal.* Make a bright, shiny metal package.

- *Is shaped like a horseshoe.* Package the product in a horseshoe-shaped package using the theme of a "dirt magnet."

- *Has two sides.* Put a cleaning product in one side of the package and a wax or shining product in the other side.

5. Select another picture and repeat steps 3 and 4.

6. Repeat step 5 until all the pictures have been used.

Semantic Intuition

Semantic intuition reverses the normal procedure when an invention is created. Instead of assigning a name to an invention, semantic intuition creates a name and then produces an invention (or idea) based on it. One advantage of this method is that it uses related problem elements but combines them in ways that help produce different problem perspectives.

Steps

1. Generate two sets of words related to major problem elements.

2. Select a word from one set and combine it with a word from the other.

3. Use the combination to generate an idea and write it down.

4. Repeat steps 2 and 3 until you have examined several combinations.

Sample Problem: HMW Encourage Employees to Stop Throwing Litter on Company Property?

1. Generate two sets of words related to major problem elements.

Things Involved with Employees	Things Involved with Litter
Working	Paper
Playing	Glass
Breaks	Metal
Bosses	Throwing
Pay	Trash cans
Benefits	Wood
Retirement	Picking it up

2. Select a word from one set and combine it with a word from the other.

3. Use the combination to generate an idea and write it down.

   • Require all employees to spend a certain amount of time each week picking up litter (from "working-paper").

4. Repeat steps 2 and 3 until you have examined several combinations.

   • Set up ball-throwing contests during lunch hour and ask participants to pick up litter around them (from "playing-throwing").

   • Require employees to pick up at least one piece of litter during their breaks (from "breaks-paper").

   • Require bosses to pick up litter to set a good example (from "bosses–picking it up").

   • Set up a recycling center that pays employees a premium price for litter they sort and turn in (from "pay–picking it up").

SIL Method

This technique was developed at the Battelle Institute in Frankfurt, Germany. The letters *SIL* represent a German acronym that translates in English as "successive integration of problem elements." It differs from most idea generation methods in that ideas are generated progressively by integrating previous ideas.

Although individuals initially generate ideas in writing, the method is not really a brainwriting technique. It was classified as a brainstorming procedure because the primary mechanism for generating ideas relies on verbal interactions.

Steps

1. A group of four to seven people silently writes down ideas.

2. Two of the group members read one of their ideas aloud.

3. The remaining group members try to integrate the ideas just read into one idea.

4. A third member reads an idea and the group attempts to integrate it with the one formed in step 3.

5. This process of reading and integrating ideas continues until all the ideas have been read and integrated.

Split-Brain Comparisons

This technique is based roughly on the concepts of analytical and creative thinking. These concepts often are compared rather simplistically with left- and right-brain thinking functions. That is, the left-brain hemisphere uses linear, logical, and analytical thought processes, while the right deals more with intuitive, holistic, and creative thought processes. In brain anatomy, the bundle of nerve fibers that joins these hemispheres is known as the corpus callosum.

The split-brain comparison technique generates ideas by designing group interactions as a metaphor of brain functioning and physiology. That is, it juxtaposes ideas from creative and analytical groups with an integrating group activity known as *corpus callosum thinking.*

Steps

1. Divide a group of twelve to fourteen people into two subgroups of primarily analytical and primarily creative-thinking people simply by asking them to classify themselves as predominately creative or analytical. One group should contain all analytical thinkers and one all creative thinkers. The groups should be as equal in size as possible. If the creative and analytical thinkers cannot be divided equally, use an approximate division.

2. Physically separate the two groups and ask them to generate ideas to solve a problem. Instruct the analytical group to consider only logical ideas and the creative group to consider only wild, off-the-wall ideas.

3. Terminate brainstorming after about twenty to thirty minutes.

4. Combine individuals from both groups to form one large group (the *corpus callosum* group).

5. Instruct the corpus callosum group to select one idea from the analytical group and attempt to integrate it with one idea from the creative group to form a new idea or modification. Continue this activity using other idea combinations until they have generated a sufficient number of ideas.

Sample Problem: HMW Improve a Flashlight?

Logical Ideas

- Use a sturdier switch.
- Use a nonbreakable lens.
- Cushion the case.
- Install a battery-life indicator.
- Make it waterproof.

Off-the-Wall Ideas

- The flashlight turns on automatically when it gets dark.
- The light brightens or dims as you wish it.
- You can lengthen the flashlight by pulling on it.
- The size of the lens increases or decreases in response to how much light there is in the environment.
- Throwing the flashlight in the air causes it to turn on automatically.

Integrated Ideas

- The light brightens or dims depending on how much pressure you apply on the switch (from "Use a sturdier switch" and "The light brightens or dims as you wish it").

- Battery life can be increased by spinning the flashlight—the spinning motion activates a small generator inside the flashlight (from "Install a battery-life indicator" and "Throwing the flashlight in the air causes it to turn on automatically").

- Make a glow-in-the-dark case. Squeezing on the case causes it to change different colors (from "Cushion the case" and "The size of the lens increases or decreases in response to how much light there is in the environment").

Trans-Disciplinary Analogy

The *trans-disciplinary analogy (TDA)* was developed by Henry Andersen, a former marketing manager at Mitsubishi Heavy Industries America, Inc. It is based on the notion that new ideas can emerge from anyone at any time. In this regard, Andersen developed the Diamond IdeaGroup, the "multidisciplinary and multinational idea generating, translating, and integrating network serving organizations and individuals worldwide." TDA is a functional translation of the Diamond Idea-Group—that is, it generates ideas by borrowing perspectives from different disciplines.

Steps

1. Form small groups of at least five people each. Each group should contain people from a variety of occupations.

2. Assign a facilitator to each group.

3. The facilitator asks each group member to select one discipline or activity of special interest to that person. This discipline or activity does not have to be represented by the person's occupation, nor does it have to be a traditional academic discipline. It may even be some activity such as dishwashing or tree trimming. However, the person selecting a discipline or activity should have some familiarity with it.

4. Each group member selects a central concept from his or her selected discipline and the facilitator lists it on a board or flip chart.

5. After all the concepts are recorded, the group selects one concept and the individual responsible for it provides a detailed description. (For instance, in one TDA group, a ballerina selected a particular dance movement as her concept. She then described the movement in detail and even demonstrated it.)

6. The group members examine the description and use it to generate ideas. They use each description as a potential idea stimulus.

7. The group then selects another concept and repeats steps 5 and 6.

BRAINWRITING TECHNIQUES

As discussed previously, brainwriting involves the silent, written generation of ideas in a group. The basic brainstorming rule of separating generation from evaluation also applies—that is, individuals should defer judgment on their ideas until it is time to evaluate them.

Brainsketching

Most of us use visual images to generate ideas. We often sketch these ideas to help us conceptualize them. The *brainsketching technique* attempts to capitalize on this ability in a group situation by allowing people to compare idea sketches. This particular brainwriting method originated during a discussion in one of my creativity classes. In 1981, Jim Pickens, a student at that time, conceived brainsketching as a variation of the *pin cards technique,* a procedure in which idea cards are passed around a group. Brainsketching modifies this procedure by passing around idea sketches.

Steps

1. Each group member individually draws a sketch of how the problem might be solved. No talking is permitted during this activity.

2. Group members pass their drawings to the person on their right.

3. These individuals modify the original drawings or add comments.

4. This process of modifying and adding to the drawings continues for about twenty to thirty minutes.

5. The group members examine all the drawings and select a final solution or construct a final solution from parts of different sketches.

Brainwriting Pool

This is one of several brainwriting approaches developed at the Battelle Institute in Frankfurt, Germany. It is relatively easy to implement and requires little in the way of leader facilitation skills. Nevertheless, it helps to generate a large number of ideas in a short time. The physical setting consists of a group of five to eight people seated around a small table.

The steps for group members to do individually are as follows:

1. Write down four ideas on a sheet of paper.

2. Place the sheet in the center of the table (the pool) and exchange it for another one.

3. Read the ideas on the new sheet and use them to stimulate new ideas.

4. Write down any new ideas on the sheet and exchange it for a new sheet from the pool when the group member needs additional stimulation.

5. Continue writing down ideas and exchanging sheets for ten to fifteen minutes.

Collective Notebook

John Haefele of Procter & Gamble developed the *collective notebook (CNB) method* to generate ideas from a cross-section of employees within an organization. A major difference between it and other group idea generation methods is that the individuals do not meet face-to-face. Instead, participants write down ideas on their own and then pool them later on. Another major difference is that ideas are generated over an extended period of time, rather than submitted spontaneously in one brief time period. About ten participants usually is enough to generate a sufficient number of ideas.

Haefele created this method in the 1960s, well before the Internet, so it represents one of the first nondigital idea management processes. Of course, the basic process still can be used without the Internet. In some instances, this may be a disadvantage due to the potential for extended incubation time.

Steps

The participants:

1. Receive a notebook containing a problem statement and background information.
2. Write down at least one idea every working day for one month.
3. Develop a written summary of their ideas, including a list of their best ones.
4. Return their notebooks to a coordinator, who reviews the ideas, categorizes them, and prepares a detailed summary to submit to management.

Professor Alan Pearson of the United Kingdom suggested a variation that should increase idea quality. He recommends that after two weeks' time, the participants exchange their notebooks with another preselected participant. They then can use these ideas to stimulate new ideas. Today, because this process is even easier with e-mail or idea management software, such exchanges might occur more frequently.

Gallery Method

This approach reverses the basic process of the brainwriting pool and pin cards techniques. Thus, instead of moving ideas around for people to examine, the *gallery method* moves the people around the ideas. It is based on the way people browse an art gallery to receive stimulation.

Steps

1. Sheets of flip chart paper are attached to the walls of a room (or flip charts on stands are placed around the sides of a room).

2. Group members silently write down their ideas on the sheets of paper (one sheet per person).

3. After ten to fifteen minutes of writing, the participants are given fifteen minutes to walk around, look at the other ideas, and take notes.

4. Group members silently write down any new ideas or improvements upon the ideas of others.

5. After about five to ten minutes of additional writing, the participants examine all the ideas and select the best ones.

KJ Method

The *KJ method* was developed by anthropology professor Jiro Kawakita when he was at the Tokyo Institute of Technology. He created this method for sequential grouping and synthesis of field observations, resulting in a clearer picture of the problem as well as new hypotheses and ideas. New ideas then are triggered by complex associations among other ideas. Although there is some verbal interaction among group members, the primary idea generation mechanism is brainwriting.

Steps

1. Individuals are instructed to write down ideas on small cards, one idea per card with a goal of one hundred cards.

2. Individuals sort the cards into categories of fifty to one hundred cards, then twenty to thirty cards, then ten cards or fewer. The categories should reflect new conceptual categories. These, in turn, help break down rigid thinking and help stimulate new ideas.

3. Individuals write down any new ideas on flip chart paper. These ideas may be related or unrelated to the problem. They also may be described graphically to increase understanding. A new conceptual picture should emerge after this step.

4. Group members read aloud groups of ideas on their conceptual pictures and write down new ideas prompted by the picture or the discussion.

The KJ method has been used widely in Japan since its development decades ago. For instance, Nippon Telegraph and Telephone used it to create a twenty-year technology roadmap, developing plans for an information network system that showed the conceptual merging of telephone, facsimile, video, and data communications.

NHK Brainstorming

Although labeled a brainstorming technique, *NHK brainstorming* actually is a brainwriting variation. The primary idea generation process involves silent, written generation of ideas. It does, however, contain some brainstorming activities. This technique was developed by Hiroshi Takahashi, of the Japan Broadcasting Corporation (NHK), hence its name.

Steps

1. Individuals write down five ideas each on index cards (one idea per card).
2. The individuals form into groups of five.
3. Each individual explains his or her idea while the rest of the group members write down ideas that come to mind.
4. All the cards are collected and sorted into categories of related themes.
5. New groups of two or three people are formed. The groups then brainstorm ideas for the themes and write the ideas down on index cards.
6. After an hour or so, each group organizes the new ideas by themes and presents them to the larger group. (All ideas are written on a chalkboard for all to see.)
7. The participants form new groups of ten people each and brainstorm improvements regarding the ideas on the chalkboard, one idea at a time.

Nominal Group Technique

The *nominal group technique (NGT)* was developed by management professors Andre Delbecq and Andrew Van de Ven in 1968 as a way to systematically structure group discussions. Because there is little verbal interaction and decisions are made quantitatively, consensus can be achieved easily. NGT has all the advantages of brainwriting and also includes an idea evaluation stage. A major disadvantage is that the written ideas are not shared, thus preventing stimulation from other people's ideas. However, new ideas can be added after the written ideas have been shared with the larger group. As with other brainwriting methods, it also could be modified and done electronically online.

Steps

1. Five to seven individuals write down their ideas without speaking.

2. Each group member orally presents one of his or her ideas without justification or elaboration. The group leader records the idea on flip chart paper (the ideas are numbered sequentially) and the next group member orally presents his or her idea. New ideas triggered by the oral presentations also may be added to the lists. This process continues until the leader has recorded the ideas—one at a time—from each group member.

3. The leader points to each idea and requests clarifying comments. No evaluation is permitted other than to eliminate duplicate ideas and to correct an idea proposer's intended meanings.

4. Group members receive index cards and rank five to nine ideas from among those listed (ratings also can be used but require more time to tally). Group members select their favorite ideas and write down each on a separate card. They indicate the idea number sequence on the upper left-hand corner of the card. Next, each member spreads out his or her priority cards and places them in order of preference by selecting the most important, then the least important, then the most important of the

remaining cards, and so forth. Finally, they record each idea's ranking on the lower right corner.

5. The leader tallies all the rankings or ratings and presents them to the group. The group examines the results and looks for inconsistencies or peculiar patterns. The leader encourages clarification of inconsistencies and solicits any information that might help members understand an idea's intended meaning.

6. If a final vote is needed, the procedure outlined in step 4 is followed.

Pin Cards

The *pin cards method*, developed by the Battelle Institute in Frankfurt, is a close cousin of the brainwriting pool. The major difference is that ideas are passed around to other group members instead of being placed in the center of a table. In this regard, the brainwriting pool may have an advantage in offering more idea anonymity than pin cards (if that is a concern). Otherwise, both procedures can generate many ideas.

Steps

Five to seven people are given a stack of sticky notes and seated around a small table.

1. Group members individually:
   - Write down one idea on a note and pass it to the person on the right.
   - Read the idea on each note and use it to stimulate new ideas.
   - Write down any new ideas on a new note and pass it to the person on the right.
   - Continue writing down ideas and passing on idea notes for ten to fifteen minutes.

2. The notes are collected and posted on a wall or arranged on a large table in logical categories for future evaluation.

TEN

Tips for Designing and Facilitating Brainstorming Retreats

Before it was possible to conduct innovation challenges online, they were conducted in face-to-face (FtF) settings known as brainstorming retreats. Online challenges, of course, do not preclude the possibility of FtF retreats. In fact, they sometimes may complement and augment each other. For instance, an organization first might want to conduct an online challenge to generate a large pool of ideas and then narrow them down to the best concepts. These concepts then could be explored more fully in a FtF retreat that would provide opportunities to interact with others in real time. Another option would be to hold an online session and follow it up with a retreat to generate additional ideas.

The type of communication environment used, however, has no effect on the need to use well-framed innovation challenges. People come to retreats with the same preconceived perceptions of challenges as when participating online. So, the same amount of attention should be given to framing challenges for FtF situations. It also is possible to introduce a competitive element into retreats by having small groups compete against one another.

More important, retreats provide a vastly richer media environment for idea generation. That is, retreat participants have more cues—both verbal and nonverbal—to use when interacting with others. And, they can use these cues in real time—although online sessions also can involve synchronous communication, of course. This means that, in person, it typically will be easier and faster to collaborate, clarify, and build off other people's ideas than is possible online. Retreats have disadvantages as well. Interpersonal conflicts and dominating individuals may make it difficult to ensure equal participation to make use of the range of insights available in a group of diverse brainstormers. However, certain group brainstorming techniques can help overcome some of these disadvantages (see Chapter 9).

This chapter is designed to provide some tips on how to design and facilitate brainstorming retreats. Parts of this chapter were taken from a similar chapter in my book *Idea Power*, also published by AMACOM. However, this chapter contains new information, although it is not intended as a comprehensive guide; other books exist on all of the specifics involved in conducting successful retreats.

Considering how to conduct a brainstorming retreat involves the same basic thinking processes and many similar activities involved in conducting online innovation challenges. Specifically, both require upfront preparation to lay the groundwork and follow-up activities to ensure successful implementation. The previous chapters in Part I of this book discussed many of these activities such as conducting Q-banks and C-banks and how to write challenges (Chapters 2, 3, and 4, respectively). Topics covered in this chapter for retreats include obtaining buy-in from stakeholders and upper management, using an in-house coordinator, assessing creativity readiness, managing expectations, creating an idea generation agenda, setting up the physical setting, choosing retreat participants, establishing ground rules, controlling pacing and timing, recording and evaluating ideas, and conducting post-retreat activities. Many of these activities also apply to online challenges.

OBTAINING BUY-IN FROM STAKEHOLDERS AND UPPER MANAGEMENT

If major stakeholders are involved from the outset with an innovation challenge, they are more likely to support the project throughout. As discussed previously in this book, involving stakeholders as participants of Q-bank and C-bank processes usually helps to ensure buy-in. However, it is important that they actually perceive and experience this; otherwise, they may sabotage later efforts or at least present minor obstacles to slow down implementation. In my experience, such buy-in typically occurs unless there are any simmering conflicts.

As with most organizational decisions, you must obtain approval for a retreat from the highest necessary level. Besides simple budget approval, management must understand and agree with the retreat's objectives. Otherwise, the outcome may be ignored or you will face an uphill implementation battle. Of course, prior management approval won't guarantee success, but it will make it easier to gain a fair hearing for the new ideas produced. The key phrase here is *highest organization level.*

Most managers recognize the importance of this guideline. In one organization I worked with, however, a personal conflict caused a manager to overlook it. Although the setting was not an off-site retreat, the incident still illustrates the need for upper-level support: My contact set up an afternoon meeting with a group of upper-level managers to discuss strategic issues. At a meeting that evening, I met the divisional director of worldwide company operations, who had not attended the afternoon meeting. I was somewhat surprised and curious about his absence; however, I just assumed he was occupied by other matters. I later learned he had been excluded intentionally by my contact. Apparently, they had a history of interpersonal conflicts, and excluding the higher-level manager clearly would send a message. Because of this slight, however, the lower-level manager found it difficult to gain support for the project. Although it may be obvious what we should do, we sometimes allow our emotions to interfere. Avoid cutting off your nose to spite your face.

In another organization, I kept pushing my in-house contact to obtain buy-in at the highest level and let me know who that person was and, most important, if that person approved of the objectives, scope of the project, and how the retreat would be conducted. And I asked these questions several times via e-mail and phone conversations over a period of several weeks. I was continually reassured that everything was fine and that necessary approval existed for conducting the retreat and for how it was going to be conducted. Now, you probably can see this coming: At the end of the first day of the two-day retreat, a senior manager walked in. He surveyed the flip charts, sticky notes, and toys we were using to provide a creative environment; and asked something to the effect of, "Who the heck approved all of this? What's going on here?" I never did learn the outcome of that event—it's probably just as well!

Another aspect of obtaining buy-in involves the specific area of buy-in. Sometimes it isn't enough to have approval at the highest necessary level with respect to conducting a retreat and the process used to generate ideas. The idea evaluation and concept formation phase of innovation challenges also requires top approval. In one company, I met personally with the highest-level-possible manager, and described the process I planned to use in detail. He approved everything I said. During the second day of the retreat, this manager showed up while the participants were evaluating ideas. He noticed that one of his pet ideas wasn't selected for future consideration and expressed his consternation that this idea wasn't chosen. I told him he was the boss and he could throw it into the idea concept "hopper" if he wanted. And he did. It later was refined by the participants, who then agreed it should have been selected initially because some modifications had improved it considerably.

SELECTING AN IN-HOUSE COORDINATOR

As with any group activity, coordination is needed to plan and conduct a retreat. An official coordinator will make it easier to conduct a successful retreat. His or her duties typically include choosing an outside facilitator, collecting planning data, choosing participants and keeping them informed, making arrangements for physical facilities, and monitoring postretreat activities. However, don't wait until the retreat to involve a coordinator. The coordinator should be appointed to oversee all retreat activities, beginning with initial planning.

Choose coordinators based on their ability to do the job and relevant experience. (Don't appoint a coordinator if his or her only previous experience was planning the company picnic!) Planning a retreat involves special skills because of its heavy task orientation and its importance to the company. The person you choose should relate to others well and be able to monitor group tasks closely. Other skills include the ability to coordinate many details simultaneously, communicate in a positive manner to encourage commitment, and be aware of the importance of teamwork and ownership of the results.

Although coordinators have an important responsibility, they may not be the best choice to serve as overall retreat facilitators. A different set of skills is needed to design a retreat and see it implemented. Unless coordinators have special expertise in these areas, you should use an outside person.

MANAGING EXPECTATIONS

Either the in-house coordinator or an external facilitator should assess expectations and clarify misconceptions. This should be done for both organizational decision makers and retreat participants.

In some organizations, high-level managers view retreats suspiciously. Their expectations and understandings may differ from those of the retreat's planners. Managers often believe that individuals are paid to solve problems and retreats are just an excuse to party. I have heard this sentiment occasionally and believe it is shortsighted thinking. A well-planned and coordinated retreat can be productive, and it can be tied directly to long-term effectiveness. Most important, retreats can provide a pool of ideas that can complement and enhance online challenges. Management usually just needs a little convincing.

After assessing expectations, the best way to clarify them is to give a balanced presentation of retreat strengths and weaknesses. You make a more convincing argument when you present both pros and cons; otherwise, the person you want to persuade may think you are hiding something. The other person also is more likely to believe he or she controls and owns the decision; therefore, commitment to the retreat and its outcome should be higher as well.

Perhaps the most important set of expectations to manage are retreat outcomes. Such outcomes typically are expressed as the quantity and quality of the ideas generated, as well as an organization learning a new process methodology to use for future idea generation projects. There is, of course, no guarantee that a challenge will be resolved to everyone's satisfaction. If the retreat is planned well, however, the odds of a successful outcome will increase dramatically.

Besides the usual rational arguments, many managers respond to the bandwagon syndrome: If everyone else is doing it, maybe we should, too (or at least take a closer look). I don't necessarily advocate this approach, but it may help occasionally. Managers learn other companies are having retreats and decide to follow suit. Monkey see, monkey do.

Although it would be disastrous to overlook managerial expectations, it also would be a mistake to neglect participant expectations. In many organizations, subordinates are not consulted about managerial decisions; thus, it is unlikely they would be contacted regarding a retreat's agenda. The high degree of employee involvement in a retreat mandates some participation during planning, however. At least one or two employee representatives should contribute to pre-retreat planning. If nothing else, give employees a chance to look over the agenda and offer opinions. And, as noted previously, some or all participants may be stakeholders who can participate in pre-retreat Q-banks and C-banks. This inclusive approach now is used more with the current emphasis on open source management.

ASSESSING CREATIVITY READINESS

Another pre-retreat consideration is to ensure that participants have *creativity readiness*. Participants should be predisposed to creative thinking; there should be no hidden agendas or other issues to deal with before idea generation. For example, some teams need basic team-building skills before they can develop a more creative climate. Matters such as interpersonal trust and cooperation often need attention before creative ideas can be generated. Groups must be able to function as a team before they can exploit their creativity. In one session I facilitated, the participants expressed a need to voice their concerns about a company administrative policy. It was obvious these concerns needed airing before any productive idea generation could take place. Once they were, the members were able to focus their attention on the purpose of the retreat.

CREATING AN IDEA GENERATION AGENDA

Retreat success often depends on how much structure you build in—generally the more structure, the greater the likelihood of success—but such structure must be used flexibly. You will have to modify almost any plan. If some groups do not respond well to one technique, offer backups. So, if you have underestimated the time needed, bring out backup techniques. For instance, schedule more idea generation techniques than time available—typically ten in total, although six or seven actually may be used. The situation is something like cutting a piece of wood to fit an area of defined length. If you make the cut too short, you can't correct it; if the cut is too long, you will have the option of trying again. So, it's better to err on the high side.

One important agenda consideration is the order in which techniques are used. I recommend starting with a brainwriting technique in which participants write down all the ideas they have brought with them to the retreat. I then follow it with one or more techniques that rely on stimuli related to the challenge, and then alternate with methods relying on unrelated stimuli. I also have found it useful to introduce a playful technique in late morning or especially near the end of the first day. One popular approach for this method is to have participants write ideas on multicolored paper airplanes, throw them to each other, and then use the ideas for stimulation to write down another idea and throw the planes again. (This is the *Fly Ajax method* listed in the sample agenda that follows.)

A detailed agenda is a primary planning goal. It should include a sequential description of major activities and the time allocated to each. However, be flexible in your approach. View an agenda as a game plan that can be modified as situations arise. A sample agenda for a one-and-a-half-day retreat is as follows:

RETREAT AGENDA
Veeblefeester Widget Corporation
Dallyshowers Resort

Thursday

8:00–8:45	Continental breakfast	Chow Chow Room
8:45–9:00	Introductions and overview	Ding-Dong Room
9:00–9:30	Brainwriting technique	
9:30–10:15	Combo Chatter technique	
10:15–10:30	Break	Caffeine Room
10:30–11:15	Product Improvement Checklist	
11:15–noon	Preliminary idea screening	
Noon–1:15	Lunch	Chow Chow Room
1:15–1:45	Fly Ajax	
1:45–2:30	Assumption Reversals technique	
2:30–3:15	Preppy Thoughts technique	
3:15–3:30	Break	Caffeine Room
3:30–4:15	Picture Tickler technique	
4:15–4:45	Preliminary idea screening	
4:45–5:00	First-day summary and discussion	

Friday

8:15–8:45	Breakfast	Chow Chow Room
8:45–9:00	Overview of the morning	
9:00–9:30	Talkin' Trash technique	
9:30–9:45	Evaluation guidelines	
9:45–10:15	Idea evaluation/Concept development	
10:15–10:30	Break	Caffeine room
10:30–11:30	Concept development	
11:30–noon	Small group reports and discussion	

I designed this retreat so that idea generation and evaluation would be separated. The participants spend most of the first day using a variety of techniques to generate ideas. They are divided into small groups and as group members think of ideas they write them on sticky notes, *one idea per note*. It is important to emphasize this point because later idea evaluation involves moving ideas around. Each group should have two flip charts with one reserved for the "best" ideas and the other for "other" ideas, so as to avoid any negative connotations. The groups place their ideas on the "other" flip chart as they write them down. After time is called for each technique, each group evaluates its ideas, places the best ones on the appropriate flip chart, and then takes turns sharing the ideas with the large group. At this time, the other participants can add to or think of any new ideas stimulated, writing down all modified or new ideas on separate sticky notes.

Once all of the groups have shared their best ideas, they place their flip-chart sheets on two different walls of the room, with one for "best" ideas and the other for "other" ideas. Participants typically vote on all of the ideas posted on the walls at the end of the first day (and sometimes at the end of the first morning). These minievaluation periods help shorten a long list of ideas, prompt suggestions on how to combine related ideas, and stimulate thinking for more ideas. Participants typically use colored, sticking dots to vote for their favorite ideas, using successive voting rounds. For instance, in the first round of voting, participants might be given ten blue dots and told to vote for their favorites (one dot per vote). Next, they might be given five orange dots and told to vote on their favorite ideas that received at least three blue dots.

I set aside the morning of the second day primarily for idea evaluation. However, I suggest using one idea generation technique first thing to capture any ideas thought of overnight. The rest of the morning, the participants should focus on idea evaluation. For this, groups should select or be assigned a highly rated idea to refine and develop into a workable concept to implement. This promotes a sense of task completion and may increase the commitment to certain ideas. It also can smooth implementation after the retreat.

I also limit the length of the retreat. There is nothing sacred about an eight-hour day. The intensity and concentration called for in retreats often make it impractical to stick to a traditional work schedule. Thus, some groups might benefit from an early finish, but if the groups are energized and seem productive, allow them more time.

Finally, it can be beneficial to stay over at least one night during a retreat. For instance, you might want to schedule informal social activities for the evening. Such experiences promote team building and contribute to a positive problem-solving climate. When I suggested this to a company vice president, his major concern was that some people would drink so much they would be useless the next day. However, I conducted a retreat for another corporation that illustrates the positive value of social affairs. The first day was not as successful as we had hoped. There was a lot of negative thinking and an unwillingness to take risks. During an evening social hour, however, several participants loosened up and suggested ideas that later were judged promising by management.

SELECTING A LOCATION AND ROOM SETUP

Although not as important as other factors, this matter still deserves attention. If resources permit, consider an off-site location removed from daily distractions. However, the location should be accessible by conventional transportation. If people must be ferried in using two-seat airplanes or portaging with canoes, you may want to rethink the location!

Be wary of hotels trying to pump up their convention business. Instead, consider resorts. Although many resorts cater to meetings, seek out those that specialize in conferences—they usually can anticipate your needs and deal with crises better. You also can use their personnel to arrange details. Always check to ensure things are done correctly, however. Sometimes, simple misunderstandings can create major frustrations. For instance, I once requested rooms with round tables only to find a classroom arrangement with straight rows of rectangular tables—perfect for a lecture, but not for small-group interactions.

Although it often is overlooked, the view—if any—from the rooms should be evaluated. Participants can be distracted by beautiful scenery if the view is overwhelming. (The only time scenery was a significant problem in one of my retreats was when the "scenery" was female. The meeting had glass walls and overlooked a swimming pool. As a result, the all-male groups in these rooms had dilated pupils for the first hours of the day.)

CHOOSING RETREAT PARTICIPANTS

People attend retreats for a variety of reasons. Usually, they attend because they work in a particular area or have special expertise. Occasionally it is a reward for outstanding performance. If you can select participants, look for those who are highly motivated by the topic, knowledgeable about the problem, and willing to generate and consider off-the-wall ideas. And, of course, people with a direct or indirect stake in the outcomes should be involved.

I generally recommend that organizations conducting retreats use both internal and external participants. Internals should include stakeholders (including employees from other divisions, if appropriate), personnel with problem knowledge, and a few participants without knowledge of the problem. Motivated and, especially, creative people from office support staff to upper management often can provide a diversity of fresh perspectives. (Such employees often receive a morale boost from being included, which can result in a more creative climate.)

There are two types of externals who should be included. I call the first type external *e-stormers* because they are not members of the organization but submit their ideas electronically, as described in Chapter 7 on idea management software. These individuals can participate from anywhere in the world and typically offer new perspectives not considered internally. As discussed previously in this book, these externals can participate with internals on submitting ideas during innovation challenges, thus significantly increasing the pool of ideas before or after a retreat. The second type of externals are what I refer to as *brain boosters*. These people work outside of an organization as creative professionals and/or as creativity consultants. I recommend including one of these individuals within each small group at a retreat. Often these individuals also have facilitation skills they can employ within their groups.

ASSIGNING PARTICIPANTS TO GROUPS

Limit groups to five or six people. Don't vary from this guideline, even if the resort sales personnel say they *always* set up tables for ten people—that just makes their job easier. It's not in your best interest. Some research suggests that five people is the ideal size, but I have had success with as few as four and as many as ten—it all depends on how their interactions are structured using idea generation techniques.

In larger groups, participation may be unequal because of cliques or simply sheer size. Cliques form when interactions among group members become difficult; it's easier to interact with four or five people than with eight or nine. Unequal participation also can occur; the larger a group, the fewer opportunities to participate. In small groups (four or five people), on the other hand, there are fewer resources to draw upon and a dominating individual may emerge.

More important than size, however, is group composition. Whenever possible, don't mix bosses and subordinates. In one retreat I facilitated, a manager insisted on being in a group with his subordinates. It didn't take long for me to figure out why the group was not generating many ideas. The boss apparently was conducting a new product idea generation session the way he conducted staff meetings. He would call on group members by name and ask for their ideas. Then he would criticize each idea as it was suggested. By dominating the discussion and criticizing ideas, he put a damper on the whole process. The subordinates were afraid to suggest any "wild" ideas. Instead, they tried to play it safe and suggested carefully thought-out ideas. It's difficult to think of carefully analyzed ideas and still be spontaneous; as a result, the ideas were few and mundane.

You also should use homogeneous or natural work units only if particular expertise is needed. Natural groups become stilted in their thinking and need fresh input from others. If you work with the same people on the same problems every day, you're likely to get the same old solutions. In contrast, groups composed of personnel from different teams can bring new perspectives. For instance, if a problem calls for engineering expertise, a natural work group of engineers may be needed. However, if the problem is more general, interdisciplinary teams will be more effective. Or, at least include people from different departments within the same groups.

In general, each small group should have one or more people knowledgeable about the challenge and one or more internal and external creative types. So, a group of five people might contain three internal experts from different departments, one external brainbooster, and one or more internals who do not work in the area of the challenge. I also advocate periodically rotating the composition of group membership, especially if most groups seem to be wearing down or are having trouble generating ideas. The afternoon typically is the best time to do this. One caution: If a group seems to be "on fire" with rapid and sustained idea generation, I would keep them together for a while longer.

By the way, one tactic to control conflict or dominating personalities is to form a group of so-called problem people. Before one retreat, we identified all the troublemakers, malcontents, and obnoxious people—and put them together in one group. We then let them fight it out and bother each other. Our attitude was that if they don't produce any useful products, at least they will not bother others. A disadvantage of this approach is that some creative individuals may be excluded. I recommend using this tactic only as a last resort; a skilled facilitator usually can deal with most disruptive behavior.

ESTABLISHING GROUND RULES

The first task of a retreat facilitator is to review the ground rules. From the outset, you should clarify expectations and establish boundaries of acceptable behavior. If people know what to expect and what the limits are of permissible behavior, they should act appropriately.

The following are some sample ground rules a facilitator might read and distribute in writing to a group:

• *Separate idea generation from idea evaluation.* Try to withhold all judgment during idea generation. Once all ideas have been generated, you will have the opportunity to analyze them. This is the most important ground rule, so remind your fellow group members if they start to violate it.

• *Do not be a conversation hog.* To benefit from all the resources represented by the group members, limit your comments.

• *Try to forget potential implementation obstacles when generating ideas.* Even wild ideas are acceptable, since they often can be modified or serve as stimuli for other group members.

• *Try to stick with the time schedule.* However, don't be afraid to deviate if needed. For instance, if one technique helps to generate ideas, don't stop using it just because the scheduled time has passed. Your facilitator will work with you on this.

• *Try to generate as many ideas as possible.* The more ideas you think of, the greater the odds are at least one will be a breakthrough.

• *Be assertive.* Your ideas are just as valuable as other people's. Even if you think an idea is impractical, go ahead and suggest it. It might prompt other ideas.

• *Have fun.* Don't worry about being silly when generating ideas.

You should establish ground rules during planning so participants won't be surprised by them; however, if you can't, explain the rationale for each rule when offered. If there are any special participant considerations, discuss and incorporate them as new guidelines if the other members agree. For instance, nonsmokers often request a smoke-free group or a limit on how many people may smoke simultaneously.

CONTROLLING PACING AND TIMING

Although planning is the primary determinant of success, the control of retreat activities runs a close second. Most of us have suffered through group experiences that can be characterized at best as aimless wandering. Avoid this problem by monitoring each group's activities and supplying structure as needed. One way to supply structure is to control the timing and pacing of activities.

Obviously, the smaller the facilitator-to-group ratio, the better that timing and pacing can be controlled. The only exception is in organizations with groups experienced with problem-solving techniques. Their experience often can substitute for facilitator skills, since experience is a form of structure.

To control pacing and timing, observe how groups respond to each technique; then move them from one technique to another based on their performance. Not all groups respond equally well, any more than individuals do to different teaching or counseling methods. Often, consensus develops within a group that a technique "just doesn't work." At one retreat, a participant responded, "This technique is a red herring." At the very next retreat I conducted, I heard nothing but positive comments about the same technique. Moreover, some groups respond so well to a technique they resist moving to another. In either case, a facilitator should allow the groups to make necessary adjustments.

Technique effectiveness depends on many factors such as group climate, problem type, and group-member motivation and experience. If a technique doesn't stimulate ideas, allow the group to move on or return to one that worked well before. But if a group is highly fluent and generates many ideas, don't break the flow and force it to learn another technique. In this case, the group climate will do more to prompt ideas than an imposed technique.

To determine proper pacing and timing, evaluate a group's familiarity with a technique and experience using it. Don't force a technique on a group if the members have little experience or familiarity with it. This is why minimal training is so important; usually a simple explanation, illustration, and short practice session will be enough. The time available also will be an important factor. More complex or time-intensive methods should be reserved for when there is adequate time.

The other activities for both retreats and online innovation challenges are the processes of selecting and evaluating ideas and implementing solutions. These topics are discussed in Chapter 11.

EVALUATING DATA

Use a systematic evaluation procedure to ensure that all ideas receive a fair hearing. This can be difficult if there are many ideas and you have little time. Many productive idea generation sessions deteriorate during idea evaluation. Faced with too much to do in too little time, group members feel pressured and choose just any idea to implement. Such an approach rarely results in a high-quality solution.

To overcome this problem, agree upon and stick with a structured evaluation approach. Although these methods vary in complexity, the evaluation process should become more manageable. For example, include a preliminary idea evaluation segment in the retreat agenda. In the agenda I presented before, group members evaluate ideas after the morning and afternoon sessions. This first screening culls out obviously unacceptable ideas, and it may stimulate thinking for new ideas or modifications of existing ones. To guide this process, use one or two major criteria. For instance, you might eliminate ideas that cost more than $1,000 and call for more than two people to implement.

A second way to structure idea evaluation is to use weighted criteria. In the previous example, cost and time criteria are equal in weight, since no mention is made otherwise—that is, cost and time are equal in importance and both should be used to judge the idea. Although equal weight may work for an initial screening, more-refined analyses call for more-refined rating methods. Because people perceive idea evaluation criteria as similar in value, rating procedures should take into consideration different degrees of importance for the criteria. For instance, when buying a car, most of us believe that gas mileage and price are more important than color and seat cover material.

One simple culling approach involves making a list of the advantages and disadvantages of each idea. You then choose ideas with more advantages than disadvantages for further consideration. Another approach is to allocate votes to each group member based on a percentage of the total number of ideas. For instance, if there are one hundred ideas and the allocation percentage is 10 percent, each member receives ten votes. The members then allocate their votes any way they want, placing all votes on one idea, dividing them equally among ten ideas, or using any other combination.

DEVELOPING ACTION PLANS

The importance of implementation action plans should be self-evident. Unfortunately, because of either time limits or distractions, we often overlook implementation during a retreat. The sun or slopes may be inviting, or group members simply may burn out from idea generation and evaluation. It is right after idea generation and evaluation that important implementation issues may arise, however. After a retreat, people may be too busy to deal with retreat-generated problems. Nevertheless, you should try to set aside time to deal with implementation.

Consider appointing an implementation monitor and assigning individuals to complete general tasks. If possible, discuss the when, where, and how of these tasks—that is, have the group specify the completion dates, locations, and details. You also might construct an implementation time line to provide an overview of the completion of each primary activity; you could develop a more refined schedule later.

PLANNING POSTRETREAT ACTIVITIES

If you sketched out an implementation plan during the retreat, it should be easy to elaborate on later. However, just because something is easy, it doesn't mean motivation and time are available. You may have to find the motivation and make the time to benefit from the retreat. Don't give up now. The four guidelines that follow will ensure that your efforts weren't wasted:

1. *Develop a final implementation schedule.* If you laid the groundwork for implementation during the retreat, a project manager can develop a more formal implementation schedule. Several software programs will simplify this task. Most are based on variations of program evaluation and review technique (PERT) charts, which compute the sequence and duration of various activities. You also can use text outlining and object-oriented graphics programs to design elementary implementation plans. They are easier to learn and much less expensive than high-priced project management software.

2. *Verify that all plans are implemented as scheduled.* Just having a plan doesn't guarantee that it will be implemented. Assign someone the role of implementation monitor. It is important that this person be detail oriented and able to oversee several activities simultaneously.

The monitor also should be skilled at motivating people to complete tasks and should work well with others.

3. *Keep upper management informed.* This guideline also should be obvious; however, internal political struggles or simple mistakes in communication with management often happen. Therefore, management may believe it is ill informed about retreat results. That is not good. Upper management probably footed the bill for the retreat and has a vested interest in it. I have attended some postretreat feedback meetings with upper managers, and they take the results seriously. You should, too.

4. *Provide feedback and involve participants.* Besides general communication complaints, a lack of feedback is probably the second most common gripe I hear from employees. Because of the time and effort they invested, you should keep retreat participants informed about outcomes. Most participants are interested in answers to the following questions:

- What decisions were made?
- When will they be implemented?
- Who is responsible for implementation?
- How did upper management react to the overall retreat?

Informing participants is a low-cost activity that yields high dividends. At the least, send a memo with results of the retreat (the most popular ideas) and postretreat outcomes (what happened to the ideas).

You also might involve some participants in implementation activities. Participants could assume direct responsibility for specific tasks or supply information and opinions. In any event, involvement creates a sense of ownership of a project and increases commitment to it.

CONDUCTING AND FACILITATING PROBLEM-SOLVING RETREATS

Feedback is a two-way street. You also should ask retreat participants their reactions. What did they like best? What worked least well? What should be done to improve the next retreat? How satisfied were they with their groups? How would they rate the performance of the facilitators? These and other questions can help planners improve future retreats.

Begin planning for a follow-up retreat. If you don't conduct retreats frequently, a follow-up may be needed. One issue rarely can be resolved satisfactorily during a short retreat. This is especially true of strategy-planning retreats, where there may be unfinished business.

When planning new retreats, consider the results of previous retreats and participant feedback. Although this may seem obvious, we often repeat mistakes. Because of the passage of time or turmoil of current events, we frequently forget what we learned. However, even simple revisions can lead to major improvements. Thus, dig out retreat evaluation data to use as a planning guide.

Depending on the problem or topic, conduct follow-ups between three months and one year later. Annual retreats also may be needed to deal with long-term issues. You'll find that follow-ups create a sense of continuity and commitment to resolving organizational problems.

ELEVEN

Evaluating and Selecting Ideas

The generation of ideas is a necessary, but not sufficient, condition of innovation. Creativity involves more than producing ideas for resolving a challenge. The ideas somehow must be reduced in number, assessed, and further narrowed down so that one or more potential solutions can be implemented. This applies to individuals as well as to groups and organizations. When innovation challenges are involved, there typically is a group of judges (for competitive idea campaigns) or at least a group of stakeholder decision makers. Therefore, this discussion will assume that at least one group will be involved in evaluating and selecting ideas.

In this chapter, a conceptual distinction will be made between the processes of evaluation and selection. Then some basic guidelines will be presented for managing these processes. Finally, several evaluation and selection techniques will be described and discussed briefly.

EVALUATION VS. SELECTION

The process of idea evaluation precedes that of idea selection. Before you can make a choice, you first must develop some basis for the choice. Then, once you have applied this basis, the selection process will fall into place, with very little difficulty involved in how final choices are made—at least, this is what *should* happen.

What often happens is that ideas are selected with little consideration given to the basis for the choice. People often select ideas without any conscious awareness of what criteria they used to guide their selections. Although such intuitive decision making can work out quite well for many types of challenges, it can be a severe liability when high-quality solutions are sought—that is, solutions with the greatest probability of resolving a problem. To increase the odds of choosing high-quality solutions, everyone involved in the decision-making process should be aware of the specific criteria being used.

In most group decision situations (as well as in individual situations), criteria used to guide idea selection will be implicit, explicit, or some combination of the two. The use of implicit criteria occurs when ideas are assessed for their potential to resolve a challenge without formally acknowledging the specific criteria used to assess each idea. In groups, this means each member individually applies his or her own criteria without sharing criteria with other members. Frequently, this lack of sharing occurs when members have not agreed on a need to share criteria or when individual members are not aware of the criteria they are using. When explicit criteria are used, the group members must formally acknowledge and agree on the standards they will use to evaluate each idea. It also is possible that criteria may be both implicit and explicit. For example, a group may agree to use certain criteria, but individual members may consciously or unconsciously apply their own criteria in conjunction with the agreed-upon criteria.

Because creative approaches typically are used when unique, high-quality solutions are desired, the use of explicit criteria is an absolute necessity. However, there will be instances in which criteria cannot be fully explored and developed. For example, if time is a critical factor, voting procedures—which use no formal, explicit criteria—may be required. This consideration and others will be discussed further in the next two sections. Nevertheless, explicit criteria should be used whenever possible.

BASIC GUIDELINES

As with most of the other problem-solving modules, idea evaluation selection proceeds more smoothly when basic guidelines are available to help structure the processes involved. These guidelines are especially important when high-quality solutions are needed. If careful attention is not given to idea evaluation and selection, the odds are diminished for transforming any ideas into workable problem solutions. The best ideas in the world will be of little value if they are not first screened and evaluated, so that the cream of the crop can be selected for possible implementation.

The use of guidelines also involves another advantage. By helping structure a process that often involves little structure, guidelines increase greatly the group members' commitment to the ideas. Even though formal techniques may be used, the outcome is more likely to result in high member satisfaction with the process when a systematic process is followed.

Although not chiseled in stone, the guidelines that follow should help groups approach the evaluation and selection process with more confidence and enthusiasm. Many people view idea generation as the most interesting and stimulating aspect of the creative problem-solving process. And it may be that it is; however, idea evaluation and selection can at least be interesting if a group approaches its task in an orderly fashion, such as using the steps that follow.

1. Assess Participation Needs

There will be times when it may be better to evaluate and select ideas alone instead of involving others; in some situations, it may be better for one or more groups to participate; and in other situations, both individual and group decision making may be better. In order of importance, the major variables that need to be assessed when making such decisions are:

a. Amount of time available

b. Importance of selecting a high-quality solution

c. Need for group members to accept the solution selected

d. Need for group members to experience the evaluation and selection process for their own personal and professional development

You should select ideas alone when there is little time available because the importance of selecting a high-quality solution is relatively low, and a group does not need to accept the solution or experience the process. Conversely, a group should participate when time is available, a high-quality solution is important, successful implementation of a solution depends on group member acceptance of the solution, and group members would benefit from experiencing the process.

However, many participation decisions cannot be made in an either/or manner. In some situations, it may be necessary for you to make some selection decisions alone and allow team members to make the remaining decisions. For example, if time is in relatively short supply, but not enough to justify excluding a group, you might select a final pool of ideas, turn these ideas over to the group, and have the group develop a final solution. Such a procedure would be especially useful when it is important for the members to accept a solution.

2. Agree on a Procedure to Use

As long as others are involved, you need to agree on a procedure for evaluation and selection. You might decide to follow the guidelines presented here, use some other procedure, or go directly to the evaluation and selection techniques. If you are working with others and they decide to ignore the guidelines described here, you still should stress the need to develop explicit evaluation criteria. You also need to decide how to narrow down the pool of generated ideas to a more manageable number. The important concern when others are involved is to agree on some procedure and avoid the temptation to proceed haphazardly.

3. Preselect Ideas

If you have a fairly large number of ideas to evaluate—for example, fifty or more—you need to reduce them to a more workable number. Some of the techniques described in the next section can be used for this purpose, or other methods may be available to you.

Whatever method is used, two major variables to consider are the amount of time available and the importance of the problem. If there is plenty of time and the problem is important—that is, the consequences will be serious if not resolved—you should devote considerable effort to this activity, assuming you are motivated to do so. If there is little time, the problem is not very important, and motivation is low, some shortcuts are needed.

An initial step you can take to narrow down an idea is to examine all the ideas with the goal of developing combinations, which are commonly referred to as *affinity groups*. When similar ideas are joined together, the overall number is reduced. You also might consider combining dissimilar ideas. Such combinations can often lead to higher-quality solutions than can be obtained from implementing two individual ideas separately.

If a group has developed all possible combinations, you should check for understanding on the part of all members. Decide whether all group members understand the logic, meaning, and purpose of the ideas. Then poll the group members to see whether they are comfortable with the list of ideas. (Examination of an idea pool will often stimulate new ideas that might be added to the list or combined with others. If this occurs, add the new ideas to the pool.)

After you select a final list, you need to decide how to reduce the number of ideas further. If time is inadequate for a thorough evaluation of each idea, two actions can be taken, either alone or in sequence. The group can organize all the ideas into logical categories according to some criterion such as problem type or potential effect. Then it can eliminate those categories of ideas that appear to have the potential as high-quality solutions. A second action is to give group members a certain number of votes. For example, if there are one hundred ideas, members could be given ten votes (10 percent of the idea pool). This is especially useful in brainstorming retreats where ideas need to be narrowed down rather quickly. An even better procedure might be to use idea categories and votes together. This can be done by voting on categories or by voting on ideas within categories. Of course, if you are using idea management software, voting procedures are likely to be built in.

These procedures can also be used if time is not a major concern. However, if the problem is very important, the group can use a slightly different method of reducing the ideas, either by itself or in combination with categories and voting. This procedure involves establishing a minimally acceptable criterion and then eliminating every idea that fails to satisfy this criterion. For example, the group might decide to eliminate every idea that would cost more than a certain sum of money to implement. (If time permits, more than one criterion could be used.)

A decision to use this approach, however, must be made with some caution. If an inappropriate or relatively trivial criterion is selected, many potentially valuable ideas could be eliminated prematurely. Moreover, what appears to be an obstacle to implementing an idea often can be overcome with a little additional problem solving. For instance, it may appear that an idea will cost too much to implement, but minor modifications may make it more workable.

Regardless of which approach a group uses to narrow down the number of ideas, it must come up with a final list of ideas that are ready for evaluation and selection. The group can consider this list tentative, depending on the particular technique or techniques used for final selection. It may be, for example, that the group finds itself with too many ideas to screen, even after preselecting ideas from the initial pool. Or, the amount of available time may decrease suddenly—a frequent occurrence in most organizations. In such cases, the group could recycle the list of ideas through the preselection phase and produce a shorter list.

Share with the group the final list to be used for final evaluation and selection. Ask group members to provide feedback concerning clarity and understanding of the meaning and logic underlying all the ideas. When a group understands and accepts the list, it can start the next step in the process.

4. Develop and Select Evaluation Criteria

Although many of the evaluation and selection methods described in this chapter use explicit evaluation criteria, there are some that do not. As discussed earlier, the quality of ideas selected without explicit criteria may be lower than that of those selected with such criteria. As a result, a group should attempt to make explicit all the criteria it will be using, whether or not a technique requires such explicitness. For example, a voting procedure relying on implicit criteria can be used to greater advantage if the group takes some time to discuss and agree on criteria that might be used to assign votes.

In developing criteria, a group should try to generate as many criteria as possible. As with idea generation, quantity is likely to result in quality. The more criteria a group thinks of, the greater will be the odds that the group will select a high-quality solution. And just as it is important to defer judgment when generating ideas, it is important to defer judgment when generating criteria. Encourage group members to stretch their minds and think of as many criteria as possible without regard to their initial value or relevance.

After a group has generated a list of criteria, it must select the criteria to use for evaluating and selecting ideas. The actual number of criteria selected will depend on the same variables used in preselecting ideas: available time and importance of the problem. When time is available and the problem is important, the group should select as many criteria as possible to use in evaluating ideas. When little time is available and the problem is not perceived as being important, the group can select a minimal number of criteria. However, if only a few criteria are used, it is imperative that the group choose relevant, important criteria that will be most likely to yield a high-quality solution.

5. Choose Techniques

The choice of evaluation and selection techniques can be as easy or as difficult and complex as you want. As with choosing idea generation techniques, many variables can be considered when choosing evaluation and selection techniques. However, in this instance, the choice really narrows down to one among voting procedures, evaluation procedures, and some combination of each. Beyond these considerations, the only other real issue is the amount of time available. Voting obviously will consume less time than group evaluation, even if the group agrees on voting criteria prior to actual voting.

The techniques in this chapter use "pure" voting methods, a criteria-based evaluation procedure that results in the selection of an idea without the need for voting, or "pure" evaluation procedures with no built-in voting mechanism or explicit criteria. There are four major criteria that can be used when selecting from among these techniques:

1. Ability of a technique to screen a large number of ideas
2. Provision for use of explicit evaluation criteria
3. Use of weightings for each of these criteria
4. Relative time requirements for using each technique

6. Evaluate and Select Ideas

At this point in the process, a group should apply one or more techniques to help it evaluate and select the ideas. It should select one or more ideas for possible implementation based on the number of ideas being evaluated, the amount of time available, and the perceived importance of the problem.

If a group selects more than one idea, it should examine possible ways to combine the ideas to produce a higher-quality solution. If the ideas cannot be combined easily (or logically) and the ideas are judged to be equal in quality, the group should consider implementing all the ideas, either in sequence or all at the same time. If the group decides there are too many ideas to implement, it can assign implementation priorities to the ideas and implement as many as possible in the time available. Or, it can screen the ideas again by using an evaluation and selection technique, but with more stringent criteria this time, in order to reduce the idea total. Regardless of what procedure the group chooses for dealing with the remaining ideas, it should constantly be aware of its ultimate objective of selecting a high-quality solution.

The group will, of course, determine the quality of the ideas before it selects any ideas for implementation. In judging idea quality, note that rating of the ideas, as used in many of the selection techniques, will result in a quality evaluation for each idea. Thus, quality will already have been considered at this point in the process. The group will need to evaluate again any ideas that survive these ratings, however, to ensure that it has selected the idea with the greatest probability of resolving the challenge. The group may have overlooked important criteria, or new information may have become available that could affect the previously determined quality ratings of the ideas.

Thus, the last step in the evaluation and selection process is to conduct a final check on ideas that survived the screening process. To do this, each group member could rate each idea (on a 7-point scale) with respect to its likelihood of resolving the problem. The group then could average the ratings or discuss them, with the purpose of achieving consensus. If the group judges none of these ideas to be of high quality, it could re-review ideas that initially failed to survive the screening process but were rated high, and evaluate them with respect to their quality.

TECHNIQUE DESCRIPTIONS

Each technique description in this section includes a step-by-step procedure for using the technique as well as any relevant information about a technique's strengths and weaknesses. As with all such techniques, modifications should be made to suit a group's particular preferences or needs.

Advantage-Disadvantage

There are several variations of the *advantage-disadvantage technique,* but only two will be described here. The first variation relies on implicit criteria and uses a listing of each idea's advantages and disadvantages. The second variation uses explicit, unweighted criteria that serve as direct measures of advantages and disadvantages.

Follow these steps to implement the first variation:

1. For each idea, develop separate lists of its advantages and disadvantages.
2. Select the ideas that have the most advantages and the fewest disadvantages.

The second variation uses these steps:

1. Develop a list of criteria to use in evaluating the ideas.
2. Write the criteria across the top of a sheet of paper.
3. To the left of the criteria, list the ideas in a single column down the side of the paper.

4. For each idea, make a check beside each criterion that is an advantage.

5. Add up the number of check marks for each idea and select the ideas with the most check marks.

These two variations can be illustrated using a problem on how to improve communications between two departments in an organization. For this problem, suppose that a few of the ideas generated are to do the following:

- Install instant messaging (IM) application on the computers in each department.

- Hold weekly meetings to discuss job-related problems.

- Assign one person the role of interdepartmental project coordinator.

- Have members of both departments attend a workshop on improving communication skills.

- Have both departments meet to identify specific communication problems and to generate possible solutions.

For the first variation of the advantage-disadvantage technique, you can evaluate these ideas using the format that follows. For purposes of illustration, only two ideas will be used. This example is shown in Figure 11-1.

On the basis of the advantages and disadvantages, the idea of using weekly meetings to discuss job-related problems might be selected because it has four advantages and three disadvantages. The first idea, using regular IM, might not be selected because although it has four advantages it also has six disadvantages. This could be due to bias on the part of the rater or knowledge of the options or the ability to think of them. Note, however, that had all the ideas been considered together, it is possible that several of the ideas would have been selected.

Using the same problem, but with all the ideas listed previously, the second variation could be set up using criteria to rate the five ideas. This analysis is shown in Figure 11-2. On the basis of the results of this

FIGURE 11-1. Comparison of two ideas using the advantage-disadvantage technique.

Idea 1: Install IM application on the computers in each department.

Advantages	Disadvantages
• Provides rapid communication.	• Some people prefer face-to-face communication.
• Easy to store and retrieve conversations.	• Might reduce productivity.
• Convenient.	• Could be used to avoid confronting other people regarding important issues.
• Fun for people who like using computers.	• Miscommunications might occur.
	• Could be used to look as if someone is working when he or she may be surfing the Web for personal reasons.
	• The network connection might malfunction.

Idea 2: Hold weekly meetings to discuss job-related problems.

Advantages	Disadvantages
• Provides for social interaction needs.	• Time-consuming.
• Allows people to better understand the motives of others.	• Conflict may arise and make some people uncomfortable.
• Problems can be dealt with by everyone involved.	• Some individuals may dominate the discussions.
• Other people's ideas can be built on to improve solution quality.	

analysis, IM would be selected because this idea has the most advantages.

Both of these variations have their own advantages and disadvantages. The first variation considers advantages and disadvantages that may be unique to each idea. However, it is relatively time-consuming to use, makes comparisons difficult due to the lack of standard criteria, does not use weighted criteria, and is subject to manipulation by its users. That is, it would be quite easy to adjust the outcomes so that one idea would be a clear winner over another. The second variation has strengths in its ability to screen a larger number of ideas in less

FIGURE 11-2. *Example of the second variation of the advantage-disadvantage technique.*

	Criteria				
	Little time	Low financial cost	Provides for social needs	Convenience	Total
Idea 1	X	X	X	X	4
Idea 2		X	X		2
Idea 3	X	X		X	3
Idea 4			X		1
Idea 5		X	X		2

time than the first variation, in its use of standardized criteria, and in the fact that its outcomes are less subject to manipulation when compared with the first variation. However, the second variation has disadvantages as well because it requires that an either/or decision be made in evaluating each idea and, like the first variation, it lacks a provision for weighted criteria.

In choosing between these two variations, you may want to use the first one when you are concerned primarily with conducting a thorough evaluation of each idea and you have the time to do so. The second variation would be more suitable when you have relatively little time and/or you wish to narrow down a large number of ideas for preselection purposes. It would be appropriate for making final selections, but it is limited by the lack of rating range and especially by considering all criteria as equal in importance. Using both variations would be another alternative to consider, which would be acceptable as long as the weaknesses of each are taken into account.

Battelle Method

Developed at the Battelle Institute in Columbus, Ohio, for screening business development opportunities, the *Battelle method* uses three levels of screens to evaluate ideas. Each level uses criteria that are progressively higher in cost. In the Battelle method, cost refers to the resource investments required to obtain information needed to evaluate an idea. Thus, ideas are evaluated first using information that is relatively easy to obtain, then using information that is more difficult to obtain, and finally information that is the most difficult to obtain. The funnel effect produced by using such screens makes it possible to reduce a moderate amount of ideas to only a few. The major steps for using the Battelle method are the following:

1. Develop lost-cost screens (or culling criteria) phrased in questions that can be answered with a yes or a no.

2. Establish a minimally acceptable passing score.

3. Develop medium-cost screens (rating criteria) phrased as questions that can be answered with a yes or a no.

4. Establish a minimally acceptable passing score.

5. Develop high-cost screens (scoring criteria) presented in the form of different value ranges—for example, poor, fair, or good.

6. Assign a weight to each criterion.

7. Establish a minimally acceptable passing score.

8. Compare each idea with each of the culling criteria questions.

9. Eliminate any idea that receives a no response.

10. Using the remaining ideas, compare each one with each of the rating criteria questions.

11. Eliminate any idea that falls below the minimally acceptable passing score for the rating criteria.

12. Using the ideas that survive, numerically rate each one against each scoring criterion and multiply that rating by the weight established for the criterion.

13. Add up the products obtained in step 12, and compare each one with the minimally acceptable passing score for the scoring criteria.

14. Eliminate the ideas that fall below the minimally acceptable passing score.

15. If more than one idea remains, attempt to combine some of the ideas or subject them to more intensive analysis.

This procedure can be understood better by looking at the challenge of improving interdepartmental communications. Using the idea of holding weekly meetings to discuss job-related problems, the Battelle method can be set up as shown in Figure 11-3. (This example uses a 3-point weighting scale, although a greater range of weights would also have been appropriate.)

According to the outcome illustrated, this idea survives all the screens and could be selected for implementation, combined with other surviving ideas, or retained for additional analysis. Note that the idea of using IM also would have been accepted by the culling screens. One

FIGURE 11-3. Example of the Battelle method.

Culling Screens					
	Yes	No			
1. Provides for social interaction needs?	X				
2. Involves members from all departments?	X				
3. Requires no new equipment purchases?	X				
Total	3	0			
Minimum yes score is 3					
Pass?	X				
Rating Screens					
	Yes	No			
1. No special training required to implement?	X				
2. No more than 20 hours required to implement?		X			
3. Will cost no more than $2,000 to implement?	X				
Total	2				
Minimum yes score is 2					
Pass?	X				
Scoring Screens (1–5 scale)					
	Poor	Fair	Good	Weight	Total
1. Projected return on investment?			3	2	6
2. Likelihood of reducing job errors?		2		3	6
3. Likelihood of reducing role conflicts?			3	3	9
Total					21
Minimum passing score is 18					
Pass?	Yes				

positive feature of this approach, however, occurs when an idea is rejected by the culling screens. Early rejection in this manner can be a strength because it makes idea screening more efficient. Some ideas are quickly eliminated at the outset, so the group can use its time more wisely for evaluating the remaining ideas. However, early rejection of ideas also could be a weakness. Answering questions with a yes or a no at the first stage can result in overlooking ways to circumvent any apparent obstacles. Thus, the wording of the questions must be considered carefully.

Perhaps the most important consideration is how the criteria are grouped together. What constitutes a low- or high-cost screen, for example, can be difficult to determine, especially when the criteria are highly subjective. To overcome this weakness, you can group the criteria into cost-homogeneous units within screens. That is, the criteria would be grouped according to similar costs of obtaining information about them. Of course, the number of criteria has to be large enough to do this. Another alternative is to use relatively low minimal passing scores, at least during the first pass through the screens. Should a large number of ideas survive all three screens on their first pass, minimal passing scores could then be raised in small increments and successive passes conducted through the screens until the desired number of ideas is achieved.

On the positive side, the Battelle method provides a relatively efficient means for screening ideas systematically. The involvement of a group in developing criteria for the screens also should increase group commitment to the final ideas selected. Finally, the use of weighted criteria in the scoring screens ensures that all criteria are not assumed to be of equal importance.

Electronic Voting

For groups that can afford it and like to jazz things up a little bit, *electronic voting*—especially via wireless keypads—may be an attractive choice. It may not be for all groups, but when time is short or a group has already spent time on evaluating ideas, electronic voting can be used quite appropriately. Note that this is different from using idea management software in which voting occurs online and participants may be in different locations; the electronic voting described here is intended for face-to-face groups.

A number of systems are available for a variety of price ranges. The major steps for this technique may vary depending on the system. Here is one approach:

1. Give each group member a seven- or nine-button remote and set up a projector and screen visible to all group members. With some systems, you might instruct the group members to rate each idea by pushing the button that corresponds to the value they would place on the idea. For example, if there are seven buttons, the first button would be used to signify little or no value to the idea, while the seventh button would be used to signify a very high value (the remaining buttons would be used to rate ideas in between those two extremes).

2. Have the group look at the vote tallies for each idea displayed on the screen.

3. Ask group members to examine the vote tallies and comment on any apparent inconsistencies. For instance, the group may note that an idea has been given a score of 7 points by three members and a score of 1 point by four members. In such cases, the inconsistency should be analyzed to help clarify why it occurred.

4. After discussing and clarifying all inconsistencies, have the group vote again and note the vote tallies that result. If no inconsistencies are observed with the second round of voting, terminate the process by selecting the highest-rated idea (or ideas); if inconsistencies are observed, repeat the procedure of clarifying and voting until no inconsistencies appear or a preestablished time limit has been reached.

The electronic voting method is very similar to the nominal group technique (NGT) described in Chapter 9. However, electronic voting has three major advantages over NGT's voting procedure. First, votes can be tabulated almost instantaneously with electronic voting; considerable time can be consumed doing the same thing with NGT. Thus, quick feedback is provided to the group members. Second, the speed with which voting is conducted and the results tabulated make it possible to process a large number of ideas more efficiently. Third, using a memory bank with electronic voting permits rapid retrieval of vote tallies should a future examination of the votes be required.

Idea Advocate

In contrast to electronic voting, the *idea advocate method*, as described by creativity consultant Horst Geschka, emphasizes evaluation over selection. The group carefully analyzes the positive aspects of each idea to ensure that no potential solutions are overlooked. The group then selects the ideas on the basis of the outcome of these analyses. Four steps are involved in using this method:

1. Give each group member a list of previously generated ideas.

2. Assign each group member to play the role of advocate for one or more of the ideas. These assignments can be made according to whether or not a group member would be responsible for implementing an idea, was the original person who proposed the idea, or simply has a strong preference for an idea.

3. Read the first idea aloud and have that idea's advocate discuss why it would be the best choice. Repeat this procedure for the remaining ideas.

4. When all the ideas have been discussed, have the group review the ideas and select the idea (or combination of ideas) that seems most capable of resolving the problem.

An obvious disadvantage of this technique is that it is not suitable for screening a large number of ideas. It will simply be too time-consuming for most groups to use for processing a large pool of ideas. The technique also may not work well if status differences exist within a group or if there are dominant personalities. Under such circumstances, all ideas are not likely to receive a fair hearing. Furthermore, the technique's focus on only the positive features of an idea may result in a distorted picture of an idea's value. If time permits, it may prove useful to incorporate some negative comments to provide a more balanced picture.

In spite of these disadvantages, the idea advocate technique can be appropriate when used in conjunction with more structured selection procedures. And it is especially appropriate when a large pool of ideas has been narrowed down to a more manageable number—for example, no more than two or three ideas for each member of a group. When only a few ideas are dealt with, each one is more likely to receive a fair hearing and a more in-depth analysis (assuming, of course, that status differences among the group members are minimal or can be controlled and that dominant personalities are not a factor).

Matrix Weighting

In contrast to the advantage-disadvantage technique, which assumes all criteria are equal in weight, the *matrix weighting technique* uses criteria that have been weighted according to their relative importance. As a result, the quality of ideas selected is likely to be higher. Matrix weighting is identical to the scoring screens used in the Battelle method (see Figure 11-3). Only the basic format used in setting up the technique is different. The steps are:

1. Construct a matrix table as shown in Figure 11-4. List the criteria down the left side of the matrix and the options being evaluated across the top. (Note that in Figure 11-2, the evaluation and selection techniques are used as examples of ideas to be weighted and evaluated.) In the column next to each option, create a *Product* column to record the mathematical product of multiplying a criterion importance rating by the rating for each option.

2. Using a 7-point scale (with 1 being low importance and 7 being high importance), rate the importance of each criterion. Use the criterion weightings column to do this. For instance, Figure

FIGURE 11-4. Example of the matrix weighting technique.

Criteria	Weighting	Advantage-disadvantage	Product	Battelle method	Product	Electronic voting	Product	Matrix weighting	Product	Nominal group technique	Product	Reverse brainstorming	Product	Sticking dots	Product
Techniques:															
Screens a large number of ideas	6	7	42	5	30	5	30	3	18	7	42	1	6	5	30
Uses explicit criteria	4	7	49	7	28	1	4	7	28	1	4	1	4	1	4
Uses weighted criteria	7	1	7	7	49	1	7	7	49	1	7	1	7	1	7
Requires little time	2	5	10	2	4	7	7	4	8	6	12	2	4	7	14
TOTAL			108		111		48		103		65		21		55

11-4 shows that "Screens a large number of ideas" is rated a 6 out of 7 in importance.

3. Using the same rating scale, rate each option (independent of the others) against each criterion. Record these ratings beneath each option. In Figure 11-4, for example, the advantage-disadvantage method is rated a 7 on its ability to screen a large number of ideas, a very favorable rating.

4. Multiply the weighting for each criterion by the rating given to each option on that criterion. Write the product in the appropriate column. For example, the criterion "Uses explicit criteria" was assigned an importance weighting of 4 and the option of the Battelle method was rated a 7 on this criterion. Thus, the product would be 28, as shown in Figure 11-4.

5. Add up all the products for each option and write the sum in the boxes in the *Total* column at the bottom of the matrix.

6. Select the idea with the highest total score and then decide if your choice reflects what might be expected. If it doesn't, re-evaluate the criteria importance ratings, the need to consider additional criteria, and the ratings given to each option.

For this example, screening a large number of ideas was viewed as being important (6), using explicit criteria was seen as moderately important (4), using weighted criteria was perceived as very important (7), and the requirement of little time was rated low in importance (2). These ratings are hypothetical, subjective, and could vary considerably depending on who is doing the ratings.

There are several cautions to observe when using the matrix weighting procedure. First, it can be a moderately time-consuming technique. It is more useful after a large number of ideas have been preselected. Second, the idea receiving the highest score may not always "feel" right to the group members. In some cases, group members may express dissatisfaction with the highest-rated idea but be unable to provide a rationale. When this occurs, additional criteria might be sought and the process repeated, or the ratings themselves might be examined to see whether any changes should be made. Finally, disagreement may arise among the group members over the ratings to be used. When disagreement occurs and cannot be resolved within the time available, voting can be used and the averages used for the ratings. Or if you have the authority, you could make the final ratings after considering the preferences of the group members.

On the whole, the matrix weighting technique is a popular procedure with many groups because of its systematic way of processing ideas for selection. In addition, the discussions about the criteria and ratings can help to clarify each group member's understanding about the ideas and what is required to ensure development of a high-quality solution. Consequently, group members are often more likely to accept the idea selected and be committed to its implementation.

Nominal Group Technique

The steps involved in using NGT have already been discussed in Chapter 9. The voting procedure is described again here because it contains the steps that deal with the selection process. NGT uses the following steps to vote on ideas:

1. Discuss each idea in turn to clarify the logic and meaning behind it. During this time, make it clear to the group members that the purpose of this step is to clarify their understanding of ideas and not to debate the merits of the ideas. In this regard, you should pace the discussion to avoid spending too much time on any one idea and to avoid heated debates.

2. Conduct a preliminary vote on the importance of each idea.
    a. Have each group member select a few of the best ideas out of the total. (The group leader should determine the number of ideas to be chosen—for example, 10 percent of the total. A number of ideas between five and nine usually works well.)
    b. Instruct the group members to write each idea on a separate 3- by 5-inch card or sticky note and to record the number of the idea in the upper left-hand corner of the card.

c.   Have the group members silently read the ideas they have selected and rank them by assigning a 5 (assuming five ideas were selected) to the best idea, a 1 to the worst idea, and so forth, until all the ideas have been ranked. Then have them rank each idea by writing the rank in the lower right-hand corner of each card and underlining it three times (to prevent confusion with the idea number).

d.   Collect the cards, shuffle them, and construct a ballot sheet. Record the idea number in a column on the left side of the sheet, and record the rank numbers given to each idea next to the idea numbers. For example, if idea #1 was given rank votes of 5, 2, and 3, this would be recorded as 5-2-3.

e.   Count the vote tallies and note which idea received the most votes (the highest total score).

f.   Terminate the selection process if a clear preference has emerged. If no clear preference is evident, go on to the next step.

3.   Discuss the results of the preliminary vote by examining inconsistencies and then rediscussing ideas seen as receiving too many or too few votes. For instance, if an idea received four votes of 5 and three votes of 1, the meaning behind the idea might be discussed to see whether there were differences in how the idea was perceived. Emphasize that the purpose of this discussion is to clarify perceptions and not to persuade any member to alter his or her original vote.

4.   Conduct a final vote using the procedures outlined for the preliminary vote (step 2).

The idea selection portion of the NGT procedure has major strengths in ensuring equality of participation and in eliminating status differences and the harmful effects of a dominant personality. The procedure also provides a highly efficient means for processing a large number of ideas. Furthermore, NGT voting concentrates disagreements on ideas instead of individuals.

On the minus side, NGT does not use explicit evaluation criteria.

The rankings are produced by group members using their own criteria, which might or might not be shared by other group members. For this reason, the NGT voting procedure might be improved by asking group members to consider a general set of criteria for all to use in ranking their ideas. If this procedure is added, there may be fewer inconsistencies in the final vote tally and less need to repeatedly discuss ideas for clarification.

Reverse Brainstorming

The classical brainstorming technique described in Chapter 9 is designed to generate a large number of ideas. *Reverse brainstorming* is also concerned with generating ideas but not for solving a problem. Instead, the ideas are couched in terms of criticisms of previously generated ideas. Thus, this technique uses a procedure opposite that of the idea advocate method: Negative rather than positive features of ideas are sought. The major steps of reverse brainstorming are:

1. Give each group member a list of previously generated ideas (or write the ideas on a chalkboard or flip chart).

2. Ask the group members to raise their hands if they have a criticism of the first idea (or each member can be systematically given a chance to offer a criticism).

3. When all the criticisms for the first idea have been brought out, ask the group to criticize the second idea. Continue this activity until all the ideas have been criticized.

4. Instruct the group to develop possible solutions for overcoming the weaknesses of each idea.

5. Select the idea (or ideas) with the fewest weaknesses that cannot be overcome or circumvented.

As with the idea advocate method, reverse brainstorming can be extremely time-consuming if a large number of ideas are being processed. As a result, it is best to use this technique when the original idea pool has been narrowed down some. Perhaps the major weakness of this technique, however, is its emphasis on the negative. Stressing what is wrong with every idea may lead to a negative climate not conducive to creativity. Although a climate conducive to creativity is more important during idea generation, the lack of such a climate during evaluation can make it difficult for the group to combine or elaborate on ideas (in a positive manner) before making the final selection.

The major strengths of reverse brainstorming are the amount of discussion devoted to each idea and the provision for developing ways of overcoming idea weaknesses. While analyzing each idea, possible implementation obstacles may be suggested and dealt with, which can ensure more successful implementation. Looking at ways to overcome idea weaknesses may reduce the negative atmosphere that often develops in a group after it spends so much time criticizing the ideas. Furthermore, looking at ways to overcome weaknesses should also increase the probability of implementation success.

Although reverse brainstorming does have advantages, it probably could be used more effectively in combination with the idea advocate technique. This would provide a more balanced evaluation of each idea and not be as likely to result in a negative climate. Of course, the decision to add another technique has to be weighed against the increased amount of time that will be required.

Sticking Dots

Sticking dots is one of the simplest, most time-efficient voting methods available. Members each receive a fixed number of self-sticking, colored paper dots with which they can indicate their idea preferences with minimal time and effort. The steps involved are:

1. Display a previously generated list of ideas on a flip chart or on sticky notes attached to a bulletin board.

2. Give each group member a sheet of self-sticking colored dots. Each member should receive a different color, and the number of dots should equal about 10 percent of the ideas to be evaluated.

3. Ask the group members to vote for ideas by placing dots next to ideas they prefer. They may allocate their dots in any way

they wish. Thus, all of one member's dots may be placed next to one idea, only one may be placed next to one idea, half the dots may be placed on one idea and the other half on another idea, and so forth.

4. Count the votes received by each idea, and select the ideas with the most votes.

Variations include the following:

1. Restrict participants to voting with no more than two or three dots for any one idea. This might help keep certain ideas in the running and prevent people from engaging in block voting.

2. Give participants three different colors of dots and have them vote using each color in succession based on ideas previously receiving votes. For instance, if twenty out of fifty ideas receive at least two votes with red dots, give the participants 10 percent of that number (two) and have them vote only on the red dot ideas using green dots. The same process then might be followed using yellow dots.

In addition to the relatively small amount of time required to use this method, there is the advantage of the sense of equal participation that it affords group members. Placing dots next to ideas is an activity in which all members have an opportunity to participate on an equal basis. Furthermore, should questions arise about the voting distribution, the color coding of the dots makes it relatively easy to ask people why they voted the way they did. And it provides an opportunity for additional discussions about specific ideas.

There are, however, several disadvantages associated with this technique. First, and perhaps most significant, the lack of anonymity may result in a certain degree of voting conformity. By seeing how the vote clusters develop, some members may feel pressured to vote in a similar manner. Second, no discussion is conducted on criteria to use in making voting decisions. Finally, there is no built-in mechanism for clarifying the meaning and logic underlying the ideas and for examining voting inconsistencies. This technique could be improved by conducting a discussion on the criteria to be used and providing time to clarify ideas and to examine inconsistencies in the voting patterns. However, the problem of voting conformity would remain.

TWELVE

Implementing Ideas

The best ideas will be of no value if they are not put into action to resolve a challenge. In some respects, idea implementation is more important than idea generation.

IMPORTANCE AND NATURE OF IMPLEMENTATION

Next to redefining the problem, this last component of the innovation challenge process may be the most critical. A high-quality idea that appears to have a high probability of resolving a problem will be of little value if it is not implemented properly. Although this statement may seem obvious, it is extremely important when you consider that it is only by taking action that a problem can be resolved. However, this action must be of the right type; inappropriate action may magnify a problem—rendering the chosen solution obsolete—or it may create entirely new problems. The key to avoiding both of these outcomes is effective implementation planning.

However, there may be resistance to taking the time to plan for implementation. Many people become impatient and lazy after they have gone through the process involving framing a challenge, generating ideas, and evaluating and then selecting the best ones. Having already devoted considerable time to dealing with a problem, organizations often are eager to terminate all problem-solving activities once they have selected a final solution. In addition, they usually have exerted so much effort in the previous stages that they begin looking for easy ways to avoid further dealings with the problem. "Let's just get it over with" is frequently heard at this point in the process. Moreover, the amount of time left to deal with a challenge may have been reduced, resulting in increased pressure to get a challenge resolved. Consequently, the attitude often is to do something, but it can leave out consideration of the consequences involved.

Although it may be normal for group members to experience such feelings, becoming impatient or looking for shortcuts at this stage could jeopardize problem resolution. Creative problem solving is a cumulative process, with each step building on the preceding one. If this is disregarded and the final solution is not implemented properly, all previous efforts may have been in vain. As much planning and care should be devoted to implementation as were devoted to the previous stages. Remember Murphy's Law: "If anything can go wrong, it will."

At its most basic level, implementation is a creative problem-solving process. A gap exists between what is and what should be—and actions are required to close this gap. In this case, the *what is* refers to the potential solution selected for resolving the focal problem and the *what should be* is the application of this solution to the focal problem. All the actions taken to apply the potential solution to the problem then constitute the implementation process.

From this perspective, a specific implementation task is a problem only if the original, focal problem is still perceived as being a problem. Problems and our perceptions of them often change over time. While a group is working on a problem, the characteristics of the problem may change over time. As a result, the solution developed by the group may no longer be adequate. Or the original problem may have changed so much that it is no longer a problem. In either of these instances, implementation would not be a problem. If the original problem has changed or disappeared, there is no reason for a group to bother with implementation.

Although this may appear obvious, it does highlight the need for groups to check on their problem perceptions periodically. Just as it is important to frame a challenge adequately at the outset of problem solving, perceptual frames must be evaluated throughout the process. This type of check is especially important immediately prior to implementation; otherwise, considerable resources may be expended unnecessarily. If it appears that the problem has changed—that is, it has been intentionally or unintentionally reframed—a group must either redefine the problem or modify the solution before implementing it. The choice will depend on the extent to which the problem has changed. However, if the wrong decision is made, then the wrong problem may be solved. Nevertheless, assuming that the original problem still exists and the chosen solution appears appropriate, you can proceed with implementation.

CHANGE AND IMPLEMENTATION

One of the first considerations in implementing solutions is the general concept of change. Most people fear change. Or, at least, they dislike it and try to resist it. "Don't rock the boat" is an expression frequently heard when any type of change is proposed.

In organizations, the issue of change is especially complex because many parts of an organization are interrelated. According to basic systems theory, a change introduced into one part may have a direct or indirect effect on one or more other parts. For example, if workers in department A have their jobs enriched in an attempt to increase their productivity and workers in department B do not have their jobs enriched, the change may backfire. Although the productivity of workers in department A may increase, the workers in department B may resent not being included and retaliate by lowering their productivity. The result might be a net loss in productivity.

Related considerations involved in implementing changes are the degree of employee involvement in a change, the extent to which employees are affected, the magnitude of the change, whether or not the change was requested, the amount of resistance to the change, and the effects of the change on employee attitudes. Because implementing ideas involves change, either directly or indirectly, groups must be aware of all considerations when planning for implementation.

If other people need to be involved in implementing an idea, they should be included in the planning process. Inclusion of others is especially important when they will be affected significantly by implementation of an idea. Broad changes that are likely to affect many people also require input from others. Furthermore, involvement of others is necessary whenever a change is not requested, since unrequested changes are more likely to be met with resistance and have a negative impact on employee attitudes and morale.

To overcome resistance to change when implementing ideas, follow these general rules of thumb:

• Involve other people in the entire problem-solving process, including implementation, whenever:

a. They need to be involved.

b. They will be affected directly by the idea.

c. The change is broad in scope, and the change is not requested.

Of course, not everyone affected by a change will want to be involved, and time or logistical considerations may limit the amount of involvement possible. Nevertheless, an attempt should be made to involve as many other people as needed.

• Be as specific as possible about the amount and type of change likely to result from implementing an idea. Nothing is more likely to create resistance than ambiguous messages about a change. Most people fear the unknown more than a specific change. Providing vague information about a change is a sure way to reduce the chances for successful idea implementation.

• When planning for the implementation of a change-producing idea that will affect others, stress the personal benefits to be obtained if the idea is implemented. If people can see some personal gain or benefit from an idea—no matter how small the benefit may seem to you—the path to implementation will be smoothed considerably.

• Whenever possible, create shared perceptions within groups about the need for a change. If the need for a change develops from within a group, it is more likely to be supported.

- Identify key opinion leaders within the larger organization and convince them to support the change. Again, just as input from stakeholders during challenge framing is critical, so it is at the end of the process as well. It is much easier to convince a small number of individuals about the need for a change than it is to convince an entire organization. Once the opinion leaders are convinced of the need for a change, they can help convince others. These opinion leaders need not be in formal positions of authority, however. Change may receive broader support if informal leaders are perceived as supporting the change.

IMPLEMENTATION GUIDELINES

The change guidelines just discussed are general considerations involved in implementing ideas. Although they are useful by themselves, successful implementation requires a more specific approach. The implementation planning process is more likely to result in a resolved challenge if a group uses more structuring than is provided by broad change principles.

Very often, an idea must be "sold" before it can be implemented. In highly centralized organizations, where lines of authority are drawn clearly, most new ideas must receive higher approval. In these organizations, all proposed changes must go through channels. And in order to move through the channels, an idea must be sold at each level. But not all ideas must be sold to an authority structure. In many cases, ideas must be sold laterally in an organization or to groups or individuals outside an organization. The process involved in selling ideas laterally or vertically is essentially the same. The only difference is the level at which the ideas must be sold.

The activities involved in selling an idea usually precede actual implementation of the idea. Of course, not all ideas need to be sold. Depending on the degree of involvement in formulating an idea, the amount of trust placed in the idea formulators, and the perceived impact of the problem on others, an idea may encounter little opposition. However, not all ideas will be accepted widely, and steps must be taken to gain acceptance.

Gaining acceptance for an idea by attempting to sell it is just as important to implementation as applying a solution to a problem. If the necessary acceptance is not gained, the idea cannot be implemented and the problem will not be solved. Thus, a group must devote some attention to developing a strategy for selling its ideas.

In general, such a strategy should go hand in hand with the overall implementation strategy. Because gaining acceptance of an idea is an integral part of implementation, the activities involved in selling an idea should flow together with those involved in applying the idea to the problem. If these activities are not aligned and coordinated, the idea may not solve the problem. Selling and implementing ideas are complementary activities that must be considered simultaneously.

In addition to the obvious need to sell an idea before it can be implemented, there are at least two reasons why selling an idea is important to its implementation. First, the feedback that a group often receives while attempting to sell an idea can provide information relevant to implementation. People may offer many suggestions that the group can use to smooth an idea's implementation. Or, someone to whom an idea is being sold may be able to provide resources to help ensure successful implementation. Second, there is the psychological support and commitment that often result from selling an idea. If an idea is sold, those who "bought" it will be more likely to support it through the rest of the implementation process. Just knowing that significant others support and are committed to an idea can help ease the task of those responsible for implementation.

* * *

The following implementation guidelines will help you develop an overall strategy. If you decide that an idea does not need to be sold, you can omit the steps concerned with making an idea presentation.

1. *Develop and evaluate goal statements.* The first task of the group is to develop goal statements that accurately reflect the purposes of the implementation process. Although group members often assume their implementation goals are understood by others, this is not always the case. Thus, it is important that these goals be made explicit at the outset and be understood clearly by all group members.

Goal statements should be specific, clear, and realistic and should

include a time schedule. Sweeping generalizations, ambiguous wording, unrealistic assessments of resources, and omitted time schedules
should be avoided. For example, the following statement for selling an
idea would not satisfy these criteria:

> To convince the board of directors that our piece-rate plan is the
> best and most inexpensive idea for improving worker productivity.

A better goal statement might be:

> By the end of this quarter, we will meet with the board of directors
> to gain approval for a piece-rate plan that is projected to increase
> worker productivity by 5 percent and to cost no more than $20,000
> to implement.

Similarly, this statement for applying an idea would be inappropriate:

> To train workers to use new computer software programs.

A better statement of this goal might be:

> By March 15, workers in departments A and B will be trained to use
> the new versions of Microsoft Office. The training will take place in
> conference room C from 9:00 A.M. to 4:00 P.M. every Friday between
> now and March 15.

Frequently, a group will need to make several attempts at developing these statements. When the group selects the final statements—one
for idea selling, if needed, and one for applying the idea—it should
evaluate them to ensure they satisfy all the criteria. Furthermore, the
leader should make certain all group members clearly understand the
statements.

2. *Assess your resources.* Implementation resources are the means
used to accomplish the goal statements. Whatever is needed to sell an
idea and apply it to a problem is a resource. Such things as information,
time, people, and physical considerations are categories of resources
that need to be assessed.

3. *Assess the needs of the people to be influenced.* If an idea needs to be sold, the group should consider the needs of the people who must buy the idea before it develops a sales presentation. Most people will respond favorably to an idea if they believe it will satisfy one or more of their basic needs. If you can determine what these needs are, you will increase the chances of getting your idea accepted.

Examples of needs you should consider are:

Power and control	Being liked
Security	Recognition
Affiliation	Impressing others
Personal growth and development	Being seen as creative or intelligent
Helping others	Task accomplishment and
Freedom	completion
Dominance	Avoiding crises

Of course, these needs are only representative of the many needs we all have. Take time to consider what other needs might be important to the person (or people) you and your group want to influence.

Assessing these needs can be a difficult task, since it usually is not possible to administer a psychological test of needs. Even if you could administer such a test, you still would need to interpret it in a valid manner—a task that would require professional assistance. How, then, might you assess needs without administering a psychological test? The answer lies in your powers of observation. Although certainly not as valid and reliable as a scientifically tested instrument, observational data can provide some clues.

The first thing you should observe is how the decision maker behaves. What patterns of behavior seem to characterize this person over time? For example, in group meetings, is the decision maker the one doing most of the talking? Does he or she tend to discount the opinions of others? If so, this person may be exhibiting signs of a need to control or dominate others. Another thing to observe is how the decision maker behaves during stressful situations, for example, in a crisis. During times of intense stress, primary motives are more likely to appear. Identify these motives and you may have another clue to the decision maker's needs.

Two additional things to observe are personal possessions and hobbies. An individual's car, house, books, clothes, and other possessions can indicate the types of things he or she values. If the decision maker drives a current Ford pickup truck, he or she is communicating values different from those of someone who drives the latest model Lexus sedan. Hobbies can reveal needs in a somewhat similar manner. A person who spends a lot of free time collecting, categorizing, and organizing radio knobs, for example, is likely to value detail work and have an inquisitive mind. (The fact that the person collects something like radio knobs also should reveal something!)

A slightly different way to assess the needs of a decision maker is to consider that all people have challenges they would like to resolve. What challenges of the decision maker could your idea solve? What problem gaps (between the *what is* and the *what should be*) could your idea help close? If you can identify these problems and structure your idea presentation around some of them, you should find the decision maker highly receptive.

4. *Assess your implementation strengths and weaknesses.* You have strengths and weaknesses that can either help or hinder the implementation of ideas. To implement an idea successfully, you first must acknowledge that you have strengths and weaknesses. Assuming that you have just strengths or just weaknesses can lead to self-defeating behavior. Once you acknowledge that you have both strengths and weaknesses, you must become aware of what they are. The only way you can have any measure of control over the implementation process is to acknowledge that some things about you will help and some things will hinder implementation. Identifying these things and assessing their contribution to implementation is the key to many successfully resolved challenges.

In group settings, the net effect of all the members' strengths and weaknesses must be evaluated. For example, if most members are proficient at planning and only one or two are proficient at carrying out plans, an imbalance may exist. However, if only one or two members are needed to carry out a plan, then there actually may be a functional balance, since the imbalance of strengths and weaknesses will not prevent successful implementation. Each group must determine whether specific imbalances will be helpful or harmful, functional or dysfunctional.

To assess a group's implementation strengths and weaknesses, you first should make a list of all activities that need to be performed. Next, have each group member list which activity is a strength or a weakness that he or she possesses. Encourage the members to be realistic. Many people tend to overrate their strengths and weaknesses. If you are the leader, you will have to make the final determination. Finally, match people with activities based on their ability to perform those activities.

Although this approach may seem obvious, it is often overlooked because of other considerations. For example, group leaders often assign some tasks on the basis of favoritism or to repay a previous contribution made by a member. Assigning implementation tasks in this way not only will jeopardize implementation but also may create ill feelings among the other group members.

Of course, all this assumes that a group will be involved in implementation. Often, this is not the case, either because there is not enough time or because the task simply does not require the efforts of more than one or two people. Selling an idea, for instance, is usually handled by the leader and possibly one or two others. In this regard, the leader and any others involved will need to assess their idea-selling strengths and weaknesses. Note that selling strengths and weaknesses may differ considerably from implementation strengths and weaknesses. As a result, separate assessments will need to be conducted for these two activities.

5. *Analyze idea benefits.* Assuming that an idea must he sold before it can he applied, you need to make an analysis of its major benefits. Not only will such an analysis help to produce a more convincing presentation; it also will help the idea presenters in understanding the idea. This understanding can prompt suggestions for eventual implementation. In addition, while the group analyzes an idea's benefits, some last-minute modifications to improve the idea's quality may be suggested.

Analyzing benefits is a divergent process similar to generating ideas.

The first step is to list all the major features of an idea while withholding all evaluation. Next, generate a list of benefits for each feature listed. The list of criteria used to select the idea may help do this. Then select the benefits most likely to persuade the decision maker of the idea's worth. If any idea modifications are suggested during this activity, decide whether you want to include them, and then reassess the idea's benefits.

As an illustration of benefit assessment, suppose that your idea for keeping drunk drivers off the highways involves mandatory installation of a Breathalyzer in every car. The assessment might be set up as shown in Figure 12-1.

6. *Prepare for the presentation.* If you must make a formal or an informal presentation of your idea, you should spend some time preparing. Nothing can doom a proposed idea more quickly than a poorly conducted presentation—except, perhaps, a poor-quality idea. Thus, any investment in preparation should result in high returns.

Some of the elements involved in preparing for a presentation are:

- *Time.* Avoid Mondays and Fridays; try to schedule the presentation in midmorning or midafternoon, but not too close to the lunch hour.

- *Location.* A pleasant, comfortable physical environment is best; if possible try to use a location away from the regular work environment.

- *Length.* Set a time limit and build the presentation around it; keep it as short as possible.

FIGURE 12-1. *Example of a benefit analysis for idea implementation.*

Features	Benefits
Compact size.	Takes up little space.
Few mechanical parts.	Requires little maintenance; unlikely to break down very often.
Ignition system hookup automatically prevents car from starting when driver's alcohol content exceeds legal limit.	Drunks cannot drive.
Alarm sounds when driver's alcohol content exceeds legal limit.	Police will be alerted.

- *Presenter.* Select the person with the best presentation skills; make sure this person is not viewed unfavorably by the decision maker.

- *Support.* If possible, cultivate advocates for your idea before the presentation. For presentations to a group, this would mean contacting the members in advance; for presentations to one person, you could try to gain support from others who are close to this person.

- *Receptivity.* Try to anticipate how receptive the decision maker is likely to be to your idea. If nothing else, you may be motivated by knowing you will be entering a hostile climate.

- *Funding.* Obtain any funds needed for the presentation; review any funding required for your idea; develop alternative approaches to funding the idea.

- *Materials and Equipment.* Inventory all materials and equipment needed for the presentation; obtain missing materials and equipment.

- *Compromising.* Decide which and how many features of your ideas you would be willing to give up in order to gain acceptance. Or, if you are willing to give up your idea, determine what other ideas might be acceptable.

- *Data.* If relevant, gather any data that might reinforce or support the value of your idea (e.g., testimonials, statistics, observations, experts).

7. *Conduct the presentation.* If you have done a thorough job of preparing, the presentation itself should be a relatively simple task. All you—or the chosen presenter—need to do now is apply the insights gained from assessing your resources, strengths and weaknesses; the needs of the decision makers; the idea benefits; and the presentation considerations. However, the manner in which you apply these insights will determine how successful you will be. Part of what is involved is style and part is substance. That is, how you present your

idea can be just as important as what you present. Before you conduct your presentation, consider the following tips:

a. *Try to adapt yourself to your audience.* If your audience is highly analytical and skeptical, structure your proposal accordingly. If your audience is more intuitive and visually oriented, make sure that you use visual aids and emphasize wholes rather than parts.

b. *Start on time.* Failure to start on time may upset your audience unnecessarily and create negative attitudes at the outset. Being prompt won't help your presentation, but starting late will certainly hurt it.

c. *Avoid memorizing your presentation.* If you speak naturally (guided only by a memorized outline), you will seem knowledgeable and be much more convincing than if you deliver a memorized talk.

d. *Be yourself.* Never try to emulate someone else's presentation style. Instead, focus on your idea and worry about how it looks, not how you look.

e. *At the outset, describe what you hope to accomplish and how you will do it.* The more straightforward you are, the more credible your idea will appear.

f. *Avoid clichés and jargon.* Unless both you and your audience use clichés and jargon on a regular basis, avoid them. If you use them inappropriately, you may come across as being more concerned with impressing others than with selling your idea.

g. *Remain loose.* Try not to be overly serious, especially when referring to yourself. Use humor when appropriate, and stay open to all comments and questions.

h. *Keep your eyes on your audience.* If you don't maintain eye contact, your audience may think you have something to hide.

i. *Avoid repetitious statements.* Although you should restate your points to get them across, try not to repeat yourself frequently. Don't linger too long in discussing any one point.

j. *Try to avoid distracting mannerisms.* Continually pulling at your collar or other obvious mannerisms may shift attention from your idea to you.

k. *Don't criticize competing ideas.* Try to be objective and non-judgmental. Both you and your idea will be seen as being more credible if your presentation is balanced and fair.

l. *Listen effectively.* Try to understand the content and feeling of what is being said to you; practice using reflective feedback. For example, "As I understand it, you think that . . ."

m. *Don't exaggerate.* Never make unsubstantiated claims about the worth of your idea. Let the idea sell itself.

n. *Respond directly to all questions.* Be as specific as possible in your answers, and be sure you deal with every question you are asked. Avoid generalities or shifting the focus of a question. You don't want to appear evasive.

o. *Try not to oversell your idea.* Once it appears that you have been successful, conclude your presentation. Otherwise, it may appear you are not very confident about your own idea.

p. *Finish on time.* End your presentation when you said you would. Finishing a couple of minutes over your allotted time is seldom a problem, especially if the audience shows a lot of interest. However, exceeding your time by very much is likely to upset the audience, most of whom probably consider their time valuable.

8. *Develop an implementation strategy.* You and your group already should have thought out the basics of your implementation strategy, and you should have included them in your presentation. For some ideas, how they are implemented may be just as important to your audience as the nature of the ideas themselves. However, if you have not already developed an implementation strategy, now is the time to do it. Or, if you have developed an outline of a strategy, it now should be filled in and developed. You must have a plan to guide implementation.

Most of the techniques described in the next section can be used for this purpose. However, the group leader will have an important decision on the way these techniques are used. Specifically, leaders need to decide whether other group members should be involved. If there is sufficient time, try to gain the acceptance of others. This is critical to effective implementation. If the others are likely to benefit either personally or professionally, you should involve them. Of course, if these conditions do not exist, you must consider implementing the idea by yourself.

9. *Implement the idea.* The last step in the implementation process is to apply the idea to the problem. If the preparation and planning have been conducted thoroughly, the problem should be resolved with little difficulty. Of course, not all implementation obstacles can be anticipated, and the problem may not be resolved as expected. When this occurs, you should review the implementation process and devise new plans. Note, however, that one of the techniques to be described, *potential problem analysis*, can avert many implementation problems. Whenever possible, use this technique before using any of the other implementation methods.

IMPLEMENTATION TECHNIQUES

With the exception of potential problem analysis, the techniques described in this section represent variations of strategies that can be used to implement ideas. Some are more complex than others, but all are capable of providing the structuring needed for implementation activities.

In selecting from among these techniques, there is one major factor that must be considered: the complexity of the idea. When an idea has multiple facets (in terms of time and activities) that you must deal with, you need to use more complex techniques. For these types of problems, PERT is most appropriate; for moderately complex ideas, flow charts are appropriate; and for relatively simple ideas, the five *W*s and time/task analysis are appropriate (the appropriateness of the copycat technique will depend on the particular method being copied).

Of course, the decision to use any of these methods also depends on the group's needs and preferences in addition to many other variables. For example, even though PERT should he used to implement a complex idea, there may not be sufficient time to do so. The group might have to use another technique instead. Or the group might decide to modify the way the procedure is used to reduce the amount of time required.

Potential Problem Analysis

Originally developed by Kepner and Tregoe and later modified by Woods and Davies, *potential problem analysis (PPA)* serves as a bridge between implementation planning and actual implementation of an idea. In contrast to the other implementation techniques, PPA is designed specifically to anticipate possible implementation problems and to develop countermeasures. As a result, you should use PPA before using any other implementation method. Based on earlier versions and with some modifications by me, the major steps for conducting a PPA are:

1. Develop a list of potential problems. Withhold all evaluation and think of everything that could possibly prevent the idea from being implemented successfully.

2. Determine possible causes of each problem listed.

3. Using a 7-point scale, estimate the probability of occurrence and the seriousness of each cause (1 = low probability of seriousness; 7 = probability of seriousness).

4. Multiply each probability rating by each seriousness rating, and sum the products. These products are known as the *probability-times-seriousness scores.*

5. Develop preventive actions for each cause. Think of what could be done to eliminate or minimize the effect of each cause.

6. Using a 7-point scale, estimate the probability that a cause becomes problematic after a preventive action is taken (1 = low probability; 7 = high probability). This estimate is known as the *residual probability.* For example, if the likelihood that a cause will occur originally is estimated to be a 6, taking a preventive action might reduce the likelihood to, say, a 2 (depending on the circumstances).

7. Multiply each probability-times-seriousness score (obtained in step 4) by the corresponding residual probability rating, and record the products.

8. For each product obtained in step 7, develop as many contingency plans as your time and resources permit.

Figure 12-2 illustrates how PPA might be applied. In this figure, the idea being implemented involves conducting an in-house workshop on innovation challenges. For this idea, five potential problems were identified and two possible causes are listed for each problem. After all the ratings and preventive actions were determined, contingency plans were developed for the four highest scores in the PS x RP column. Of these plans, the most important ones appear to deal with the potential problem of participants losing interest.

The usefulness of PPA is exemplified best by the maxim: "An ounce of prevention is worth a pound of cure." The amount of resources consumed in the systematic anticipation of potential problems and development of countermeasures will be well justified if the idea is implemented successfully. For relatively important implementation tasks, the short-run costs of PPA will be offset, in most cases, by the long-run benefits. Another major advantage of PPA is that it can be used easily by both individuals and groups. Furthermore, the ratings can be obtained in groups quite efficiently by using averages whenever time is not available to achieve consensus.

A disadvantage of PPA is that it is not always possible to identify all potential problems and likely causes. Leaving out just one major problem cause could doom implementation success. As a result, considerable care must be used to generate as many potential problems and causes as possible. A second disadvantage of this method concerns the amount of time expended relative to problem importance. Spending time to do a PPA must be weighed against the costs of not solving the problem. If a group decides to use PPA, it will need to balance the amount of time spent against both the need to solve the problem and the likelihood of encountering major obstacles. It would make little sense to spend several days on an implementation task that involves a

FIGURE 12-2. Using PPA to anticipate workshop problems.

Problems/Causes	P	S	PS	Preventive Actions	RP	PS × RP	Contingency Plans
1. E-mail not understood:							
a. Assumes background information is known	1	7	7	Test assumptions.	1	7	Have several people read it.
b. Ambiguous wording	3	7	21	Have someone else read it.	2	42	
2. E-mail not received:							
a. Spam filter on	1	7	7	Send individual e-mails.	1	7	
b. E-mail not checked	2	7	14	Ask someone else to remind.	1	14	
3. Workshop equipment not available:							
a. Already reserved	4	3	12	Reserve well in advance.	2	24	
b. Broken	3	5	15	Lease equipment.	1	15	
4. Location not available:							
a. Already reserved	3	5	15	Reserve well in advance.	2	30	Reserve backup locations.
b. Not large enough	2	6	12	Specify size when reserving.	1	12	
5. Participants lose interest:							
a. Boring lectures	7	7	49	Use multimedia.	4	196	Use participant exercises.
b. Material not relevant	4	7	28	Use relevant examples.	2	56	Before workshop, ask participants to check relevancy of workshop material.

relatively unimportant problem and comparatively few major obstacles.

Copycat

If your idea is similar to one that has been implemented before by other groups or individuals, you can be a *copycat*. Instead of trying to reinvent the wheel, you can borrow someone else's implementation strategy. However, before you do this, make sure that the strategy you borrow will work with your idea. Even a relatively minor difference between your idea and another one could preclude using a borrowed strategy. Nonetheless, there will be many situations in which only a few modifications will be required, and thus considerable savings in time and effort will result.

Five *W*s

In addition to being useful for reframing challenges, the *five W*s technique can be very useful for implementing ideas. For relatively simple implementation tasks, this method provides an efficient and orderly means for seeing that an idea is applied to a problem. (It also can be used quite easily in conjunction with other methods.) The major steps are:

1. Ask *who, what, where,* and *when* in regard to implementation tasks. For example, you might ask: Who will implement the idea? What will they do? Where will they implement the idea? And when will they implement the idea? Then answer each of these questions, being as specific as possible.

2. Ask *why* for each of the preceding questions and answer each question. For example: Why should these people implement the idea? Why should they do what they are going to do? and so forth. (By asking why, you provide a rationale for each implementation action and ensure that no major activities are overlooked.)

3. If asking why reveals any overlooked implementation activities, revise the implementation strategy.

4. Implement the idea.

Flowcharts

When a sequence of activities is required to implement an idea, *flowcharts* can be used to guide the process. Similar to the diagrams computer programmers use to depict the operations needed to carry out a program, flowcharts provide an efficient means for structuring implementation activities. The basic elements of a flowchart are activities, decision points, and arrows for activity indicators. Using these elements, a flowchart can be constructed as follows:

1. State the objectives to be achieved, including the desired end result.

2. Generate a list of all activities needed to implement the idea.

3. Put the activities in the order in which they must be performed.

4. Examine each activity and decide whether any questions must be asked before the next activity can be completed.

5. Write the first activity at the top of a sheet of paper and draw a box around it. Draw an arrow from this box to the next activity or decision point. (Draw a diamond shape around questions at decision points.)

6. Continue listing each activity and decision point in sequence until the terminal activity has been reached.

7. Using the flowchart as a guide, implement the idea.

Examples of flowcharts can be found in Chapters 2 and 3 in the figures used to illustrate the Q-banks and C-banks. The best way to learn how to make flowcharts is to practice using them. Always make a rough sketch first and don't be afraid to add your own modifications. For instance, many people find it helpful to add time estimates for each activity. Moreover, software programs now exist to facilitate drawing them.

PERT

The *PERT method* (program evaluation and review technique) was developed by the military in the 1950s to facilitate the development of a new missile project. It is a relatively complex implementation procedure and requires the use of a computer for large projects. However, it can be adapted for smaller implementation projects and set up without any computer assistance.

The basic steps are similar to those used to construct flowcharts, except that time estimates are an essential part of the PERT method. In addition, the terminology differs somewhat. With PERT, activities are work efforts that consume resources. Activities are represented by arrows. Those places where activities begin and end are known as *events* and are represented by circles. Dummies are activities of zero duration that consume zero resources and are used only to maintain the logic between events and activities. Dashed arrows are used to represent dummies.

To construct a relatively simple PERT network, use the following steps:

1. Define the implementation objectives, including an end product.

2. Generate a list of all activities needed to implement the idea. Whenever possible, list subactivities as well.

3. Put the activities in the order in which they must be performed, and assign numbers to them to indicate their order. If two or more activities need to be performed at the same time, assign each of these activities the same number.

4. Construct the basic PERT network by connecting the events and activities. Place event numbers in the event circles. Write activities above the arrows.

5. Review the network and make any modifications needed to ensure the network is complete.

6. Estimate the amount of time needed to complete each activity (hours, days, weeks, months, years) and write these estimates beneath the activity arrow.

7. Review the network as close as possible to the implementation target date (the time of the first event). Update the network if any information has become available that requires changes.

8. Implement the idea using the PERT network as a guide.

The actual construction of a PERT network should be guided by certain rules. The most important of these rules are:

- A previous activity must be completed before a new event can begin.

- Only a single event can be used to begin and end a network.

- All activity arrows must be used to implement an idea.

- Any two events can be connected with only one activity. When more than one activity connects two events, a dummy activity is required.

- A previous event must occur before a new activity can begin.

A PERT network is presented in Figure 12-3 to illustrate how PERT might be applied to the workshop example used for PPA. The activities involved and their assigned event numbers are:

1. Develop the workshop.

2. Write a memo describing the workshop.

3. Send the memo to the participants.

4. Reserve required equipment.

5. Request snacks for breaks.

FIGURE 12-3. Using PERT to implement a workshop.

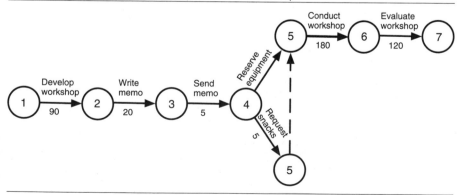

6. Conduct the workshop.

7. Evaluate the workshop.

These event numbers and descriptions of the activities are shown in Figure 12-3. A time estimate (in minutes) for completing each activity can be found below each activity arrow. Because reserving equipment and requesting snacks are seen as activities to be performed at about the same time, a dummy activity has been included to preserve the network's logic.

Note that Figure 12-3 presents only a very elementary PERT network. Implementing ideas that require more precise time estimates and that are more complex than the one represented here involves using much more sophisticated networks. For example, there are a variety of methods for calculating time estimates for individual activities to increase the accuracy of the time estimate for the entire process. The reader interested in these more advanced PERT procedures should consult the numerous books and software programs available on this topic.

Time/Task Analysis

One of the simplest implementation techniques is *time/task analysis (T/TA)*, also known as *Gantt charts*. Similar in purpose to PERT, T/TA is used by relating time requirements to implementation tasks and constructing a graph to depict the flow of events. The major steps for conducting a T/TA are:

1. List every task that must be completed to implement the idea. Be as specific as possible and try not to leave anything out—even relatively simple tasks may be critical for implementation success.

2. Estimate the amount of time available to implement the idea. Make this estimate as realistic and accurate as possible.

3. Determine how much time will be needed to complete each task. Again, try to be realistic and avoid underestimating the time required. Make sure that the time required for completing all the tasks does not exceed the total amount of time available.

FIGURE 12-4. Using T/TA analysis to select an engineering candidate.

	February	March	April	May	June	July
1. Develop criteria						
2. Advertise positions						
3. Receive applications						
4. Conduct interviews						
5. Select candidates						

As a rough rule of thumb, remember that most tasks take longer to complete than people originally think they will.

4. Construct a graph showing the relationship between each task and its time estimate. Plot the tasks on the vertical axis and the time on the horizontal axis.

5. Implement the idea using the T/TA as a guide.

Suppose, for example, that your idea involves recruiting minority personnel to fill various engineering positions in your company. To implement this idea, you could develop a chart such as the one shown in Figure 12-4. With this chart, it is easy to see which tasks overlap each other, which ones must be done after the previous one has been completed, and the relative amount of time required for each one. As with PERT charts, more information can be found in books and online.

Bibliography

Barlow, Christopher M. "Deliberate Insight in Team Creativity." *Journal of Creative Behavior* (2000) 34 (2): 101–117.

Bateson, Gregory. *Steps to an Ecology of Mind: Collected Essays in Anthropology, Psychiatry, Evolution and Epistemology*. San Francisco: Chandler, 1972.

Battelle, John. "1.2 Trillion Buck Chuck." *Business 2.0,* March 2006, 101–102.

Bower, Joseph L., and Clayton M. Christensen. "Disruptive Technologies: Catching the Wave." *Harvard Business Review* (1995) 73: 43–53.

Burke, Raymond R. "Virtual Shopping: Breakthrough in Marketing Research." *Harvard Business Review* (1996) 74 (2): 120–129.

Bryson, John M., Andrew H. Van de Ven, and William D. Roering. "Strategic Planning and the Revitalization of Public Service." In *The Revitalization of the Public Service,* ed. Robert Denhardt and Edward T. Jennings, Jr. Columbia: University of Missouri Press, 1985.

Cheesbrough, Henry William. *Open Innovation: The New Imperative for Creating and Profiting from Technology*. Boston: Harvard Business School Press, 2003.

"Crowdcasting." *Business 2.0,* November 2006, 86–87.

Damanpour, Fariborz. "Organizational Innovation: A Meta Analysis of Determinants and Moderators." *Academy of Management Journal* (1991) 34 (3): 555–590.

Doblin Inc. "Special Report—Get Creative! How to Build Innovative Companies." *Business Week*, August 1, 2005, 72.

Entman, Robert M. "Framing: Toward a Clarification of a Fractured Paradigm." *Journal of Communication* (1993) 41: 6–25.

Ghanem, Salma. "Filling in the Tapestry: The Second Level of Agenda Setting." In *Communication and Democracy: Exploring the Intellectual Frontiers in Agenda-Setting Theory,* ed. Maxwell E. McCombs, Donald Shaw, and David Weaver. Mahwah, N.J.: Lawrence Erlbaum Associates, 1977, 314.

Goffman, Erving. *Frame Analysis: An Essay on the Organization of Experience*. Cambridge, Mass.: Harvard University Press, 1974.

Hallahan, Kirk. "Seven Models of Framing: Implications for Public Relations. *Journal of Public Relations Research* (1999) 11 (3): 205–242.

Hamilton, David L., and Mark P. Zanna. "Differential Weighting of Favorable and Unfavorable Attributes in Impressions of Personality." *Journal of Experimental Research Personality* (1972) (6): 204–212.

Hamm, Steve. "Innovation: The View from the Top." *Business Week,* April 3, 2006.

———. "Two Pillars of IBM's Growth Look Shaky." *Business Week,* August 1, 2005, 67.

Hart, Christopher W., and Christopher E. Bogan. *The Baldridge: What It Is, How It's Won, How to Use It to Improve Quality in Your Company.* New York: McGraw-Hill, 1992.

Holmes, Stanley. "Inside the Coup at Nike." *Business Week,* February 6, 2006, 34–37.

IBM Corporation. "Speed Innovation." Retrieved January 19, 2007, from http://www-306.ibm.com/e-business/ondemand/us/index.html?P_Site=S500).

Kaplan, Robert S., and David P. Norton, II. *The Strategy-Focused Organization: How Balanced Scorecard Companies Thrive in the New Business Environment.* Cambridge, Mass.: Harvard Business School Publishing Corporation, 2001.

———. *Strategy Maps: Converting Intangible Assets into Tangible Outcomes.* Boston: HBS Press, 2004.

Kepner, Charles H., and Benjamin B. Tregoe. *The New Rational Manager.* Princeton, N.J.: Kepner-Tregoe, 1981.

Luthje, Christian, and Cornelius Herstatt. "The Lead User Method: Theoretical-Empirical Foundation and Practical Implementation." *R&D Management* (2004) 34 (5): 549–564.

MacCrimmon, Kenneth R., and Ronald N. Taylor. "Decision Making and Problem Solving." In *Handbook of Industrial and Organizational Psychology,* ed. M. D. Dunnette. Chicago: Rand McNally, 1976.

Maier, Norman R. F. *Problem Solving and Creativity in Individuals and Groups.* Belmont, Calif.: Brooks/Cole, 1970.

Mintzberg, Henry, Duru Raisinghani, and Andre Theoret. "The Structure of Unstructured Decisions." *Administrative Science Quarterly* 21 (1976) (2): 246–275.

Mitroff, Ian. *Smart Thinking for Crazy Times: The Art of Solving the Right Problems.* San Francisco: Berrett-Koehler Publishers, 1998.

Mucha, Thomas. "How to Ask the Right Questions." *Business 2.0,* December 10, 2004.

Novak, Joseph D., and Alberto J. Canas. "The Theory Underlying Concept Maps and How to Construct Them." Retrieved July 23, 2006, from http://cmap.ihmc.us/Publications/ResearchPapers/TheoryUnderlyingConceptMaps.pdf.

Nutt, Paul C. "Framing Strategic Decisions." *Organization Science* 9 (1998) (2): 195–216.

Osborn, Alex. *Applied Imagination.* New York: Scribner, 1963.

Pillar, Frank T., and Dominik Walcher. "Toolkits for Idea Competitions: A Novel Method to Integrate Users in New Product Development." *R&D Management* 29 (2006) (3): 289–302.

Pratto, Felicia, and Oliver P. John. "Automatic Vigilance: The Attention-Grabbing Power of Negative Social Information." *Journal of Personality and Social Psychology* (1991) 61: 380–391.

Premier, Inc. "Nonprofit Hospitals and Health Systems: Caring for Our Communities, a Charge to Keep." Retrieved August 12, 2006, from http://www.premierinc .com/advocacy/issues/nonprofit/06/policy-position-nonprofithospitals-06 .pdf.

Quinn, James B. "Managing Strategic Change." In *Strategic Management*, ed. Arthur Thompson, William E. Fulmer, and Alonzo J. Strickland, III. Homewood, Ill.: Irwin, 1989.

———. "Outsourcing Innovation." *MIT Sloan Management Review* (2000) 41: 13–28.

Ries, Al, and Jack Trout. *Positioning: The Battle for Your Mind*. New York: McGraw-Hill, 1981.

Russo, J. Edward, and Paul J. H. Schoemaker. *Winning Decisions: Getting It Right the First Time*. New York: Currency/Doubleday, 2002.

Schoemaker, Paul J. H., and J. Edward Russo. "Managing Frames to Make Better Decisions." In *Wharton on Making Decisions*, ed. Stephen J. Hoch, Howard C. Kunreuther, and Robert E. Gunther. New York: John Wiley & Sons, 2001.

Scholey, Cam. "Strategy Maps: A Step-by-Step Guide to Measuring, Managing, and Communicating the Plan." *Journal of Business Strategy* 26 (2005) (3): 12–19.

Schon, Donald. *Beyond the Stable State*. New York: Norton, 1971.

Starbuck, William H. "Organizations as Action Generators." *American Sociological Review* (1981) 48: 91–102.

Toubia, Olivier. "Idea Generation, Creativity, and Incentives." *Working Paper*, Columbia Business School, New York, 2005.

Treacy, Michael, and Fred Wiersema. *The Discipline of Market Leaders: Choose Your Customers*. Cambridge, Mass.: Perseus Books, 1995.

Trochim, William M. K. "An Introduction to Concept Mapping for Planning and Evaluation." Retrieved October 9, 2005, from http://www.socialresearchmethods .net/research/epp1/epp1.htm.

Turrell, Mark. "How to Connect Corporate Objectives and Investment in Innovation." *Innovation Tools*. Retrieved November 25, 2005, from http://www.innovation tools.com/Articles/EnterpriseDetails.asp?a=202.

Tversky, Amos, and Daniel Kahneman. "Rational Choice and the Framing of Decisions." In *Rational Choice: The Contrast Between Economics and Psychology*, ed. Robin M. Hogarth and Melvin W. Reder. Chicago: University of Chicago Press, 1987.

VanGundy, Arthur B. *Idea Power*. New York: AMACOM Books, 1992.

———. *Managing Group Creativity: A Modular Approach to Problem Solving*. New York: AMACOM Books, 1984.

———. *Techniques of Structured Problem Solving* (2nd ed.). New York: Van Nostrand Reinhold, 1988.

VanGundy, Arthur B., and Addys Sasserath. "The End of Fuzzy: The Fuzzy Front End in New Product Development. Paper presented at Brandworks University, Racine, Wis., 1999.

von Hippel, Eric. *Democratizing Innovation*. Cambridge, Mass.: The MIT Press, 2005.

Womack, James P., and Daniel T. Jones. *Lean Solutions: How Companies and Customers Can Create Value and Wealth Together*. New York: Free Press, 2005.

Index